MW01251130

Hemingway

The Grace and the Pressure

Hemingway

The Grace and the Pressure

Aubrey Dillon-Malone

Robson Books

We find little in a book but what we put there,
but in great books the mind finds room to put
many things.

Joseph Joubert

First published in Great Britain in 1999 by Robson Books, 10 Blenheim Court, Brewery Road, London N7 9NT

Copyright © 1999 Aubrey Dillon-Malone

The right of Aubrey Dillon-Malone to be identified as author of this work has been asserted by him in accordance with the Copyright, Designs and Patents Act 1988

British Library Cataloguing in Publication Data

A catalogue record for this title is available from the British Library

ISBN 1 86105 290 1

Printed in Great Britain by Creative Print and Design (Wales) Ltd

Contents

Acknowledgements

With special thanks to:
John Whelan, Michelle Walker and Aoife Hart for their
sterling labours on typesetting, Sarah Fordham for her
invaluable assistance in sourcing material, and Alan
Goodrich of the John F. Kennedy Library in
Massachusetts for all his help and advice concerning the
illustrations.

Introduction

If I could have made this enough of a book it would have had everything in it.

It would have had the war, the last gentleman's war, and all the good thoughts Papa had about his life during it, and the early fincas and deep sea fishing and nights outside the cafes in Paris when no one asked you what you wanted to do with your life and you didn't ask yourself either because you were just going through the day and it was pretty and beautiful and the buildings were fine and there were many good friends and it was a treasure to have them there by your side swopping talk about the metier and brave bullfighters and men and women who knew life wasn't easy but took the right chances at the right time.

The early years on Horton bay where you lost your heart to women who mightn't have even known it, and the wind coming up sharp and cool in the long mornings afterwards to remind you of that, or even to help you forget.

Waking up to the sun in Key West and feeling as if it was the first day of your life, or maybe the last, and the way the sea would look when it was cold and hard and inviting you into it with a sly elegance, and all those Cuban trips and the drinking and stories afterwards even if half of them were false, and the good feeling you had about all the writing you were doing and how it was such a hell of a thing not to feel guilty that you didn't have a proper job. But this was the proper job even if your mother wouldn't have thought of it that way or your father either.

Going hunting with him in Michigan and being shown how to trap wild animals, watching the sun go down on the bay afterwards and carrying all your dreams with it, and all your hopes and fears as well. Coming home late at night when the lights were on the river and the leaves falling from the trees and telling stories that were still good and true even if the person that told them wasn't you anymore and anyway it was a long time ago and in another country so it might not have been that important but it still might have been.

It would have Gertrude Stein throwing her head back and laughing raucously at yet another clever riposte by the young Chicago man, and then berating him for his insolence. Or Hemingway taking Hadley to Fossalta in 1922 but seeing no remnants of the war there at all, only the shell of past glory.

It's a pity we don't have him fishing for trout in Michigan or salmon in the Loire, relaxing with a book afterwards as he lay down with Hadley under the stars, marvelling at how lucky he was to have found a woman so pure and giving, and a life that allowed him to go anywhere he wanted without anyone breathing down his neck for deadlines anymore, or telling him who to interview, or how to write.

And Papa with new wife Hadley in 113 Rue Notre Dame des Champs above the sawmill, she worried about money as he sweated over the stories. Going to bicycle races with Dos Passos to get your mind off all the rejection slips as you wondered what it was you had to do to get famous.

It would have had Scott and Zelda calling to the Paris apartment at four in the morning and proceeding to throw toilet rolls from the top of the stairs to the bottom, then laughing wildly with the influence of the drink...and the happy look that came into Zelda's face because she knew Scott wouldn't be able to write now.

My God, you could not get in the stories behind the big books, many of which shouldn't be told but what the hell, and the writing you went at again and again until you got it right, the hard work nobody knew about because they always thought Papa was too busy chasing tigers to care about his craft when the truth of it was that he cared almost too much about it to talk about it.

It would have had discussions about how to write in a way that people would appreciate, getting to the point of things quickly before they lost interest, but not giving them too much either, just enough.

Realising too that life would always be more important than writing about it or being famous, even if after a while no one saw anything except those goddamned newspaper reports and maybe they didn't even read the books any more, only the reviews with the lies in them, written by hacks who hadn't read the books either but knew enough about Papa to get by on the bullshit stuff.

You could have had him shooting himself in the knees when trying to kill sharks, and *mano a mano* bullfights, and breaking the comb for Adriana Ivancich in Latisana in 1949 and meeting Marlene so many years earlier when she wouldn't sit at a table of thirteen people because, like Papa, she was superstitious.

We would have had him shooting the tips off cigarettes held in the mouths of his friends in Spanish bars for fun, and parties that went on all night, and dancing in the square with senoritas and wrestling little bulls to the ground by their horns.

Bumby should have been in it, cutting a half moon in Papa's eye with his fingernail in Montreux. And the agonising pain. (But maybe a bit of laughter too).

This book doesn't have the skylight crashing down on top of him in Neuilly in 1928 and him needing nine stitches to stop the bleeding from his head, but being amused by the absurdity of it, as he would be amused by his plane crashes a quarter of a century later, because, what the hell, we all had to go sometime, and maybe the more you suffered the easier the pain got.

Also include the Alpine idylls and cats in the rain and the *riau riau* dancers in Pamplona.

It would have had him telling his parents he was engaged to the movie star Mae Marsh even though he never met the woman. Or the day he broke Wallace Stevens' jaw after Stevens called him a sap. Or shooting duck with Coop in Wyoming, or the boxing bout with John Huston that never happened. Teething pains with Martha and pretending they weren't there because other distractions stopped you seeing the problems, or wanting to.

It's not enough of a book to have him hanging Miro's 'The Farm' in his Paris apartment for the first time, and afterwards learning how to write from it, along with the works of Klee and Cézanne and Picasso.

It would have him drinking at La Floridita and pontificating on how it was when his luck was good and the wind blowing from the right quarter and the sun coming up on the waves and hills like white elephants in the distance as he hooked another marlin with Miss Mary. Maybe things weren't quite as good now as they had been with Hadley in the sawmill when he was starting out, but he could forget this if the writing and the fishing were going well, and if he felt he could leave something true for his children, or the world at large, to savour.

Why not have Papa going to Italy with Mary in the forties with the intention of defecating on the spot where he had been wounded, but settling instead for placing a thousand lira note there, something Colonel Cantwell could never have done?

It would have the snow melting in the Abruzzi as the troops marched by, and the wind knifing through him as he climbed a mountain in search of a new nirvana, or a new kill.

He would be writing his later books in a standing position laying off the sauce during the composition and not talking about what he was doing either for fear he would talk it all out of himself. And re-doing it and re-doing it until it was right, as if it was a mathematical formula, or a key you turned in a lock.

It would have had him standing in front of Henry Strater in Bimini in 1935 after Strater had hooked a 500-pound marlin, looking at it as if it was his own catch, the way he always had to have the biggest fish, and the most attention.

And of course Hemingway breaking John O'Hara's blackthorn stick over his own bare head, much to the amazement of O'Hara, and possibly himself. But then this would also be the head that would butt its way out of a burning aircraft in 1954...

What about him borrowing books from Sylvia Beach because he

couldn't afford to buy them, but building up some mighty good ideas that way, and some kind of a goddam library too?

Or even when he interviewed Lloyd George in Canada on the very day Bumby was born, getting carpeted by Harry Hindmarsh afterwards for spending too much time at the hospital when he should have been writing stories.

It would have sex and death and murder in an almost mystic union. It would have the U-boats of World War Two and the taking of the Ritz via the Rambouillet route. And the lions that Santiago dreamed of, and the frozen leopard on Kilimanjaro, and living in coldwater flats that charged only sixty francs a month, and ski-ing in the Vorarlberg and how he felt when Boni & Liveright said they were taking *In Our Time*.

We could have him standing in his shorts and loafers in the Finca Vigia, his typewriter on a shelf opposite him as he wrote dialogue, leaving it aside whenever he had a descriptive passage to essay. Or getting to know Hadley in Paris and thinking it was going to be always like this, struggling to find the right words for the feelings, and writing damn good stories even if they weren't selling enough to keep you in food.

Papa smuggling copies of *Ulysses* into the States and telling Ezra Pound that someday somebody would appreciate his gesture.

And marriages that looked to be good ideas when he started them but things changing when he got greedy or selfish or successful or whatever, and not knowing who to blame and not wanting to blame himself but sad too to be parting because each time a marriage died a part of him died too and then it seemed to get easier to end them, and for lesser reasons. You had to return to the books for solace; a book wouldn't betray you. Only the critics did that. Or friends you trusted before they got sucked into telling stories about you.

It would have him writing *The Fifth Column* in 1937, and staying cool under fire, but still not managing to produce a work of literature that would last, perhaps for that very reason.

We should have put in Aaron Hotchner meeting him for the first time in La Floridita, his favourite Cuban bar, so that he could write an article on 'The Future of Literature', which was subsequently scuppered, to their mutual amusement.

Or maybe the excitement of seeing his name in print before he was famous, even if it was only in a cuckoo literary magazine that paid peanuts.

Tracking a lion or shooting and fighting with John Huston. Catching fish with his father and learning what to do with them afterwards. Being intoxicated with Pauline and not knowing whether to give in to it or not. Imagining he would be the greatest writer of all time, and then cutting down on that ambition. Going a couple of rounds with Shakespeare and the Russians before he found his own voice.

Or playing the role of a writer for a time rather than writing, living off the fat of the pen before he shook himself up for those late surges.

Or even have him interviewing Mussolini twice, and both times seeing through his bluff when no one else did. Or giving boxing lessons in Kenilworth Avenue as his mother did her singing classes upstairs. (Now there was a contrast).

Rushing away from Key West to sleep with Martha, and Pauline knowing something was up but not being able to say what. Going to Spain with Martha but feeling bad about the relationship even before things had properly begun. Or maybe being fascinated by Duff Twysden and unable to do anything about it, like Jake Barnes, but for a different reason.

It would have him running with the bulls in Pamplona, and meeting Dominguin and Ordonez and making these people his heroes just as writers were his heroes, the way it all seemed to gel into one master plan. At least until the war wound, or all those freakish accidents, or the plane crashes. And then there was all that stuff in the Mayo Clinic which was the worst place in the world for a cult hero to be, making love to Mary, or trying to, in a room that anyone could walk into if they felt like it.

The pills the doctor had that made you feel strange, but the not taking them being worse. A black mood with no cause and no respite.

It would have had the first time he knew he could write novels and not just stories, and the rush you got when it was going well for you, and then it was on the best seller list and then another one was, and suddenly you knew that what you were doing was important and would last, so you celebrated with one too many glasses of wine and afterwards your nerves were shot to pieces and you couldn't write afterwards again for a while as a result. But what matter. The books were out there and many were reading them and full of admiration and there were more where they came from, even though other problems were making the writing of them more difficult than you wanted, and also there were people who would never be able to write books themselves telling you the bad things about them, or making up bad things that weren't even there because they were jealous and small-minded.

This book should have had Hadley and Bumby in Paris, and Hadley playing the piano as Papa wrote, but Papa not being a good papa when Bumby was young, but this wasn't because he didn't love him, just because he was busy writing and he knew he could make it up to him when he grew up and they could go hunting together like he used to do in Michigan before things went bad with his father.

How could we forget Papa falling into a bush fire two weeks after his plane crashed and not minding, or at least not seeming to, and not suffering any long-lasting symptoms either, though they said that after the crashes too even though there was a lot of damage nobody knew anything about.

Or Papa being shelled in the Florida Hotel, the ceiling falling down on top of him but the minor tragedy causing him only mild surprise as everyone around him frantically picked pieces of plaster from their hair.

We could have had him sitting on *The Pilar* watching how the fish were running, the sun beating down on him as he tested the tension of his fishing line, boasting afterwards about the size of his catch like an adolescent, but aware too in a deeper part of himself that such things didn't really matter. They didn't matter any more than winning the Nobel did, or marrying four times, or wanting to bed Mata Hari even though she was dead, or even capturing the Ritz, of downing all those bottles of Valpolicella in the Hotel Gritti. No, all that mattered when you came down to it was living your life from the ground up like Dominguin or Ordonez and taking the chances when they came, be it at the feria or in a secret part of your heart, the part where the magic resided, or maybe the demons, or maybe the magic and demons together in some rabid communion that sucked his inspiration into a vignette that was - Yeats would know - as cold and passionate as the dawn.

How could we have missed him telling people not to write too much or too quickly, pacing yourself like an athlete until there was always something left over for the next day, some departure point that would set the juices going rather than writing yourself out in an empty flourish. Or brutally editing his own work, the early sketches that were too insubstantial and the late ones that were overly self-indulgent, all the while in search of that one true sentence with a simplicity that hid its own depth.

Ernest could be fishing along the Irati, or watching the sky change colour on the Spanish sierras, or looking at Ordonez going in over the bulls on muggy afternoons in San Fermin. He could also be shooting lighted cigarettes out of Ordonez' mouth at his sixtieth birthday party, the cigarette getting shorter with every shot but his aim still millimetre perfect, even under the influence of tequila.

It would have had him happy as hell boxing with Ezra even though Ezra was not a good boxer, and meeting Gertrude Stein and Ford Madox Ford and Alice B. Toklas. Or boozing with Jimmy Joyce when fights broke out and Papa treating him like a little boy, the same way he treated Scott Fitzgerald. It would have had him playing doctor to Scott and then making fun of his crack-up even though his own would come too, and it would be a much worse one when it did.

There should also be Stein thanking him for publishing parts of 'The Making of Americans' in the *Transatlantic Review*...and then telling him to give up journalism because it was taking the juice from him that he could have been using for 'the other stuff'.

Or maybe the plains of Lombardy, or the Caporetto retreat, or those endless games of *jai-alai* in Cuba, or bringing Hadley to Lake Walloon for the first time, or travelling to Lyons with Scott Fitzgerald...or even that early weekend with Pauline in Paris when he wanted and yet didn't want her. All this could have been here, and more besides.

Or what about the ranch and the silvered grey of the sage brush, the quick clear water in the irrigation ditches, and the heavy green of the alfalfa? Should they not have been here too if the book was good enough?

He would have had to be in it at Schruns, or the Abruzzi, or even the Huertgen Forest, beating his chest like Tarzan over yet another novel, or yet another wife. And then going into his tent to commune silently with *nada*.

He should have been doing carefully and slowly and well all the things that had been taught to him at the *Kansas City Star*, and also in Toronto and Paris, even if he changed these things as time went on, or if his personality intruded on the writing, or vice versa. But of course you had to make allowances for that, and anyway who was the final arbiter when what you were really talking about was capturing reality as only you knew it and that was fine but you had to be careful to angle it to the reader so he wouldn't know too much and also that there wouldn't be hollows in the writing. Wasn't that right? Gaps were fine but they had to be pregnant ones and if they were done right and true and cleverly the people reading them would know what to put in and maybe they would fill them with their own experiences if you were very lucky or very good.

A better book would have him sauntering round the Finca Vigia like a benign tyrant, admiring the animal heads adorning the walls or lost among his books and his cats, those little tigers that may have reminded him of larger ones on mountain peaks he could not dream of scaling now, or outdoor hunting scenes he had loved almost from the first moment he drew breath.

The smell of smoked leather should have been here, and the smell of frozen roads, and the blue steel of the sky in the early morning shoots at Sun Valley. Or the rush of excitement at the first kill. And the thrill of telling about it afterwards. But not too soon - and not too damned much either.

It would have him waking up early in the morning in Paris to do his writing, the old military discipline standing to him as Hadley turned around for the second time. There would be few people about as he looked out the window during a break from his labours, only the goat-herds and an occasional hobo, or maybe small pockets of people huddled round the braziers, warming their hands off the embers as their breath fogged the air. It would have him waking Hadley to show her what he had written even if it was only a few lines, proud like a child at some turn of phrase or abstruse insight into society's forgotten people, the ones he loved because he was one of them, and the ones he hoped never to desert if he became rich and famous. He would become both, and critics would say he lost sight of such a society in his lust for grandeur, but always there would be an empathy with the peasant in him, even if he was America's pre-eminent literary pariah.

Or how about Ernesto putting priests aboard *The Pilar* during World War Two to kill Krauts or disguised Franco-philes, and even if that didn't happen they had a good time trying, didn't they? Maybe he ended this war as he did the first one, on an anti-climax, having tried equally hard to get involved, with his self-styled U-boat, and his self-styled guerilla persona...and a crew as wild and woolly as himself.

But was he ever any other way? And wasn't it better than staying back at the Finca Vigia abusing Martha? And neither did he end up this time with his knee exploded into hundreds of pieces, or in love with a woman who would throw him over for a dope...

We would have to have him cutting Mary's vein when her Fallopian tube ruptured and thus saving her life, or telling Lillian Ross that he felt so awful about the First World War that he couldn't write about it for ten years afterwards, or arguing with Dos Passos when he drifted to the left in the thirties or telling Leicester that cats had 'absolute emotional honesty', or Leicester himself saying that Papa's real ambition in life was to be 'Superman's older brother', or Hadley's brother Jamie committing suicide in 1930 at the age of fifty-two, or Grace telling Carol that his writing 'bastardised a noble art', or Gregory feeling guilty about the money he inherited after Pauline died, or Jinny Pfeiffer telling Pauline to screw him for every cent after he divorced her, or Hadley feeling like 'an old hag of thirty' on their honeymoon at Horton Bay, or the night Papa used a marlin he caught that day as a punchbag, or the night he made a promise that he would 'break one lousy critic's jaw every two years.'

It would have had these things in it, and also the day Hadley placed a bet on a horse at 120/1 and nearly won, and Papa sneaking away from Pauline in Key West to sleep with Jane Mason in Cuba, and Stein using a bloodhound to keep him away from her when things went bad between them, and Martha getting on so well with all his sons, maybe too well for his liking, and the ordinary nights in Chicago with Y.K. Smith and Doodles, and maybe even his belief, oft-stated, that women had their brains between their thighs.

It would have to have such details in it to give justice to Hadley's description of him as being more complicated than geometry.

There would have to have been something in it about Papa and Winston Guest conspiring to help Bumby lose his virginity to a lady named Olga in San Francisco de Paula, not being aware that he had already done so the evening before. Or Picasso reading his poetry to Gertrude Stein at her studio and an unimpressed Stein telling him that if that was the best he could do, he better go home and paint. Or Stein telling Hadley not to buy clothes but rather paintings, or Hadley being packed off with Alice B. Toklas while she engaged in more intellectual chatter with her gifted husband. Or maybe Papa getting Alice's last name wrong, or being secretly disgusted by her lesbianism, and Stein's, but not saying anything because Gertrude was his friend, and possible career ally.

It should have him getting excited about Sara and Gerald Murphy, and then tired or their vapid wealth and the life they represented...and tired of Jane Mason in the same way, even if he had more aspects of these people inside him than he might have cared to admit. And it should have good old John Dos Passos, the Quiet Man in his life and the one he loved and hated just as Dos loved and hated him, but a man he could never forgive after that horrific car accident that all but decapitated his old friend Katy Smith.

He should also be declaiming in The Floridita about J. Edgar Hoover and Franco and the Loyalists, and every other s.o.b. who tried to cramp his style or muzzle him, including the All-American Bitch who laid his father low. And almost himself.

And he should be talking about how drink proved both his nirvana and his nadir at different times of his life, giving him the courage to go on for a while, and then stiffening that very courage when the grip got too great.

It would have had indian camps and clean well-lighted places and hunting in Sun Valley...and how the weather was.

And it would have had the thoughts that were in his mind when he tried to kill himself, and especially on July 2 1961 when he succeeded, if that's the word.

But it is not that kind of a book, nor would it hope to be. There are just a few things to be said, that is all.

There are just a few practical things to be said.

War and Peace

Hemingway was born at eight o'clock on the morning of July 21 1899, into a world of horse-drawn carriages. He died in the decade in which his country would put a man on the moon.

Born into an upper middle class family in the idyllic midwestern community of Oak Park, Illinois, he was the younger brother of Marcelline, who would be a rival of sorts to him right through his childhood. After him came three more girls - Ursula (his favourite), Carol and Madelaine (aka Sunny) and finally another boy, Leicester, though he arrived far too late to be the male buddy Ernest always craved.

The robins sang their sweetest songs on the night he was born, his mother claimed.

Oak Park was a country retreat ten miles west of Chicago, a broad expanse of nature with rolling fields. Hemingway's obstetrician father Clarence, in fact, did his house calls on horseback, continuing to use this method of travelling even after he bought a car. The four-legged animals didn't have engines that broke down in an emergency, he reasoned. Neither were cars able to find their way home if he had to leave them in a hurry.

Hemingway would witness not only two World Wars but also a Civil war and countless other skirmishes. And when wars weren't happening at some corner of the globe, he would make some for himself. A man who was as fascinated by violence as he was emotionally gutted by it, he experienced death early from accompanying his physician father on his rounds, and also by going hunting and fishing with him, where death was in some way controlled.

Oak Park, he claimed, was full of 'wide lawns and narrow minds'. A suburb where cinemas closed on Sundays and the sale of alcohol had been forbidden since the 1870s, it wasn't really ready for Ernest Miller Hemingway. Indeed, his mother's twee philosophy was a microcosm of an area that had the soubriquet 'Saint's Rest' tagged on to it.

No prostitutes resided here, nor punch-drunk fighters nor contract killers nor alcoholics nor matadors nor thieves. No, Kenilworth Avenue was as dull and predictable as its architecture. It was full of houses, as Hemingway's future friend James Joyce might have put it, conscious of the decent lives being lived inside them.

Rude language wasn't allowed in Oak Park, and if anyone used it, their mouth was washed out with soap. Drinking and smoking was forbidden in most houses - including the Hemingways - and the word 'virgin' was even deemed too contentious to appear in school text books.

The people of Oak Park were cossetted from the earthier realms of life, from the darkly phobic characters who would people Ernest's future fiction. It was a suburb with a virtually nonexistent crime rate and a tight set of social strictures. Hemingway wouldn't have been allowed to legally buy cigarettes until he was eighteen, for instance, nor drive a car - or even own a cap gun within the village limits.

Both of his parents were devoutly religious, adhering to strict disciplinarian codes. The fact that Hemingway came from such a Bible-thumping background, of course, made him an unlikely candidate for becoming standard-bearer to a generation of disaffected, agnostic dilettantes. His roots lay in the heart and soul of Middle America.

He inherited his love of the outdoors from his father, but little else. He certainly didn't inherit his drinking habits from him (Clarence was a teetotaller), nor his left wing views, nor his sexual infidelity, nor his fondness for expletives, nor his sense of humour.

From his mother he got his bad eyesight and probably some more of her character traits as well. Like pugnacity, for instance. And recalcitrance. And self-righteousness. This pair of enemies were much more similar than either would admit to. Maybe this was the reason they repelled one another so much.

His upbringing was more Scott Fitzgerald than Damon Runyon, but the young man whose character and priorities were formed by Mark Twain's Huckleberry Finn was determined to amass some of Huck's roguishness and implicate it into his own flimsy bad-boy repertoire. In his mind, at least, he could re-write history and make the fashionable suburb of Oak Park into a Skid Row of sorts. And he himself, if not quite an anti-christ, at least someone who flirted liberally with the *demi-monde*. Right through his life he would be this sheep in wolf's clothing.

One of the many myths of Hemingway's youth - probably propagated by himself - was that he ran away from home to become a prize-fighter. The early sallies of his imagination - he would subsequently tell his parents he was engaged to be married to screen siren Mae Marsh - were every future biographer's nightmare. After a time, not even Hemingway himself seemed sure where fact ended and fantasy began.

His domestic problems began on the day of his christening. He always hated being called Ernest, associating it with Oscar Wilde's play *The Importance of Being Earnest*. And all the effeteness that that implied.

Actually being called Ernest was one of the most disturbing elements in the young boy's life, considering he hated the name so much because of its distinctly unmacho overtones. Couple this with the fact that his mother would probably have preferred him to be a girl so she could realise her fantasy of having twins, and his childhood rage was almost complete. Could these two events, trivial and all as they may appear now, have caused him to over-react to the extent of creating a persona that would be the polar opposite? But whatever damage his mother did to him was more than compensated for by the hunting and fishing expeditions his father organised for him. The irony, of course, was his father too was under the thumb of Grace Hall Hemingway.

With a mother like Grace, a name like Ernest, and a houseful of sisters, Hemingway could well have turned out to be as ineffectual as his father if he hadn't worked hard at developing his masculinity. Whether he overdid it is another question.

Grace's over-protectiveness towards her son, and her continuous efforts to subdue his buoyant moods, only drove him further and further away from her, and closer and closer to an identification of virtue with virility, and cowardice as the greatest possible vice. Her fussiness in this regard drove him to war instead of to college.

When Ernest was asked at the age of five what he was afraid of, he replied: 'Fraid a nothing'. Over the next fifty-nine years, to greater or lesser degrees, he would continue to repeat that statement in various forms.

When he was four years old, his mother used to sing him to sleep by trilling 'Onward Christian Soldiers', but the young Ernest wasn't too impressed with her choice of lullaby. 'I don't want to be an Onward Christian Soldier when I get to be a big boy,' he moaned, 'I want to go with Dad and shoot lions and wolves.' The child, truly, was father of the man.

Hemingway's father may have been his superficial role model in the sense that he gave him his love of hunting and fishing, but a deeper and more influential one was his grandfather Anson, who fought in the Civil War. Clarence may have liked to shoot, but he never shot at anything that could attack him, unlike his father and (subsequently) his son.

The habit of telling tall tales - which would be a feature of his entire life, both on and off the printed page - began early. At the age of five he told his grandfather that he had stopped a runaway horse single-handedly. Fraid a nothing indeed. His grandfather commented: 'With an imagination like that, you'll either end up famous or in jail.' (Come to think of it, the fact that Hemingway never spent a night of his life behind bars is one of its most intriguing phenomena.)

By the age of six he's alleged to have known the names of more than 250 birds in Latin. In years to come, his photographic memory would stand him in good stead. He would say to Leicester in later years: 'I have always made things stick that I wanted to stick. I've never kept notes or a journal. I just push the recall button and there it is. If it isn't there, it wasn't worth keeping.'

Ernest was born a year after Marcelline. His mother had wanted another daughter, so she tried to make him into one as much as she could by twinning the pair of them. An early photograph of him carries the caption underneath it: 'Summer Girl'. He always feared that such a photograph would surface in some magazine during his lifetime. Thankfully it didn't or his buccaneering image would have taken a huge tumble.

The fact that Ernest was twinned with Marcelline may strike us today as worthy of Freudian analysis but in the early years of this century it was regarded as an innocuous practice to dress siblings of different sexes similarly. Where Grace differed from most mothers of the time was in continuing to dress Ernest in female attire after he passed the age of two or three.

Another theory behind her twinning of Marcelline and Ernest is more oblique. She herself was two years older than her brother Leicester when he arrived in her own house, and she may well have felt herself neglected as a result. Fearing history would repeat itself in the next generation, she could well have tried to obviate the possible tension by treating Ernest as another female, thus protecting Marcelline's sense of importance even as her own had been whittled away some forty years before.

Grace twinned Marcelline and Ernest by giving them similar clothing and hairstyles, and kept Marcelline in kindergarten an extra year so she could be in the same High School class as her brother. After Marcelline reached five the twinning process was reversed and Grace dressed and coiffed her daughter as a boy. This was something he never spoke about in his life. Indeed, it was a proviso of his financial support for Grace after his father committed suicide that she wouldn't allow herself to be interviewed about his youth.

When Grace went shopping she bought two of everything, thus paving the way for both Ernest and Marcelline to have identity crises of huge proportions in years to come. They slept in the same room in twin white cribs, had dolls that were similar, and played with china tea sets that had exactly the same pattern. During their High School years Grace did everything in her power to encourage them to be social partners, even to the extent of forbidding Marcelline to go to parties with other boys so that Ernest would be forced to accompany her. Whatever her intentions, however, her actions only succeeded in driving both siblings farther and farther apart. Familiarity bred contempt.

Grace wanted to keep Ernest as a little boy for all of his days. She gave him a cello, but his father gave him a fishing rod and a rifle. He appreciated the latter items more, but he did inherit his artistic side from his mother, in however eccentric a form.

At the age of three Hemingway was already aware of the fact that all was not right about the cross-dressing, and told his mother he was worried Santa Claus might not recognise him at Christmas. He was perhaps afraid that he would be given a doll instead of a pop gun. He didn't so much want to be 'Dutch Dollie', her pet name for him, as 'Pawnee Bill'.

If we look at photographs of Hemingway from his mother's scrap album, there's a staggering difference between the way he looked in 1902 where he could easily have been mistaken for a little girl in his long pink dress, and one of a year later in Lake Walloon where he stands on top of a boat with a toy rifle in his hand, looking for all the world like Huck Finn in the offing.

Hemingway's fascination with his heroes and heroines having the same style and colour of hair, going from *A Farewell to Arms* through *For Whom the Bell Tolls* to *The Garden of Eden,* would seem to have had its embryology in his own youth with Marcelline. As would his need to prove his virility over and over again...

His mother's main ambition was getting him to play the clarinet.

No big game hunting sprees were on her horizons, but Ernest had other ideas. If she was Aunt Sally he was Huckleberry Finn, a young man who would crawl out from under her apron-strings to become America's foremost chronicler of fortitude in adverse circumstances. 'Grace under pressure' was the term he used, but pressure under Grace might have been equally apt.

She made Ernest play cello in the school orchestra even though he evinced no flair for this. He liked to tell people she kept him out of school for a year just to practise it, but this was yet another of his yarns, as Marcelline made clear in her memoirs. It was actually she who was kept back in school so that the twinning with Ernest, who was a year younger than her, would be complete.

'A music nut' was the way he would describe Grace Hall Hemingway to his wives, but her influence cut deep into him. You can always tell a lot about a man from his mother and Hemingway was no exception. She sowed the seeds of resentment for females in him - particularly powerful females. And she gave him a hatred of anything effeminate, which would manifest itself in almost every act he performed after he left home, and which became a focal point of the famous Hemingway code of honour.

The best time his family ever had in Oak Park, he said, was the time his mother was laid up with typhoid fever and everyone had a free run of the house - which was, for once, free of her reign of terror. That might be a strong way to put it, but it was how he saw things. One is almost reminded of the Angela Lansbury character in *The Manchurian Candidate*, a woman who would try to brainwash her son into following her pursuits to the letter. Her daughters largely acceded to this gameplan, but taking Ernest Hemingway out of the woods to practice a cello ranks up there with bringing John Gielgud on a commando raid to Entebbe.

In many ways, she was a woman before her time. She had already raised a few eyebrows when she cycled down the streets of Oak Park on a bicycle some years before. She made little secret of the fact that, while marriage to an obstetrician might have been a step up the social ladder for some women, for her it was more like a hiccup to a musical career (she had a promising contralto voice) that had been cut short due to defective vision in her left eye, a problem exacerbated by theatre lights in concert halls.

Not only did Grace teach music, she also wrote poetry, gave lectures on literature, painted and composed songs. She acted as if 'mere' housekeeping was beneath her - but not beneath her husband, who seemed somehow intimidated by her past, if not her personality. Whatever, to him fell at least half the domestic chores, whenever he could squeeze them in between his rounds, or those outdoor weekend pursuits which seemed incongruous with her domination over him. Or did he seek out the woods and streams simply to get away from her nagging?

There was nobody to bully him in the woods. Here he could breathe freely and release his tensions shooting wild birds and eating food that didn't necessitate washing up afterwards.

Clarence promised Grace before he married her that he would do his share round the house in order to allow her to pursue her own interests in music. He was as good as his word and never shirked domestic chores, going overboard on occasion by bringing her her breakfast in bed as well as attending to the normal routines of the house.

Grace's power over Clarence started even before they married. Into the marriage she carried the aura of the young woman who 'sacrificed' her career for Clarence, though this wasn't strictly speaking true. She also paid for the Kenilworth Avenue house with the inheritance from her father's estate, which didn't do much for Clarence's confidence in himself as a provider. And she designed the cottage they owned on Walloon Lake.

Hemingway said his father was married to a woman with whom he had no more in common 'than a coyote has with a white French poodle.'

Grace made it clear from early on in her marriage that the Hemingway household was her show. Clarence, sadly, didn't have enough backbone to take her down from her pedastal.

What surprises one most of all about the situation is the fact that, considering Ernest was having similar problems with Grace as he was - i.e. being bullied by her - the pair of them didn't join forces and assert themselves in a concerted display of male power.

Clarence was a decent man who worked far beyond the call of duty, going out on calls at all hours of the day and night and not asking for payment from those patients too cash-strapped to be able afford his fee. He was also, however, a hugely nervous man prone to a Jekyll & Hyde personality, his high good humour reverting to sullenness or naked rage in an instant. A man who needed to control his children but who was in turn controlled by his wife, maybe the seeds of his eventual depression were sown by such emotional instability. It's even possible that he vented his rage on those children out of frustration at being afraid to stand up to his wife. Many cowards are also bullies, and Clarence Hemingway had elements of both in him.

But he was also a very human man, more sinned against than sinning, and in many ways his own worst enemy. In 'Fathers and Sons', Hemingway captured his contradiction when he said he was 'both cruel and abused.' A househusband before that term was coined, he busied himself with household chores as his wife, a suffragette of sorts, continued her musical career within the marriage by conducting family concerts and teaching music to pupils who came to the house.

His authority was being steadily deflated in the same way as Ernest's masculinity was being undermined. Both events were equally subtle, and both masterminded by the one woman.

A diva even off the stage, she exuded something of the aura of a Tallulah Bankhead as she walked down the street. In the absence of a singing career she made her family her audience and her house her concert-hall. The music room in Kenilworth Avenue was like her shrine. It was here she planned to give a new generation of Grace

Halls to the world. Ernest too would be commandeered into it to play that cello - that is, if she could drag him away from his boxing exploits next door.

Grace didn't fancy cooking or household chores or changing diapers or anything else she regarded as cutting in upon her artistic or idealistic pursuits. It was Clarence who had to break off his house calls to remind her to put the roast in the oven. If there was a family crisis, she ran from it to her room, pulling down the shades and turning off the lights so that she could rest in the dark. When Clarence said he would like to practice medicine abroad, she said no, that wouldn't be feasible. She had after all sacrificed her own singing career for him, so the least he could offer her was this domestic stability.

So Clarence continued shooting, hunting, curing, and taking bullets from people's legs in indian camps without anaesthetics as Grace pasted photographs of her progeny into family albums or lectured in ladies halls on music, decorum and how to practice love and understanding...though not necessarily in that order. The young Ernest watched all this and took it in, setting his mother's hypocrisy off against his father's silent suffering. Inside himself he vowed that his own life would be different; that he would never marry a woman like Grace, and if he did he would do something about it very soon, before the wound festered. He saw his father administering poultices to the needy anywhere he saw them, but he knew, even if he couldn't verbalise it, that it was a case of 'Physician, heal thyself'.

Ernest had an ambivalent relationship to his father. His admiration for his authoritative bearing was compromised by the bullying he saw him getting from his wife. Neither did the young Ernest respond well to being disciplined by the older man. In fact he told his friend Bill Smith he often sat in a shed they owned, aiming a loaded shotgun at his father's head if he had been punished by him. Such oedipal thoughts were rare, however, his deeper resentment being foisted on his mother.

Maybe Clarence tried to undo the damage Grace caused to

Ernest's masculinity by giving him an early exposure to the world of nature and its harsh, exciting rigours. Whatever his motive, the effect worked and the pupil eventually outdid the master.

If we're looking for a psychological explanation for why Hemingway's life went the way it did, we may find it in this convoluted set of domestic circumstances, where traditional roles were almost totally reversed. His mother, in many ways, was the male element, even though she sat in her drawing-room pontificating about music and the arts, whereas his father, even though he spent much of his time in the woods hunting and fishing, was the female one. When he returned from his outdoor exploits he found himself performing menial chores as Grace retired to her chambers. It might be difficult for us to believe a man with a rifle in his hand could be dominated by a woman with a tuning fork, but such was the case.

The fact that Ernest was getting these kinds of confused signals could have given rise to the strong theme of the transmogrification of sex roles in his work. It may also explain why he set such store by a life of action: it was, after all, a way to escape from Mother. He couldn't escape from his own sensitivity, however, or the love of art he inherited from that woman, and which fed its way into his writing. It's this intriguing mix that gave it an extra dimension, so maybe we should be grateful to Grace Hemingway after all. She didn't so much create doubt in the locker-room as doubt in the home. But Hemingway, like his father, carried such doubt everywhere he went. He was never quite as relaxed with his exploits as he led people to believe.

Asked once what was the main reason for his success, he chirped: 'I owe it all to the idle hours I spent in the music room playing 'Pop Goes the Weasel' on my cello.'

In later years, Hemingway would go fishing and shooting not to escape his mother, but his *fans*.

That would be a long time into the future. As for now, he was busy trying to hold on to some semblance of dignity with his mother. And an older sister who, whether she realised it or not, was totally cramping his style.

Writing gave him his first opportunity to exhibit his personality in all its puckishness. In the school magazine for which he wrote prolifically he was short of a feature one week so he invented a Boy's Rifle Club to fill the space. Each week afterwards the paper carried a column about the (non-existent) club. When it came time for the School Yearbook to be printed, Hemingway borrowed a set of shotguns and placed them in the hands of many of his friends, whom he subsequently photographed for inclusion in the photo.

He would always be grateful to his teachers for pointing him in certain directions, but he knew at best that they could do little more than lay texts before him for his perusal, never furnish him with a creative seed. 'What does one learn about writing in high school?' he said once, 'You're lucky if you're not taught to write badly.'

Hemingway was unexceptional in class. Neither did he excel athletically. There was always more clout in American society in being exemplary on the playing field rather than the killing fields, but Hemingway was an indifferent, even clumsy, footballer. He had creative prowess to be sure, but it would be a prescient critic indeed who would see in his juvenilia the birthpangs of a man who would become America's pre-eminent literary stylist; it was far easier to dismiss his scribblings as so many preppie outpourings in the Horatio Alger mould. His writing had a definite pellucid edge even then, but his individualistic stamp had yet to be born. That would only come when experience became the crucible in which his ego fostered. Or, depending on your point of view, festered.

One would imagine his good looks and continuous exposure to girls (from having all those sisters) would have increased his confidence for dating but it didn't work that way. Either he was slow to develop sexually or, which is more likely, he had the bashfulness of many writers. Such bashfulness, incidentally, he would retain to the end of his days, even after negotiating four marriages and numerous affairs.

Even in married life years later Hadley would say that she would often be in the middle of an embrace only to realise that he was reading a newspaper over her shoulder. Hardly what one expects from one of the supposed great lovers of our time...

Marcelline believed that it was *because* he had so many sisters hovering round him in his early years that he was slow to seek out girlfriends.

Contrary to popular belief, Hemingway was anything but the local town stud in Oak Park. He didn't have his first date until he was fifteen, and probably didn't lose his virginity for another five years after that. The fact that Marcelline was both taller and stronger than him for many years, and also brighter academically, couldn't have done much for his confidence. A winner by nature, both Marcelline and his mother seemed to be doing everything in their power to thwart him, which was a bitter pill for him to swallow.

Hemingway liked to tell people that before he met Hadley he had already slept with Agnes von Kurowsky - the nurse he met after being wounded in Italy - as well as Kate Smith and Marjorie Bump, but all three of these women denied his claims. A more likely possibility is that his only sexual experience before Hadley was a one-night stand with a waitress from Horton Bay and an equally brief dalliance with Prudence Bolton, an Indian girl who worked as a cook for the Hemingways. Ernest would later tell his fourth wife Mary that Prudence was 'the first woman he had ever pleasured'. (The verb is probably a euphemism from Mary of a more Anglo-Saxon term beloved of her husband). 'Prudy' also appears in his story 'Fathers and Sons' as the woman who 'did first what no one has ever done better.'

In 1914 he had his first official date with a girl called Dorothy Davies, and afterwards took a shine to Frances Coates, but neither of these developed into relationships. One imagines he was more comfortable in the presence of his male friends. What dances usually meant to him was acting as a chaperone for Marcelline, a terminally boring activity to a young man who missed the smell of the campfire and the feel of the forest underfoot.

Bashfulness with women was only one of the reasons he shied away from dances. Another was the fact that his big feet made him as clumsy on the dance-floor as he was on the football pitch.

Nobody in Oak Park, however, had a more engaging personality than he had. Not only was he devilishly handsome and well-built, he also had charisma and a ready wit, and could converse knowledgeably on sedentary pursuits like literature as well as boxing and baseball.

Most of Hemingway's classmates, if not his own family, had a feeling he would make his mark on life in some shape or form. Even if his talents in some areas were deficient he was willing to give anything a whirl, and his literary juvenilia in the school magazines had enough potency to show that he might one day find his own voice. If he didn't, there were any number of blue collar posts he could take up as he searched for the lifestyle that would define him and release all that dormant energy.

1914 was the year his appearance changed for good, much to his relief. From being a mere five feet four inches in May, he shot up to five-ten by September, finally outgrowing Marcelline for once and for all, and laying that particular ghost.

Something else happened in 1914 too: the First World War. Hemingway followed it with interest, particularly when his own country became part of it.

He flirted with journalism in *The Kansas City Star* from 1917, but the war was a bigger draw by far. It was like the ultimate football game to him and he was determined to get a place on the military team by hook or by crook, even if it meant sitting on the sub's bench, or playing on the B-side. 'I can't let a show like this go on without getting into it,' he told Marcelline, the use of the word 'show' being indicative of the way he perceived it.

On April 6 1917 America declared war on Germany. Two months later Hemingway graduated from school. He disappointed his parents by informing them he had no interest in going to college, but he was too young to be drafted.

A post with the Red Cross eventually proved his gateway to glory. His defective left eye looked set to keep him out of the action (he cursed his mother for the inheritance) but when a colleague from the *Star* who had a glass eye - the result of a golf ball hitting him after rebounding from a tree - managed to sign up as an ambulance driver in France, Hemingway followed suit.

It was ironic that the defective vision in his left eye would effectively deny him military service as seeing things like nobody else could was what would subsequently make him famous. (Vanity precluded him from wearing glasses except when it was absolutely necessary, but he was myopic for most of his life.)

Based in Italy rather than France - he would later say his reasons for this was that he felt there was less chance of getting killed here - he experienced his first rush of adrenalin in the presence of death.

He drove an ambulance for the Red Cross in Schio, a town situated in the foothills of the southern Alps. This was a step in the right direction but he wanted to get closer to where the action was. The frontline was at Fossalta, on the Piave river, and he asked to be moved to that location. It was here on July 8, just a couple of weeks before his nineteenth birthday, as he was cycling towards the troops with some cigarettes and candy, that an enemy mortar knocked him off his bicycle and killed one of the soldiers standing beside him.

Seeing another man writhing in agony, he tried to lift him to safety but was hit by machine gun fire into his left leg. He continued carrying the soldier to the trench and then collapsed.

For back-packing the injured man back to his dug-out, Hemingway was awarded not only awarded the *Croce di Guerra* but also the much more prestigious *Medaglia d'Argento al Valore*. He said later, with typical self-deprecation, that he threw them into the bowl beside his hospital bed 'with all the other scrap metal' i.e. the pieces of shrapnel that were taken from his leg. The aw-shucks style of the comment hardly masked his huge delight.

On his nineteenth birthday, as he lay wounded in hospital in Milan, his mother wrote to him saying it was 'great to be the mother of a hero' and reassuring to know her boy was 'every inch a man'. In years to come he would become more than a man than she would wish for. More, in any case, than his father, who had moulded him in his image only to see him supersede him in almost every department of virility.

Hemingway's experience at Fossalta was dramatically similar to the plane crashes he would be involved in in the fifties in the sense that two accidents followed one another in rapid succession. Nobody has ever been able to explain how he was able to carry a man to the safety of a dug-out after his knee had been shot to pieces, which has caused much sniping among biographers about the deservability of his medals. Agnes Kurowsky, whom he would fall in love with after she nursed him in hospital, said she never heard anything about him carrying a wounded man to safety. Neither did Frederic Henry, his alter ego in *A Farewell to Arms,* carry anyone on his back after his wounding, being too immobilised by the shell to do so.

It's possible he did carry a wounded soldier to safety after being hit himself, but considering his wounds numbered 227, it strains credulity somewhat to imagine he could muster that kind of energy in his condition, no matter how gallant he felt.

The incident, in any case, should never have happened.

The plain fact of the matter is that he shouldn't have been where he was. The last thing a Red Cross Lieutenant handing out chocolates and cigarettes to the troops expected was a shell from a trench mortar bursting above his head. He was a boy in a man's environment, an accidental victim of circumstance.

The reality of the situation was that he was decorated by the Italians because they needed an American hero to ensure US support for them in the war, and in him they found an ideal one because of his high profile.

Apart from dispensing cigarettes and candy, his role was largely cosmetic. The idea was that if the Italian soldiers saw an American uniform it would increase their morale, making them feel reinforcements were on the way.

After the trench mortar narrowly missed him he claimed he was disappointed he hadn't been wounded, a comment that speaks volumes to us about his need for exposure on the world's stage. As he convalesced he removed his Red Cross uniform and replaced it with a military Italian one. Already he was learning to play the role of the *poseur.*

He wrote to his parents shortly after the wounding and said: 'Maybe you didn't appreciate me when I used to reside in the bosom.' The war had made a nobody into a somebody. He added that the experience was 'the next best thing to getting killed and reading your own obituary' - the latter reference an ironic foreboding of what would happen to him thirty-five years later in somewhat different circumstances.

The hospital patient was attended to by no less than eighteen nurses, but only one took his fancy: the aforementioned Agnes von Kurowsky, a flighty damsel who gave a new dimension to the term 'bedside manner'.

Agnes was the daughter of a Polish aristocrat who had emigrated to the United States after his family went bankrupt. Hemingway was impressed with such details.

He was eight days in hospital before he took a turn for the nurse. She specialised in night duty, and night-time was when his demons struck, when he felt himself in need of some old-fashioned mothering. He would look for the same soft care from Hadley Richardson in the not-too-distant future.

He fell head over heels in love with her and believed such love was requited. He felt sure they would continue their romance back on home soil and she gave him no reason to believe any differently.

Hemingway was always taciturn about Agnes, as is evidenced by the fact that he never mentions her in any of the letters he wrote home around this time. (They go into graphic detail about his wound, and many other more inconsequential matters). They're the most affable letters he would ever write to Oak Park, as if he had suddenly come of age and sloughed off not only his adolescent callowness but also any grievances he may have had against Clarence or Grace. Such, alas, wasn't to be the case.

Kurowsky's attitude to Hemingway is dramatically different in her letters and her diaries. The letters were meant to be read by just one man, Hemingway, whereas the diaries were probably designed for more public consumption. To that extent, she was much safer here in her outpourings, writing of her fling with him as little more than a casual dalliance. In the letters, however, we see the kind of passion that would be reprised by Hadley soon afterwards. Why did she trivialise the relationship? A more common phenomenon in cases like this is to dramatise a contact with somebody who subsequently became famous. One wonders why this lady insisted on playing it *down*.

In one of her (fairly frothy) letters to him written at this time she signs herself, 'Yours Till the War Ends'. It's a significant phrase, whether she meant it this way or not. Could it be that Hemingway was merely filling in time for her until something better came along? Perhaps. But if so, she deserved an Oscar for the enthusiasm evident in the letters, which she wrote to him on an almost daily basis - sometimes even sending him two on the one day.

On one occasion she wrote to him, 'No letter from you since Sun. afternoon, so I'll probably expire gaspingly tomorrow if none is forthcoming by noon'. Can this be the same woman who wrote only a few months later, 'Dear Ernie, you are to me a wonderful boy, & when you add on a few years and some dignity and calm, you'll be very much worth while. I only fear all the Chicago femmes will be willing you away from your night nurse.' Here she seems to be damning him with faint praise, letting him down gently under the auspices of making him think the opposite is the case. 'I'm looking to you to do big things, she continues, 'Don't worry & fret over me & get silly ideas in your imaginative brain, but carry on and you'll get farther than you would if you sat down & thought of me all the time.' What she's really saying here is that he probably only imagines he's in love with her, which was quite possibly true. The letter, in any case, was written a full two months before her final one to him, so he shouldn't have been as shocked as he was by the rejection when it came.

There are various possible reasons for the incongruity between the tone of the diaries and letters. She may have been simply flattered by his attentions and indulged him temporarily, not having the courage to tell him directly how she felt about him, or she may actually have had a change of heart between the two forms of communication - though they do overlap chronologically. In one of her letters she says she hopes he doesn't think her a 'hopeless flirt', which may be a Freudian slip. On the other hand she doesn't hide anything from him with regard to the attentions she has received from other men. On the contrary, she appears to flaunt this type of information.

If we wish to be especially generous to Agnes we could say that by rejecting Hemingway she was really protecting him from himself. Though she gave him a ring - which he wore as proudly as his military attire - she basically saw him as a crazy, if affectionate, mixed-up kid. Indeed, this very term of endearment ('Kid') along with 'bambino' and so on, shows she was all too well aware of the age gap between them. Unlike Hadley Richardson, whom he would soon meet and marry, Agnes' seniority to him was more pronounced because she was the type of woman to let her head rule her heart, and also because he matured quite a lot in the relatively short time between meeting Agnes and Hadley.

We may also surmise that he was looking for a mother substitute in these two women, in the absence of having had, in his eyes at least, any actual mother love. In the Dear John letter Agnes wrote to him on March 7 1919, she said, 'I know that I am still very fond of you, but it is more as a mother than as a sweetheart'. Her feelings were obviously fortified by the nurse/patient context in which their relationship blossomed. It's possible she might not have seen him in quite this light if she had met him, say, in a bar, like Martha Gellhorn, or at a nursing function. Lying immobilised on one's back at the age of nineteen wasn't exactly the ideal way to try and seduce a worldly wise woman like Agnes, as he learned to his cost.

Having said that, she was hugely impressed by his natural charm and his zest for life. She rightly saw that he would make his mark on life some day, but wasn't quite sure precisely how.

The fact remains that Agnes wrote him no less than fifty-two letters between September 1918 and March 1919, when she dropped her thunderbolt on him. Many of these are well-nigh indistinguishable from the kind of missives Hadley would soon compose, both in their sense of playfulness and also their gushy tone. Their frequency is also similar. What we must be aware of, however, is that letter-writing was one of Hemingway's favourite hobbies right through his life, as was letter-reading, so it's possible he put pressure on Agnes to be more forthright in this way than she might have wished. This is the only way one can account for the discrepancy between the earnestness of the correspondence and her subsequent disenchantment with everything he stood for. 'You certainly are the champion love-letter writer, old furnace man,' she wrote to him at one point. (Sadly, his own letters to her haven't survived.)

Sometimes she signed off as 'Mrs Kid' and 'Mrs Hemingstein', which is either an example of leading him up the garden path or a case of not knowing her own mind. Either way, Hemingway took it all as seriously as he would the missives he would send to Adriana Ivancich some thirty years hence - the age gap would be much more dramatic here, with Hemingway now the senior party - where he signed himself 'E. Ivancich'.

On another occasion she dubbed him 'The Light of my Existence', and on another occasion still emoted that he was 'about the nicest man I know, or ever will know.' All we can deduce from such details is that Agnes seemed to be just about as mixed up as her would-be suitor when it came to matters of the heart, despite (or possibly because of) her relentless soul-searching.

Hemingway stayed in Italy as he recuperated, watching military developments from the sidelines and limping from battlefield to battlefield like an old general as he wrote incessantly to Agnes, who had by now been transferred to another hospital in Florence.

Eventually he went home, feeling secure in the knowledge that she would follow soon after and they would continue where they left off in Milan. This was either as a result of adolescent naivity or a triumph of optimism over experience.

Back home he was accorded a hero's welcome. The young man with such an obvious lack of direction seemed to have suddenly become focused. Such a focus was a relief not only to him but his parents as well.

Clarence referred to his wound as a 'miraculous deliverance', with a fairly typical nod towards divine intervention. As far as his son was concerned, the divine intervention was almost the explosion itself.

When Hemingway went back to his *alma mater* to tell his former teachers and fellow pupils about his war experiences they lapped them up with ill-concealed relish, gasping audibly when he passed his blood-spattered uniform round for them to examine. A year earlier he would perhaps have been too shy to brag like this, but he had done a lot of growing up in Italy. According to Leicester, he was like 'a scoutmaster coming to talk to a new class of Boy Scouts'. Most of his classmates had graduated and were in jobs by now, making him feel disoriented even in this, his pre-eminent moment of glory.

The war gave him standing, though. Before it he had been a drifter and a layabout in his mother's eyes. In a sense his wounding was little more than an 'industrial accident' which he couldn't have foreseen, but how it happened wasn't as important as *that* it happened. It was his *entrée* into the public world he dreamed about, a piece of publicity he couldn't have orchestrated better. Each piece of shrapnel was like a brownie point he would notch up on the way to becoming

America's best known war hero...and he wasn't even a soldier. But how he loved talking about it.

He would exaggerate the story as the weeks went on to boost his morale. The number of pieces of shrapnel lodged inside him would grow, as would the number of operations necessary to get them out.

In the manner in which he beefed up apocryphal incidents from the war, we were witnessing the beginning of the Hemingway myth - what his spiritual godson Norman Mailer would call 'Advertisements for Himself'.

He kept his uniform on through all the weeks of recuperation, just in case anyone might forget what he had been through. He also gave a speech to a civic group in Petoskey dressed in it, allowing himself to be photographed afterwards. His boots were probably important for him to wear to support his wounded leg, but the rest was sheer spectacle.

The truth of the incident was that he had only been injured from the knees down. He hadn't been hit by 237 pieces of shrapnel. There were twenty pieces of mortar shell inside him, but the idea that he was one of the most severely wounded Americans in the war was a classic piece of mythmaking he would disavow only many years down the road when he had other wounds to boast about.

In fact it's arguable that Hemingway himself is one of those whom Colonel Cantwell inveighs against in *Across the River and Into the Trees:* freeloaders who 'profit quickly from the war they never fought in'.

His fascination with his hero status may also be gleaned from smaller details like the fact that he went fishing in Michigan after he recuperated dressed in his Italian service beret and combat boots.

Just as he wasn't to be a rifle-bearer in World War Two - for a reporter to do so would have breached the Geneva Convention - neither was he here. He was a rolling canteen worker cum ambulance driver who had overstepped the mark. He would deck himself out in a soldier's cape in the months to come, but a soldier he never was.

This is neither to impugn against his bravery or to emphasise it; merely to state a bald fact. What Oak Park didn't know wouldn't bother it, however, and he was more than willing to embellish the facts of the matter - or have others embellish them for him. It was all grist to the mill for a young man who had been rather anonymous in High School, having had trouble even securing his place on the Varsity football team. That made his new-found fame all the sweeter.

He told the *Oak Parker* newspaper that he had received thirty-two .45 calibre bullet wounds, twenty-eight of which were removed without the benefit of an anaesthetic. An inveterate spinner of yarns, he was able to land such statistics on unsuspecting auditors and still keep a straight face: a characteristic that would stand him in good stead in the years to come when the Hemingway legend took off in earnest and he became seduced by the bitch goddess of fame. To his friend Guy Hickok he phrased it in more Cartesian fashion: 'I felt my soul or something coming right out of my body like you'd pull a silk handkerchief out of a pocket by one corner. It flew around and then came back and went in again and I wasn't dead anymore.' This reads like one of the vignettes from *In Our Time* where violence is described almost impishly.

Though Hemingway played the role of the Hard Man after his wounding at Fossalta, the fact remains that he experienced deep psychological traumas from the incident right through his life, having to sleep with a light on for a long time after it happened, and possibly developing a life-long insomnia problem as a result of it as well. He believed that if he fell asleep in the dark he would never wake up. This was a classic example of what we now call shellshock; he writes about it in some detail in the partly autobiographical story, 'A Way You'll Never Be'.

The war guillotined any chance Hemingway's parents had of making him live something approaching a white collar existence. In *A Moveable Feast* he wrote that once you have lived in Paris you're changed forever, but so also did being shelled by an enemy mortar in a dug-out as a Red Cross ambulance driver. The fact that this baptism of fire was followed by a crash course in puppy love from a heartbreaker of a nurse in effect made him do all his growing up in a few months, and gave him a lifelong need for rapidfire gratification of whatever need he felt at a given moment. In contrast to this, a life in 'Saint's Rest' with all the Grace Hall clones must have struck him as something close to purgatorial.

His post-war excitment, however, was followed by a period of inertia. The practical reality was that he had no job, his school friends were already on the way to different careers or university, and his stories weren't being accepted by the magazines he sent them to.

The honeymoon ended soon. When the allure wore off he was like Krebs from 'Soldier's Home', a beached whale who had to invent lies to keep his adrenalin going so he wouldn't slide back into being a nobody again. Nothing was more boring than war heroes who outstayed their welcome. It was like somebody regaling you with the gory details of their gall bladder operation. There was a life to be lived, a direction to take. He had to use the experience rather than let it use him.

Grace, predictably, wanted to know what he was going to do with the rest of his life, and so did he. He wanted to be with Agnes instead of this harridan of a mother breathing down his neck. You could only live so long off a war wound, but what else was there?

Hemingway wasn't long home when he received the rejection letter from his beloved Agnes. It would be the first major blow to that huge ego, and perhaps laid the foundation to a philosophy of love that would be the cornerstone of all his work: If you gave too much of the heart to any woman she would be taken away from you in one way or another and you would die emotionally.

When people speak of his 'war wound' maybe they should be talking of Agnes as much as Fossalta. The two events devastated him equally. They were his twin baptisms into love and death - the two themes that would be synonymous with his writing from here on in.

Agnes said she eventually became tired of his egotistical nature, which makes you wonder why she led him on to the point of him believing he was engaged to her. She later claimed that she only pretended she loved him to get rid of him. If she hadn't given him an undertaking that she would marry him, she claimed, he would have hung round Europe and plagued her.

Hemingway threw up after he received the letter. He said he felt like 'a hermit crab in its borrowed shell'. He felt inconsolable, but the experience made a man of him just as Fossalta di Piave did.

Agnes, in many ways, became the mother he never had. In 'A Very Short Story' he tells us her letter focused on the fact that the dalliance was merely a 'boy and girl affair', but it would be truer to say that it was actually a mother/son one.

Afterwards she became engaged to an Italian artillery officer who was heir to a Neapolitan dukedom. This liaison also came to an abrupt end, however, when the officer's mother decided Agnes wasn't quite worthy of her soon-to-be-titled son. For Hemingway it was poetic justice that she too was jilted. More surprising than the rejection of Agnes, perhaps, were her sudden 'notions' that she could attach herself to nobility this readily. Of course Hemingway had given her immense confidence in herself in the few short months he knew her - in the same way, as he would soon do to Hadley Richardson. (This was part of his charm in those days: the ability to make women feel capable and confident, as if they were the only person in the world when he talked to them. It was only in his flabby middle years and his tragic last ones that such a gift deserted him.)

Hemingway knew full well that Agnes' engagement was more than instrumental in her dismissal of him. Up to now she had been keeping her options open, as if the gauche war hero would 'do' if nothing better turned up. Now she was set up, however, and could speak of their relationship in the most utterly banal terms imaginable. He would never forgive her for this, and never seek out her company again. This was unusual for a man who would be renowned for the manner in which he remained amicably disposed to his ex-girlfriends and even ex-wives, but Agnes had hit him at the pit of his being. It would be four years before he could even write about it. He would do so in the aforementioned 'A Very Short Story' - the *Farewell to Arms* that wasn't. (In the early drafts of this the nurse's name is Ag, but it was subsequently changed to Luz - and the narrative voice goes from the first person to the third.)

Hemingway once told Arnold Samuelson: 'Most writers keep on writing about their childhood until they're forty. They spend their youths concealing their love affairs and their old age revealing them.' Something like this happened between Agnes and Catherine Barkley, between 'A Very Short Story' and *A Farewell to Arms*. Or rather vice versa. He used the hurt to create poetry, but then came back to the original pain to write a different kind of poetry, a more brutal and literal type.

In retrospect, Agnes was probably right about Hemingway's feeling for her being a 'boy-and-girl' thing even if he couldn't see it like that at the time. She owed him more than a curt letter, but she must have realised that he wasn't so much in love with her as with love itself. She was the perfect footnote to his war excitement; she rounded off the equation. 'He knew he himself was nothing,' he would write many years later in *For Whom the Bell Tolls*, '(but) with another person (he) could be everything.' In this sense Agnes was more a symbol than a real woman. She was like another trophy to put on his sideboard and show off to the Oak Park faithful. A testament to his newly-won manhood just like his damaged kneecap.

Kurowsky never saw him again after he left Italy. She had fond memories of him but it didn't go deeper than that. His literary success meant little to her. She was unimpressed by his reputation as a *bon vivant* and neglected to visit him any time she passed through Cuba, having heard stories of his legendary drinking habits and being reluctant to test their veracity at first hand.

'He didn't know what he wanted,' she would say afterwards, 'he hadn't thought out anything clearly.' She liked him immensely, but felt he still had a lot of growing up to do. She also felt he was a loose cannon emotionally, and could go into a psychological decline after the war ended. This was all eminently insightful. The one thing she didn't predict was that he would go on to be the most famous author in the English-speaking world. (Amazingly, Agnes moved to Key West after the war and spent fifteen years living less than a mile from Hemingway, even though the two of them never met in that time. 'Ernest never forgave me for deserting him,' she would say jocularly, but why did the murderer return to the scene of the crime, as it were, unless she was in some way fascinated by the man he became after such a desertion?)

After she rejected him his nervous system went to pieces and he developed a fever as a result. Pain changed to rage however and it wasn't long before he expressed the hope (in a letter to his friend Elsie MacDonald) that when Agnes returned to New York he hoped she would trip on the boat and knock out all her front teeth. Frederic Henry, indeed, went through a similar process after losing Catherine Barkley in *A Farewell to Arms*. Grace under pressure often means *anger* under pressure, as we may glean from the final pages of that novel. Hemingway himself said he 'cauterised' Kurowsky's memory out of himself with a course of booze and other women - which was how he dealt with most problems in life, be they failures in love or anything else.

Literature also became a form of therapy for him. He started to feel his way in the short story form, using the succinct delivery he employed in his journalism for dramatic effect. Some years later, as already mentioned, he would microscope the relationship between himself and Kurowsky in wry but incisive form. Later again, he would romanticise it out of all proportion to become the guts of *A Farewell to Arms*. But that would be many years down the road. For now it was journalism that was providing whatever money he was earning from blackening pages. It wasn't, alas, very much.

Neither of his parents saw writing as a job. Hemingway himself didn't see himself making a living out of it either, which is probably why he entered journalism as a halfway house, or a stopgap. He would later call it whoring, but it paid the rent. Unlike the stories he wrote which kept coming back to him in those early years, summarily dismissed as being mere anecdotes rather than authentic literature.

His mother also displayed tunnel vision in seeing him as a loafer even as he was composing fiction that would shape the thinking of a generation. The irony, as he subsequently stated in a letter to Pauline Pfeiffer's mother which he would write during the composition of *Green Hills of Africa*, was that non-writers saw writers as loafers when they were writing, which was physically draining, and then when their books were published and hopefully lauded, they were championed... just as the point of their lives when they really *did* loaf.

Before he became famous his mother regarded him as a dredge on the community, someone who would probably never convert his writing into a job or career. She saw him frittering away whatever small amounts of money he earned and berated him for 'trading on your handsome face to fool gullible little girls'. She also importuned him to remember his duties to 'God and your Saviour Jesus Christ'.

Grace's frustration with her son's idle ways, as she perceived it, boiled over in 1920 when he was enjoying himself at the family cottage in Windemere with his friend Ted Brumback. She wanted him to do more housework and less loafing, and when he defied her, that was effectively that. She ordered him off the premises like, as he saw it, the hired help. Thus was their relationship severed forever. It was a decision Grace would learn to regret with time, but one the Victorian prude with the work ethic still had to make.

On that occasion she also accused him of corrupting Ursula and Sunny. She wrote him a long-winded didactic letter comparing love to a bank account on which he had overdrawn. His own reading of the situation was that his mother had been emotionally bankrupt all her life so she was hardly in a position to comment either way.

All that happened was some innocent horseplay at a midnight picnic - the kind of feisty excitement that might be expected of any fullblooded All-American youth, but Grace's reaction made it appear as if he had breached some sacred law. His mother's disapproval was hardly surprising, but when his father commented that 'suffering alone will be the means of softening his Iron Heart of selfishness', he had the right to be aggrieved. 'Mother was glad of an excuse to oust me,' he told his friend Grace Quinlan, 'ever since I opposed her throwing two or three thousand seeds away to build a new cottage for herself'. He would have preferred if the money were used to send some of his siblings to college - an unusual attitude for one who would later frown on anything to do with formal education. 'Mother' told him she would only welcome him back into the family fold when he had learned not to curse and swear at her 'whether it be in this world or the next'. She wasn't to know it then, but it wouldn't be in this one...

She banished him from the cottage he loved so much, the location where he had composed so many of his early stories, and where he went to escape from the stuffiness of Oak Park. He had spent every summer of his life here thus far. Now that was all going to change forever.

His days 'up in Michigan' were drawing to a close. Illinois was about to be replaced with Italy, and Petoskey by Paris, a city where loafing had a licence and the sedate life of the writer a guaranteed prestige.

Leicester said he was never sure just how deeply the expulsion affected his brother. 'The injured war hero was jilted by the woman he loved,' he told author Denis Brian, 'and then kicked out of his home practically on his twenty-first birthday. He was an over-sensitive man. How long do you think this stayed with him? Maybe ten minutes, maybe years. I think he held pieces of it in his heart until the day he died, but I don't know how big the pieces were.'

For the rest of his life, he would return to Oak Park only five more times, one of which would be to his father's funeral. He would be as much of an exile as Ireland's James Joyce, and would carry an equal amount of bitterness as Joyce into his life and work.

Oak Park gave him an axe to grind. He saw it as a place where the principles of the inhabitants were as sturdy as oaks themselves. Graham Greene once said that an unhappy childhood was the best possible breeding-ground for a writer. Hemingway didn't have an unhappy childhood as such, surrounded as he was by sisters who doted on him and a father he revered, but if he had grown up in some urban sprawl, one feels his desire to rebel would have been somewhat lessened. The fact that Oak Park wore its decency on its sleeve gave him a structure to tear down, particularly since he saw a microcosm of that structure in his own mother, who spoke often of love, but seemed only capable of it on her own terms, or when the objects of such love were in some way beholden to her.

By driving him away from home, Hemingway's mother probably made him a better writer than he would otherwise have been. Everything he achieved after that became intensified by the knowledge that he was creeping out from under her shadow - and, in a vicarious way, punishing her by letting her know that if she and her kind didn't appreciate him, the greater world outdoors would.

Nelson Algren put it well when he said Hemingway would have been an expatriate even if he had never left Oak Park. 'His exile,' Algren contended, 'wasn't from a land, but from the living. His need was not for a country, but for the company of men.' And, of course, women. (How could Mr Algren forget that?)

'There was no place on earth he wasn't at home,' wrote E.L. Doctorow, 'except perhaps his birthplace. His parents' Middle Western provincialism made independence an easy passage for him.'

He didn't want the white picket fence, the family dog and the 2.2 children in leafy suburbia. Not for him the girl-next-door. Or even the girl-next-state.

The rainbow's end, to be sure, seemed to be waiting just round the bend for the young man who was determined to have 'the good times now'.

The Toronto Star beckoned, as did Paris, the place he would make into the first of his many adoptive homelands, and also where the young Illinois tyro would finetune the writing talent that would revolutionise the face of literature for a generation, divorcing it forever from its rarefied niceties.

A young man who made it his avowed ambition to cock a snook at convention, he was always going to be more Jesse James than his namesake Henry.

A Terribly Fine Article

Hemingway was hardly over the heartbreak of Agnes when he met Hadley Richardson, the woman who was to become his first wife, and the one he loved more than any other to his dying day if we're to believe his letters and memoirs. Hadley was a St. Louis girl, which almost seemed to be a prerequisite for being one of his wives. She met him while visiting her old school friend Kate Smith to recover from the trauma of having nursed her mother through a terminal illness. Kate, who would later marry Hemingway's friend John Dos Passos, was a free spirit who lived in a hotel room and hung around in the company of writers. Hadley, who had lived a sheltered life up to this, was looking forward to coming out of her shell with her.

After her traumatic experience at their mother's terminal bedside she was ready for someone to, as she put it 'hit my soul's centre'. She would certainly find that man, and hit his soul's centre as well.

The attraction of Hadley to Ernest wasn't too difficult to understand. He was handsome, he had vitality, he was full of mirth and yarns. Intelligent as well as charismatic, and as good a listener as he was a talker, he was one of the most eligible bachelors about.

He was also much more confident than he had been when lying on his back in a hospital bed in Italy, needless to say. The man Agnes met, while full of potential, hadn't realised any of it as yet.

Hemingway was already something of a poseur when he met Hadley, but in an engaging manner. She was attracted to his mind, his body and his charismatic personality. In her, meanwhile, he saw class, culture and refinement. (It also helped that she hung upon his every word).

She was like a breath of fresh air to him, a timely antidote to everything that had gone before. The only thing she shared in common with the other major female influence on Hemingway's life thus far (i.e. his mother) was her love for the piano. He described her as 'a sort of terribly fine article'.

He was still wearing his Italian officer's cape on the night she met him, but she sensed he was a shy soul behind it all. Her main worry about him was that he was seven years younger than her. This was to be a cause of some concern to him as well, especially if others commented on it, but he imagined their love could over-ride it. Nevertheless, he sometimes added a few years onto his own age to make the gap less noticeable.

Hadley deflected the age issue by telling Hemingway (sincerely) that she felt he knew more about life than she did, despite his tender years, and that she would enjoy learning from him. On the other hand, he had suffered so much at the hands of his mother it's possible that one of the things that attracted him to her was the fact that he saw her as a mother substitute who could undo the damage Grace did to his ego.

If he was older than his years, she was younger than hers because she hadn't really started to live yet, having all that repressed energy harnessed inside her waiting to explode. That made the chronological difference between them effectively unproblematic. At least so far.

When they got to know one another better, they discovered that they had more than a little in common. Hadley's mother, like Hemingway's had had six children. She was also a bully, if not a bitch, and she had had a promising musical career cut short by marriage. Her father had shot himself when he couldn't cope with her browbeating (or his failing finances) any more. This would also be the fate of Clarence Hemingway in a few short years.

In addition to financial problems (he had lost most of his money as a result of unwise investments in the stock market) Hadley's father also suffered from alcoholism, insomnia and migraine. As would be the case with Hemingway's father, he felt that his suicide would ensure his family's financial security because they could now cash in on his life insurance. Listening to all this, Hemingway must have felt he was hearing about a Clarence clone, right down to the domination by his inconsiderate wife.

Hadley would probably have had a deep relationship with her father if he had lived longer because they were alike in temperament. Both of them were witty and slightly eccentric, in contrast to the severity epitomised by her mother and sister Fonnie, who seemed to gang up on her after her father's suicide. (Hadley's family gynaecologist, amazingly enough, was the father of Martha Gellhorn, who would also marry Hemingway in time. And her mother had died of Bright's disease, like his own grandfather.)

Both of their mothers also had suffragette leanings, which no doubt increased the tendency to be assertive with their husbands. Not that there was anything wrong with that, but considering the husbands in question were meek in temperament anyway, this in effect became tantamount to bullying.

Hemingway also sympathised with Hadley's traumatic youth. When she was a young girl she fell out of a window and was wheelchair-bound for a year after the accident. Three of her family also died, two in infancy and one in a fire, and Hadley herself had suffered many emotional problems. Her mother had always treated her like a cripple since her accident, and her beloved sister Dorothy had died in a fire when she was young, which compounded her distress. She also had a failed romance with her piano teacher (conducted mostly in her imagination) and had experienced much pain when a rumour flew around St. Louis that she had lesbian leanings.

Hemingway had much to identify with in all of this turbulence. He had felt he was an emotional cripple after Agnes, as had Hadley after the death of Dorothy, and then her mother. They were both coming to the relationship - like so many of his fictional creations - from a position of being wounded.

Hemingway only saw Hadley seven times in the nine months of their courtship that was to follow but they communicated heatedly through letters. In these nine months they would write each other over a thousand pages of correspondence. (Such epistolary zeal would also be a feature of his early relationship with his second wife, Pauline Pfeiffer). He liked to have a letter from Hadley each day - sometimes even more than one - so she threw herself passionately into the composition of same. We must remember that this was in the days before airline travel (or even long distance telephone calls) were commonplace. And what better way could a writer communicate with his inamorata than through words?

'Oh Mr Hemingway I love you,' Hadley wrote in one of her more breathy missives, sounding resoundingly like Charlotte Bronte's *Jane Eyre*, 'How exciting you are. What a lot of things happen round you...I love the way you love me.' It was undercut by a prescient insight, however, when she said, 'Maybe your work calls for another, harder wreckage, but you're not going to get it from me.' She might have been referring to Agnes here.

In the following months Hemingway gave Hadley a life that was light years away from what she had experienced in St. Louis, where she did little but read and play the piano. She also adorned his own one.

In an unpublished story from this time he wrote, 'Those days to me were wonderful, for I was awakening from a sleep which I thought was everlasting.' This almost sounds like something Hadley might have said rather than he. (The common perception of the Hemingway of 1920 was anything but a dreamer.)

She mellowed him at a time of his life when he was an Angry Young Man with a certain amount of 'attitude', and many resentments about his past as well as frustration about the way his writing was going. She was 'the chink in his armour of telling the world to go to hell.'

Like Cathy and Heathcliff they spoke of being not only similar, but parts of the one person. Such identification patterns would find their way into much of Hemingway's fiction in the future, all the way from *A Farewell to Arms* to *For Whom the Bell Tolls*. Those two novels would also have submissive heroines partly modelled on

Hadley. The last thing he wanted was a woman like his mother. The other main woman in his life to date, i.e. Agnes, had also called the shots. Hadley was different. 'What you want,' she would say, 'I want.' She was the ideal woman for him in so many ways: attractive, refined, graceful, intelligent and sensitive. Almost single-handedly, she renewed his faith in women. She was, as he said, 'the best and truest and loveliest person that I have ever known'.

She was a late bloomer, which made such blooming all the sweeter. Her handsome authorial suitor, despite his apparent lack of prospects for such a refined young lady, was to be the catalyst for such a transfiguration.

Hadley always had an admirable *joie de vivre*. Hemingway evinced the same thirst for living in all his gung-ho pursuits, even as far back as the midnight picnic incident with his sisters which resulted in the decline of his relationship with his mother. Both of them were people who wanted to attack life, but who, for one reason or another, had been prevented from doing so until they met up. Now they could do it together.

When Hemingway brought Hadley to meet his parents they were predictably relieved and excited. The potential ne'er-do-well had finally come up trumps, settling for a 'nice girl' from St. Louis. Not only that, but she even played the piano.

Hadley's basic nature was to treat everyone cordially, regardless of past misdeeds, but it would have been a brave woman who tried to form a harmonious relationship both with Ernest Hemingway and the woman he most despised on the planet.

Grace fawned over Hadley but Hadley found it difficult to warm to her after Ernest's stories of suffering at her hands. They remained courteously distant from one another.

On September 3 1921, Ernest and Hadley were married in a Methodist church in Horton Bay. The ceremony passed off without much note, except for Hemingway being unable to kneel properly in church due to his trick knee. As they left the church he inadvertently stepped on one of Hadley's white slippers which she felt to be a bad omen though she said nothing about it at the time.

They honeymooned in Windemere Cottage, which Grace and Clarence had built in 1904 and where Ernest had spent every summer since then, except for 1918 when he was busy getting wounded in Fossalta di Piave.

Hadley later described the honeymoon as a flop. Both of them were sick, the weather was overcast, and anyone they met seemed to focus on her seniority to her new husband, making her feel like 'an old hag of thirty'. Hemingway spent a lot of his time introducing her to some of his former girlfriends (like Grace Quinlan and Marjorie Bump) as if to let her know what she had to live up to. He thought she would be impressed by seeing women he threw over to marry her but she regarded the whole experience as a childish exercise in vanity.

Afterwards they moved to a Chicago apartment. For both of them it was like the beginning of a new period of stability in their lives. They were both thin-skinned individuals who had been victims of a misunderstanding world, but now they planned an 'onslaught of love' on that world. Their main problem, as Hemingway saw it, would probably be financial. He wanted to chuck in journalism and try to live off his creative writing, but that was hardly feasible considering he had little or no published work behind him. Hadley, however, had a Trust Fund worth $3,000 a year which helped enormously, and a month after they got married an uncle of hers died leaving her a further $8,000. This was like manna from heaven for both of them.

Hemingway's reliance on Hadley to be the early breadwinner was like a direct replay of his parents' marriage, where Grace's earnings from singing exceeded those of her physician husband. The difference was that Clarence Hemingway allowed this powerplay to be a feature in all the years they spent together. His son wouldn't make the same mistake.

Hadley occupied the traditional role of mother and wife in a way that neither of his subsequent spouses would. She provided an ideal working environment for him in the sense that she continually subjugated her wishes to his. She was also the inspiration behind his major fictional heroines, all the way from Lady Brett to Catherine Barkley to the Maria of *For Whom the Bell Tolls* - even if hers wasn't the only influence behind them.

She advanced his 'artoostic kareer', as she dubbed it (the pair of them played with words all their lives), no end. She also made it possible for him to entertain his dream of living on the continent, where he felt he would find the ideal millieu for his burgeoning literary talent to flower. Not long after they were married he started saving whatever money he earned from his journalism and converting it into foreign currency so he could make what he called 'the bold dash' to Paris - the place where, as Gertrude Stein so succinctly put it, 'the twentieth century was'.

He probably didn't know it then, but he was about to define that century just as much as it would define him.

The American in Paris

Imagine if we had been born at a time when we could
never have had Paris when we were young.
Ernest Hemingway

It had to be only a matter of time before America produced a major talent who came to writing, if not from left field, or a football field, from *Field and Stream*. Hemingway's first priority in life was to learn to hunt and shoot well, with some literary dabbling on the side in high school magazines. After the war he prided himself on being a fighter rather than a writer, and he would always try to be both to some extent, but after he went to Paris and met up with those at the cutting edge of the *avant-garde* he thought he could embody both worlds equally effectively.

Unhappiness with his environment led him to seek out adoptive parents in people like Ezra Pound and Gertrude Stein, and adoptive homelands everywhere from Italy to Spain to France to Africa to Key West - the latter of which he dubbed 'the St. Tropez of the poor'. He would go wherever his wanderlust led him - and whenever he met somebody like James Joyce, another disturbed soul who had to travel from his birthplace to do justice to his art, he would identify and empathise.

In Paris, Henry James wrote, the very air was suffused with style. Hemingway would have agreed. Almost from the moment he arrived in it, armed as he was with letters of introduction from Sherwood Anderson to Gertrude Stein, Sylvia Beach and Ezra Pound, he was seduced by its radical milieu. He told Anderson he was going to launch these letters 'like a flock of ships' - and he did. At every harbour he could find.

'You know I was born to enjoy life,' he wrote to his parents in 1918, 'but the Lord neglected to have me born with money - so I've got to make it, and the sooner the better'.

He wasn't getting anywhere with his writing in 1922, which was why he was more than delighted to have Anderson's letters of introduction. He was clued in to the writing scene enough to know that who you knew was at least as important an ingredient in literary success as how well you wrote. On the other hand, he was shy to approach the people Anderson had referred him to - particularly Stein and Pound, both of whom had reputations for being eccentric. Pound would be a useful contact though, despite this, because he had already established himself as a friend to struggling writers as well as being an intelligent editor of their writings. T.S. Eliot called him *Il Miglior Fabbro* after his herculean work on *The Waste Land*. Hemingway didn't have too much respect for that abstruse poem, but he knew that Pound was probably his best shot at getting known to the right people, and having his work evaluated fairly and sympathetically.

The Paris of 1922 was awash with literary hopefuls and rich dilettantes. Between 1920 and 1927 it was estimated that as many as 35,000 Americans emigrated there, seduced by its bohemian air and the ubiquitous sense of freedom. It was also relatively cheap to have a good time there, the dollar being worth fifteen francs in 1920. Apart from the fact that the cheapness of the franc in comparison to the dollar made it attractive to an indigent scribe there were also the cafes and the fruit markets and the restaurants and the wine - not to mention the entertaining chatter of *boulevardiers*.

It had also been a port of call to Hemingway's maternal and paternal grandfathers in the latter quarter of the nineteenth century - and Hemingway himself had passed through the city on his way to the war in 1918. 'If you are lucky enough to have lived in Paris as a young man,' he wrote, 'then wherever you go for the rest of your life, it stays with you, for Paris is a moveable feast.' He referred to it as his mistress. Not only was it the epicentre of bohemianism; it was also a melting-pot where the budding literary talents of the time could come to compare notes, philosophise about their books, backbite one another...and drink.

He saw it as a state of mind as much a a place. A conduit for the countercultural expatriates of the time, it provided the young Hemingway both with an endorsement of what he had already done and the promise of better things to come under the tutelage of his literary heroes. 'Paris was always Paris,' he wrote cryptically, 'and you changed as it changed'.

Though hardly a veteran of war, Hemingway was fêted as such in this hotbed of creative fervour. On the surface he denigrated his contribution to the war effort, but he was chuffed by the attention it brought, and was more than willing to milk it for whatever capital it might store up for him among his peers. He may not have seen combat as such, but he had stood up to a challenge and not been found wanting. They also served who only stood and delivered candy and cigarettes.

Paris was also the nerve centre of chic. What the likes of Sartre and Camus were attempting in a philosophical realm, Stein and Pound practised in their fiction and poetry. 'In each shape and gesture and avenue and cranny of her being,' e.e. cummings wrote, the city was 'continually expressing the humanness of humanity.'

Nobody doubts that Hemingway had a fine time in Paris, and he also met an inordinate amount of fascinating people there, but perhaps he over-romanticised it because of the contrast it posed to where he had come from. Stanley Kauffmann has described this syndrome as 'reverse provincialism' - an exaggeration, no doubt, but nonetheless a point worth taking on board when we succumb to the temptation of romanticising this phase of his life out of all proportion.

It wasn't all plain sailing for the fresh-faced author beavering away in the carpenter's loft he rented with Hadley. In years to come he would tell his friend A.E. Hotchner some of the traumas he experienced at this time when rejected manuscripts would come through the slot in the door of the bare rooms where he lived over the sawmill. 'The rejection slip is very hard to take on an empty stomach he told

Hotchner, 'and there were times when I'd sit at that old wooden table and read one of those cold slips that had been attached to a story I had loved and worked on very hard and believed in, and I couldn't stop crying.'

Hadley kept his spirits up, as did his belief that one day the world would sit up and take notice of his crude, harsh style. In the meantime he would write journalism on and off for *The Toronto Star* as its foreign correspondent and, in between assignments, sample the good life of Paris in whatever manner his limited budget allowed.

For that newspaper he covered everything from troutfishing in Europe to the effects of inflation on the German mark. He brought a whimsical style to topics that might not have lent themselves to an offbeat approach heretofore. In his laconic asides and generally puckish approach readers were witnessing the emergence of a man who even then was bigger than what he wrote about, and doing whatever he could to turn it into his own personality. His interview with Benito Mussolini at a time when that demagogue was being exalted by so many showed that Hemingway's inbuilt crap detector was functioning even this early. 'There is something wrong.' he wrote, 'even histrionically, with a man who wears white spats with a black shirt'. Tailors may not make men, as Shakespeare knew, but Mussolini's naff dress sense seemed to hint at a more insidious buffoonery for the young Hemingway. And how posterity proved that intuition to be true.

At this point of his life he was a *tabula rasa* upon whom life would write its instructions. He wasn't just a sponge that would soak up every *experience* that life would present to him, but also every literary influence. In his High School days he was known as Ring Lardner Junior, but a few years afterwards it was difficult not to hear the voice of Sherwood Anderson speaking through his lines. And then came Gertrude Stein, who gave an edge of eccentricity to his mock-illilerate ramblings and stark vignettes. Hemingway would subsequently disavow any debts he owed to the above, perhaps too stridently, as if the accusations hit a nerve.

He met Stein in March 1922 armed with Anderson's letter. (Anderson himself had received a letter of introduction to her from Sylvia Beach some years earlier). She was more impressed by his personality than his writings, but they formed an unlikely friendship. After a time she visited him in his dingy flat above the sawmill. Neither was she impressed by this. She lectured him on writing while Hadley was paired off with her live-in love Alice B Toklas. When he showed her his work she told him he needed more discipline - which was rather ironic considering he was perhaps the most fastidious American writer of his time, and she herself a veritable model of indiscipline.

He sat at her feet listening to her declaiming about art and life. He was getting a hands-on, rollercoaster ride through literature from the ground up - and loving every minute of it. It was like going ten rounds with Gene Tunney and holding your own. He was still only a *parvenu,* but being treated like an old friend. Oak Park was never as welcoming as this.

He visited her house at 27, Rue de Fleurus on a habitual basis once he got to know her, almost foaming at the mouth for advice about the *metier* and his own efforts to master it. Stein, he said, looked like an Indian but spoke like an angel.

From her he learned the art of 'conscious omission', the thinking being that 'the omitted part would strengthen the story and make people feel more than they understood.' If journalism had taught him that a spade was a spade was a spade, the dadaists preached something else entirely. Having been apprenticed in a hard school where no excess literary baggage was countenanced, he could now spread his wings and experiment.

Hemingway didn't only get his penchant for repetition from Stein, but also his quirky phraseology and wilful awkwardness. Journalism honed his literary skills into a compressed format, but Stein forced him to unlearn the stern dictates of newspaper reportage.

Though she liked to say 'a rose is a rose is a rose', her own lapidary style - and Hemingway's too, in gestation - told her readers it was anything but that.

The fact that Stein became his adoptive mother wasn't without its ironies, for Hemingway had often referred to his real mother as 'Mrs Stein' (in the same way as he liked to dub himself 'Ernest Hemingstein'). Both also had similar personalities, liking to dominate conversations and enwreath auditors in their respective webs. The fact that one was talking music and the other literature was beside the point. Even though Ernest hung on Stein's every word in his early days in Paris, it's probable that if he had been her actual son he would have tired of her self-indulgent rantings much sooner than he did. Stein's attachment to Alice B. Toklas could also be compared to the relationship between Hemingway's mother and her close Oak Park friend Ruth Arnold - with no prizes for guessing which women occupied the power position over their partners.

Stein fulfilled the role of surrogate mother in the same way as acolytes like Ingrid Bergman and Ava Gardner would become surrogate *daughters* to Hemingway in years to come. Neither of his wives would bless him with a real daughter, and, in his own mind, he never had a 'birth' mother worth talking about.

Toklas took to Hadley but not Ernest. For her he was 'an opportunist concerned only with creating and nurturing his own legend' - an interesting insight, but one that perhaps applied as much to Stein as Hemingstein.

He also met James Joyce at this time. He had read *Dubliners,* like most young turks who were sculpting syllables for a living, and became entranced by its poetic rhythms and the ominous air of tension that hung between the lines. He was surprised at Joyce's wry sense of humour - as Joyce must have been at his. The pair of them didn't socialise often in the years to come, but Joyce was one of the few writers he didn't fall out with in his life - perhaps for that reason.

Meeting Ezra Pound was another watershed in his life. Like

Joyce, Pound was an eccentric who was more concerned with 'getting it right' on the page than selling out his vision for the reader's shilling, and this appealed to Hemingway, who would probably have liked to be more like this himself. He even took to Pound's irascibility, preferring it to the hypocritical stances of the superficially sweet.

He was two months in Paris before he approached Pound. When he did, he found he was more interested in talking about politics than writing. Pound sounded off about the ills of society in typically acerbic fashion and Hemingway was more bemused than impressed.

Pound, like the older Hemingway, had a crusty, outspoken demeanour, but he was as soft as putty inside. He built up a genuine, no-holds-barred affection for Hemingway which was reciprocated in kind. The pair of them spent much of their time boxing together. Pound was no expert in this field but enjoyed it for the hell of it. Hemingway appreciated such laidback abandon.

He also liked Pound's iconoclasm and his choice expletives. And he learned something from his imagistic style of writing, which wasn't altogether antithetical to Stein's or Joyce's. They were all pioneers in their way, and Hemingway knew he needed some colour to flesh out his own blunt style.

He taught Pound to box, throwing himself into the challenge with the same enthusiasm he brought to his writing. In time to come he would speak - metaphorically - about 'going a few rounds' with the likes of Turgenev and Chekhov. It was all grist to the mill. The perfect fight was like the perfect story or novel. There were winners and losers outside the ring as well as inside it. What mattered was perfecting your trade and outlasting the opposition. If war and boxing were both blood sports, so was the activity of putting words on paper for a living.

At this time he also struck up a camaraderie with Ford Madox Ford, the expatriate British author he would subsequently satirise in *A Moveable Feast*. Ford was editor of *The Transatlantic Review*, which would be the outlet for much of Hemingway's fiction (as it would be for Gertrude Stein's) in the years to come.

'I did not read more than six words of his,' Ford later stated, 'before I decided to publish anything he sent me.' This was heartening stuff for a writer who had experienced as much rejection as any struggling scribe in their callow years.

'One of his pages,' Ford commented, 'has the effect of a brook bottom into which you look down through the flowing water. The words from a tessellation, each in order beside the other.'

A generation of critics would say much the same thing in a variety of different ways in the years to come, but for now Ernest Hemingway was just one of many young hopefuls who was having a limited degree of success in self-important, self-serving magazines largely ignored by the reading public.

No more than Joyce with Dublin, he seemed to be able to see Michigan more clearly when he was out of it. 'Never write about a place until you're away from it,' he would tell his Cuban fishing friend Arnold Samuelson, 'because that gives you perspective. Immediately after you've seen something, you can give a photographic description of it and make it accurate. That's good practice, but it isn't creative writing.' What he was really saying here was that there was a point where the novelist took over from the journalist. He went into that grey area, that twilight zone where reportage became alchemised into the stuff of art.

Hadley continued to tell him his work was marvellous but a lot of it went over her head. She appreciated its veracity, but not its hardbitten edge. She liked her reading to be more lamp than mirror, and maybe her husband's stories cut just that little bit too close to the bone for comfort. Which wasn't to say that she didn't appreciate him. She loved his writing because it was he, her darling Ernest, who was doing it rather than anything endemic in the writing itself. Her natural preference was for tame scribes like Henry James. (Hemingway would agree with William Faulkner that James was 'the grand old lady of American letters'. He was insulted to be mentioned in the same breath as him).

Hadley praised the 'clean muscular freshness' of his style, and his refusal to deal in the fancy effects so prevalent in young writers anxious to make an impression too fast, but her attitude to his writing was always tinged with her own psychological orientations. She would forgive mushiness more than any future Hemingway wife, would forgive even *Across the River and Into the Trees* because of her sympathy for its vulnerable anti-hero. Ethics over-rode aesthetics in her book.

With her by his side, in any case, Hemingway felt the world was his oyster. He wrote, boxed, played tennis and talked literature with his peers, and she stayed on the sidelines like the dutiful wife she was.

Living in Paris with the woman he loved and soaking up the milieu of erudite expatriates with a common interest in writing literature that would push back the boundaries was the stuff of which fairytales were made, and these were indeed fairytale years for a young man who had been rescued from a life of provincial mediocrity first by a war wound and now by a literary career that was set to blossom like that of no American before or since.

From another point of view he must have felt some guilt at having, as some would subsequently see it, married for money as much as love, if not moreso. He would say in *A Moveable Feast* that he was 'very poor and very happy' with Hadley, but there were a lot of writers starving in Parisian garrets as Hemingway and Co. swilled wine in Left Bank cafes. According to the legend he fought with seasoned boxers for ten francs a round and on another occasion smuggled a pigeon out of a public park under a baby's blanket so he could bring it home to cook, but these stories are possibly apocryphal. Hemingway at one time chortled at the idea of James Joyce moaning about poverty and then dining out with 'the whole celtic crew' in fashionable restaurants, but in reality he too seemed to be able to find the wherewithal to dine (and live) lavishly when he wanted to - even if both he and Hadley dressed scruffily by Parisian standards.

It was, to be sure, an upside-down life. Hadley's trust fund paid for the necessities, i.e. gambling, fishing, wine and ski-ing holidays in Austria, whereas Hemingway's meagre proceeds from writing took care of the luxuries - like food and clothing.

Being 'very poor' in effect meant having their own cook, dining out with famous writers, nipping over to Spain for bullfights when the desire arose, and going to the races locally.

The truth of the matter is that they were both rich *and* poor in these years. As Hemingway explained in a letter to his friend Bill Horne, 'Sometimes we'd have to wait a month from the time I'd send in my expense account to *The Star*, and we'd live on ten francs a day, then be rich as hell when the five or six hundred seed would come.'

Apart from being denied creature comforts for much of the time (even if he overstated their poverty in *A Moveable Feast*) they both experienced many bouts of loneliness: Hemingway as he sat in cafes poring over blank sheets of paper and Hadley as she waited in the empty rooms of a draughty loft for her husband to come home from foreign conferences, or gyms.

She didn't exactly relish their lifestyle but she put up with it for his sake. If her man was happy, she was happy. He was giving her life and vivacity and she was willing to put up with the occasional sacrifice. For Hemingway, who had watched his mother's monetary extravagance cripple his father, it was a felicitous reversal of his own domestic history.

In fact the raiment of the struggling Montmartre writer sat well with the image of himself Hemingway liked to peddle to posterity, if not his Parisian contemporaries. Chucking in 'the day job' definitely meant he had to cut his cloth, but the permanence of Hadley's fund meant he wasn't leaping without a safety net. He felt he had far too many important things to be doing with his life than to have to spend his time worrying about filthy lucre, but another part of him felt that Hadley's 'easy' money prevented him from communicating properly with his muse in the way that some of his poverty-stricken forbears had done. He was grateful to her for allowing him to hone his craft without having to worry about starving when his work was rejected, but in December 1922 an incident took place which almost put him 'out of business' (to use one of his own favourite expressions) for good.

Hadley was travelling from Paris to meet him in Lausanne for a ski-ing holiday and took all of his writings with her so that he could work on them. She stuffed everything into a valise, carbons and all, and once aboard the train, left her compartment to buy some Vittel water. When she came back, to her horror, all the manuscripts were gone.

She had left the suitcase unattended only for a few moments in the Gare de Lyon, but it was long enough for some thief - who probably threw it away afterwards when he saw it contained 'only' papers - to help himself to it.

He claimed she lost a total of eleven stories as well as an unfinished Nick Adams novel, but it's likely that the themes which he explored in these writings eventually surfaced in some form in his later work. If the stories that survived - 'My Old Man', 'Up in Michigan' - are anything to go by, he was at the height of his literary powers at this time, so the blow must have been doubly hard to take. Some critics have suggested that she lost them deliberately, feeling depressed about the fact that he had started to concentrate more on his writing than on her and fearful that he would drift away from her emotionally if more fame came his way. This is a patently ludicrous theory.

When she met Hemingway at Lausanne she was so upset she couldn't speak, which caused his imagination to work overtime as to what could be so terrible. Perhaps she had had an affair with a black man, he mused, in a rare example of racism on his part. When she eventually told him what had happened he forgave her, expressing only mild surprise that she had packed the carbons as well as the originals. Inside himself, however, he seethed. He immediately returned to Paris to see if anything was left behind; sadly it wasn't. To make her feel better he told her it would be good discipline for him to start his work afresh, but he knew it had been irresponsible of her. Leaving his manuscripts unattended was bad enough, but having packed the carbons as well added insult to injury. Nevertheless, to suggest she lost them deliberately to make her husband more dependent on her displays a total misunderstanding of her character.

Shortly afterwards he wrote to Ezra Pound to tell him all that remained of his writings were 'three pencil drafts of a bum poem' - which was later scrapped.

'Up in Michigan', the story Gertrude Stein described as being *inachrocable* (i.e. unhangable, like a painting) was saved because it was on the way back to him in the post when Hadley left the flat, having been rejected (thankfully!) by yet another editor. 'My Old Man' was also in the hands of an editor, as was 'Out of Season'. Apart from these, all the stories he had slaved over were gone; he was finished before he properly got started. And all because of a casual oversight on the part of his wife.

Clearly, Hadley's priorities were markedly different to his own. It would be two more marriages down the road before he would find a woman who regarded literature as being as important as life. (Martha Gellhorn, to his amusement, would compare *For Whom the Bell Tolls* to a child - in their biologically childless marriage).

There was method in her madness, however. She knew that Ernest was going to edit and therefore needed to work on the originals and carbons simultaneously in this respect. He couldn't see the logic of this. To him her decision smacked of putting all his eggs in the one basket. And now that basket was gone. Probably forever.

The fact that Hadley lost his prized writings could well have caused any friction there was between them before this to boil over into naked aggression. Some commentators and biographers have argued this, but Hemingway himself told A.E. Hotchner; 'Poor Hadley was so broken up about it I actually felt worse for her than for having been robbed of everything I ever wrote. I never really blamed her. She had not been hired as a manuscript custodian, and what she had been hired for - wifeing - she was damn good at.'

He said to Arnold Samuelson that she had actually done him a favour by losing the valise because it meant the critics would never know what he wrote first and therefore couldn't trace his development. 'It's none of their business that you have to learn to write,' he told Samuelson, 'Let them think you were born that way.'

Hemingway never wrote about the situation directly, but in *The Garden of Eden* Catherine Bourne burns her husband's writings in a gasoline drum. He describes the loss as being 'like coming around a curve on a mountain road and the road not being there and only a gulf ahead.'

Whatever way we look at it, the incident was a watershed in their relationship. It paved the way for Pauline - a woman who would never have brought the carbons as well as the originals. And who wouldn't have left them unattended in a train carriage as she went for a glass of water.

Another event that caused friction between them at this time was Hadley's pregnancy. Having lost the literary offspring he craved, in January 1923 she told him she was expecting a baby, which news caused him not a little concern. In a panic he ran to Gertrude Stein, telling her he was 'too young to be a father'. Ezra Pound, who had a pronounced bias against children, told him the baby would change his life irrevocably and Hemingway was inclined to agree with this dour prognosis. (After Pound's mistress had a daughter some time before this pronouncement, the pair of them gave her to a peasant woman to raise as her own.)

Hadley played tennis and other vigorous sports during her pregnancy, which wasn't advised by the doctors. Hemingway himself, who wouldn't have been too perturbed if she miscarried, certainly wasn't going to be the one to deter her from such pursuits.

He was busier than ever with his writing at this time, and finally starting to get some of his 'stuff', as he called it, between covers.

Editor Robert McAlmon brought out his first book *Three Stories and Ten Poems* in August. It only had fifty-eight pages and no more than 300 copies were printed, but already the Hemingway stamp was there, albeit writ small. Edmund Wilson, who would become a confidante in time, and one of the few critics he respected, was lavish in his praise for it, giving the struggling author a much-needed fillip.

Printing privately was in vogue in Paris in the twenties and Hemingway was glad to be a part of that scene. Not because he was a conformist (the words 'private' and 'Hemingway' should always have a respectful distance from one another) but because it was a shortcut to the readers he knew in his bones he would one day find.

The three stories in *Three Stories and Ten Poems* were 'Up in Michigan', the most sexually daring vignette of his early career, 'My Old Man' (his alleged debt to Sherwood Anderson) and 'Out of Season.' These had a special sentimental significance for Hemingway considering they were the three which had survived Hadley's Gare de Lyon debâcle. By printing them now he was ensuring the world would see them, whatever others perished at the ill-fated train station. The poems, which were quality-studded, looked somewhat incongruous beside them, but all of the writing had a stark quality. The book could have been accused of being slight so Hemingway insisted that blank pages be included at either end to flesh it out. This it did, and it was well received as a result, even if it only reached a coterie readership. These were his letters in a bottle to souls as sensitive (and desensitised?) as his own, so many postcards from the edge sent out by a young man who brought an elegiac lyrical quality to life's compromises and tragedies.

The proximity of being a father however presented him with a more pragmatic problem...

Hemingway decided he would need a steady job to support his soon-to-be born child, so arranged to move back to Toronto before the end of the year to work again for *The Star*. Hadley also felt she would receive better ante-natal care in Canada.

The move to Canada was practical, but Hemingway's spirits

weren't too high here. He was as unhappy with Hadley's pregnancy as he was with the loss of his manuscripts, and neither was his work with *The Star* going to plan.

His boss here was Harry Hindmarsh, a man who felt the young journalist was something of a prima donna (he was partly right) so he lost few opportunities to bring him down a peg or two, landing him with humble assignments like writing obituary notices when Hemingway wanted to be at the cutting edge of current affairs. One day he sent him 600 miles away to investigate a mining problem near Georgian Bay.

Hindmarsh, the son-in-law of *The Star's* owner, did everything in his power to bring the cocky young Hemingway down to earth, making him realise it wasn't only the Grace Halls of the world who could be downright nasty when they wanted. He seemed to have gone from the frying pan into the fire, and wrote to Gertrude Stein to say, 'I have understood for the first time how men can commit suicide simply because of too many things in business piling up ahead of them that they can't get through.' This was a dramatic over-reaction to his workload and an early reference to a preoccupation that would plague him during every crisis (and mini-crisis) of his life.

Hindmarsh gave him not only an endless litany of graveyard shifts but also a range of dead end commissions guaranteed to ensure the greatest geographical inconvenience he could muster. As envious of Hemingway's journalistic expertise as he was resentful of his self-confident swagger, he did his utmost to destroy both qualities by such bullyboy tactics. He didn't bargain on the cub reporter's resilience, however, or his thirst for an exclusive. So Hemingway soaked up the pain. After a few months, however, he realised he was going nowhere fast career-wise. And also, more importantly, that his boss was blunting his creative edge as well as his appetite for influencing the public with Words That Mattered.

Just before the baby was due to be born Hindmarsh sent him on an assignment to New York and from there to Canada to interview the

British statesman David Lloyd George. He accepted the task reluctantly and Bumby was born while he was away, much to his chagrin.

Hemingway did his best to play the father figure, though the erstwhile hunter/boxer/soldier/fisherman wasn't ideally cut out for this role. 'The baby has taken to squalling and is a fine nuisance,' he wrote to his father in less than ecstatic tones, 'I suppose he will yell his head off for the next two or three years. It seems his only form of entertainment.'

Such yelling not only threatened his mental health, he told Hadley, but also his livelihood. He would tell Aaron Hotchner in years to come; 'To be a successful father, there's one absolute rule. When you have a kid, don't look at it for the first two years.'

He had a short fuse as far as Bumby was concerned, and frequently fled the house to do his writing, taking his notebook and pencil to nearby cafes to seek out the proper ambience to get 'the juice' flowing.

He went back to Oak Park for Christmas with a few copies of *Three Stories and Ten Poems* which he intended to give to various members of his family as presents, but a row shortly after he arrived made him re-think this course of action. Instead he slipped a copy of the book quietly to Marcelline. She wasn't impressed by it, especially after reading the story 'Up in Michigan', which she found 'sordid'. It was a good thing, she opined, that it wasn't being published in America. ('Up in Michigan' has often been used as a stick to beat Hemingway by critics who deem his style crude and sexist, but the fact remains that this is a story written from the point of view of the victimised *female*.)

Hemingway received this blunt critique of his work with wry detachment. It was obvious that fame hadn't altered the friction between himself and his older sister one whit. If anything, it only served to fan the flame. (He would always insist that Marcelline more than any of his other siblings was wildly jealous of him).

The Hemingways returned to Paris in January 1924 with the

young Bumby, living on Hadley's income as Hemingway sweated on his stories and also busied himself working as sub-editor of *The Transatlantic Review* under Ford. Then in March his second book, *in our time*, was published by Three Mountains Press. This was little more than a group of violent vignettes, but its publication paved the way for another book of the same name (albeit without the pretentious absence of capitals) which would hit the shelves eighteen months later.

In the winter of that year Hemingway went with Hadley to the Austrian ski resort of Schruns, having sub-let their Paris apartment. It was here he received the news that *In Our Time* had been accepted by Boni and Liveright - his first letter of acceptance from a commercial publishing firm. The advance of £200 was hardly a princely sum but he was understandably over the moon at the news.

The book let readers know in no uncertain terms that a striking new voice had arrived on the literary scene. A compilation of material already presented in his two previous books, it neatly encapsulated his work to date and gave him a window to a wider reading public than had been his lot heretofore. The title was derived from the chant in the Common Prayer Book, 'Give us peace in our time, o Lord' - with obvious irony considering his choice of subject matter.

It was a title which demonstrated the fact that Hemingway wasn't just interested in providing his readers with isolated glimpses of life, but rather a document, however piecemeal, for his generation. Right from the first sentence of 'On the Quai at Smyrna', ('The strange thing was, he said, how they screamed every night at midnight'), the reader is hit for six by the casualness of the violence, and the author's assured, knowing tone. There's no attempt to explain who 'he' or 'they' are. We're plunged into the story *in medias res*, without any of 'that David Copperfield stuff', as J.D. Salinger's Holden Caulfield would put it in *The Catcher in the Rye*.

These are stories that always want to tell us more than they're doing, but resist the temptation. They scream at us almost with their mouths shut. In many of them there's no development of either plot or character, with people speaking to one another in cryptic mono-syllables or epigrammatic ambiguities. The sensation achieved is something like speaking to someone under water, or in a bubble. It's the literature of profound non-communication, the bland bromides and dog-weary clichés picking up the slack.

'Any part you make will represent the whole if it's made truly', he often said, like a mantra, and that was how he wrote, giving you the part, however flimsy, but indicative. In previous eras readers had been spoon-fed with extraneous details, flowery adjectives and spidery subordinate clauses. Hemingway's brief was life itself, without the appendages.

Notwithstanding their superficial nonchalance, these early stories contain any number of incendiary devices that explode as much in the reader's head as they do on the page. Little is said but much shown and it's left to us to join the dots where characterisations are left incomplete, or merely hinted at.

The strain is continued in 'Indian Camp' where a man slits his throat after he sees a doctor deliver a stillborn baby from his scream-ing wife without an anaesthetic. Here we're introduced to Nick Adams, who will be Hemingway's *doppelganger* for many years, and a useful conduit through which he will filter muted shock. Nick has witnessed the death beside his physician father and is understandably numbed, and his father is 'terribly sorry' he had to see it. He ends by being 'quite sure' that he himself will never die. The 'terribly' and 'quite sure' are arrestingly laconic considering what we've just witnessed. Hemingway is undercutting violence by ironic asides that only serve to intensify the effect, the violence trivialised by the fact that Dr Adams seems to be more annoyed that his son has witnessed the suicide then by the suicide itself.

Hemingway deleted the first few pages of the original version of 'Indian Camp' which features Adams being afraid of being alone in the woods at night. Is this an exemplification of the trauma from Fossalta that he didn't want to be advertised around the world?

In 'Soldier's Home' he writes of life in Oak Park for one of the few times in his career, even if he sets the story ostensibly in Oklahoma. The friction between himself and his mother is captured almost verbatim in the manner in which Kreb's mother castigates him for his post-war lassitude, and we even have a reference to Ursula's almost incestuous fascination with Hemingway in the flirtation that goes on between Krebs and his sister Helen.

Krebs, like Hemingway himself, who suffered a subdued form of shellshock after his wounding in Italy, tries to console himself that things are 'fine' in the classic tradition of Hemingway heroes in denial. He immerses himself in trivia (like the Nick Adams of 'Big Two-Hearted River'), to deflect attention from his burgeoning depression. The mind-numbing boredom of the provincial backwater in which he lives becomes the objective correlative of that depression.

'Soldier's Home' is probably a closer inspection of Hemingway's life in Oak Park - both before as well as after his wounding - than we get anywhere else in his published work. The domestic friction becomes the subtext of his quiet desperation as he busies himself with trivia to counteract the shock he's feeling but won't admit to. The glow of being a war hero has worn off for Krebs (as it must have done for Hemingway) and now there's a life to be lived; it's just that he's not quite sure where to start. Watching his sister play indoor basketball is hardly the ideal place.

In 'The End of Something' we have another theme that will figure largely in his output: the end of a romance. Nick doesn't quite know why being with Margie 'isn't fun' any more, and the story ends in mid-air, like most of Hemingway's early stories, making unseasoned readers wonder if a page mightn't be missing. The following story, however, 'The Three-Day Blow', picks up where 'The End of Something' left off. Again the tone is disarmingly low-key, and we're two-thirds of the way through it before we realise why Bill and Nick are getting drunk. 'The Three-Day Blow' also gives us the beginning of a negative view of marriage that will run through Hemingway's *oeuvre* when Bill says that married people 'get this sort of fat married look' which makes them 'done for'. Things suddenly don't look too well for Ernest and Hadley.

D. H. Lawrence compared the end of the love-affair in 'The Three-Day Blow' to throwing a cigarette end away; it's an image worthy of the story itself.

'A Very Short Story' has, in miniature, the relationship between Hemingway and Agnes which was to become expanded out of all recognition in *A Farewell to Arms*. It's also the story which, more than any other in the collection, was responsible for Hemingway's father returning to the publisher the half dozen copies of *In Our Time* which were forwarded to him. He didn't think he had raised a son who would write about people who contracted gonorrhoea in taxis, let alone indians who cut their throats after a stillborn birth.

'My Old Man' is an impressionistic fable employing a kind of stream-of-consciousness narrative technique. Its main interest comes from the fact that the reader realises at a certain point that he knows much more about the old man and his shady exploits than his own son, who tells the story, does.

When Edmund Wilson, a critic Hemingway respected more than most, said that 'My Old Man' reminded him of the race-track stories of Sherwood Anderson, Hemingway responded that while the matter may have been the same, the manner was his own, adding, somewhat irrelevantly, that Anderson's recent work seemed to have gone to hell 'perhaps from people in New York telling him too much how good he was.' Hemingway himself would know that feeling a few years down the road.

'Mr and Mrs Elliot' employs the satirical strain Hemingway would soon use in *The Torrents of Spring*. Even from the names of the characters (Hubert and Cornelia) we may know what to expect. The idea of trying hard to have a baby, and crying when things go wrong, becomes the stuff of high farce. The fact that Mrs Elliot is 'quite' happy at the end is about as convincing as the fact that Nick Adams is 'quite' sure he will never die at the end of 'Indian Camp'. Whenever Hemingway uses this particular term, we can take it as read that what he means is the precise opposite. In 'Mr and Mrs Elliot' we can see a clear example of Hemingway's 'necklace' style of writing, where each sentence has a hook word that leads into the next one.

In the first sentence we establish two chains of the necklace: 'Mrs Elliot' and 'tried'. These are repeated in the second one. 'Tried' is repeated in the third, and a new chain introduced: 'boat'. Then 'boat' gets repeated in the next sentence, where 'sick' becomes the new hook. This is how Hemingway creates his mesmeric effect. People talk often about his use of repetition, but it's more elaborate than he's usually given credit for. Every time he repeats a term he adds something new beside it to give him ammunition for more repetition. It's a very elaborate structure, like a jigsaw puzzle.

His sentences cascade down upon one another in marginally varying form - somewhat like those notebooks we had as children where we drew slightly different pictures and then flapped the pages to create the illusion of movement; a very makeshift piece of DIY animation. Hemingway practises the same sleight-of-hand, like a trainee cameraman.

One commentator on this story has gone so far as to suggest Hubert Elliot is Hemingway's anti-self...because the initials of his name are an inversion of Hemingway's. The nadir of litcrit would appear to have been reached in such speculations.

'Big Two-Hearted River,' which closes the collection, is a story in which nothing happens twice - if I may borrow the classic phrase Hugh Kenner used to describe *Waiting for Godot*. Most critics are intrigued by it, as was Hemingway himself, but there really is less to it than meets the eye. The coy references to the war, or some other crisis Adams is having a problem coming to terms with, are too flimsy to make an impact, which means that it's difficult for the reader to care what, if anything, they mean. As Gertrude Stein might have said, remarks are not literature. If Hemingway had dropped broader hints as to Adams' state of mind, or took the trouble to inject some decent human interest into a story which never becomes more than a solid piece of descriptive narration, it could well have become one of his most memorable stories. As it stands, however, Nick's 'other needs' go for nothing, leaving us with the impression that all that decent writing would have fared infinitely better as a chapter in a novel where the characters were already established. Indeed, it reads suspiciously like many descriptive passages from *A Farewell to Arms*, but without the involvement of context. It also jars with the foregoing stories, knocking the collection out of sync.

Scott Fitzgerald said of the story that there was no tail on it, 'no sudden change of pace at the end to throw into relief what has gone before'. This is a comment that could apply to every story Hemingway ever wrote, but it doesn't make this one any better in this writer's view. One senses Hemingway is already limbering up for some of the great descriptive passages in the novels, but it still remains a non-event of a story and one wonders why he set such store by it. Only he could know what wasn't being said, so the creative pleasure in this instance was unshared.

The secret Nick Adams has to hide here, no doubt, is the fact that (again) he's shellshocked. This is fair enough, but good suggestive literature hints at what it's hiding, otherwise the concealment just becomes self-serving. The shellshock of Jake Barnes, with its physiological overtones, will be infinitely more effective, because less pretentious, in *The Sun Also Rises*.

The story is impressive in its construction, but has been taken far too seriously by those literary critics Hemingway always despised - people who analyse it for its Fisher King undertones and neo-modernist nods to the likes of T.S. Eliot.

Hemingway himself informed his colleagues that he was pleased with the fact that he hadn't mentioned the war in it. But surely if we're to understand that this is indeed what it is 'about', then we need more clues. Conscious omission is fine as long as there are lucid and cleverly-worked clues, but for all we know of the Nick Adams of this story, he could just as well have carved up his parents and fed them to the family pets than been traumatised after the war.

Here, as elsewhere, Nick has cut off his fundament of feeling as a protection against being hurt. This seems to be evident in the manner in which he throws himself into the concrete, preoccupying himself with the minutiae of the river. In 'The Three-Day Blow' he gets drunk to deal with the break-up of his romance with Marge, which is the way Hemingway himself probably dealt with the rejection of Agnes von Kurowsky after their relationship ended.

The collection, of course, was mainly significant for introducing the reading world to Nick Adams.

Adams is like Mr Junior America; a young man who's outdoorsy and resourceful, but added on to this is his vulnerability. Somebody once said of Marlon Brando that he brought doubt into the locker room. Adams, in the same way, undercuts the Jock stereotype by embodying many of the characteristics of the contemporary existential hero. He's like Huckleberry Finn crossed with Holden Caulfield as described by Bret Easton Ellis. He served as a useful conduit for Hemingway himself in his quest for a linking persona who would be partly himself and partly someone upon whom he could hang a thematic hook. After a time, however, Adams would seem to have outlived his usefulness, having become an all-too-instantly recognisable fixture in the stories to the extent that whatever individualistic surge they may or may not have possessed was compromised by actions (and reactions) Adams could be guaranteed to have associated with him.

Slotted in between all the stories of *In Our Time* are so many italicised vignettes, almost all of which focus on violence, which was to fascinate Hemingway all his life, right up to his final act. The vignettes are about physical violence; the stories themselves about the domesticated war between the sexes. He saw them as 'interchapters', comparing the effect to that of watching a coastline from a ship, first with the naked eye and then with binoculars.

The fragmentation and cross-cutting techniques owed as much to the cinematic montage of Eisenstein as they did to the collages of Miro and Cézanne. Hemingway had never made any secret of his love for abstract painting, nor of the fact that he sought to reprise its chaotic structure on the printed page.

The interchapters are beset not only with violence but the threat of further violence. The fragmentary structure *in itself* carries the sense of dissonance and fear.

Maybe the main surprise of *In Our Time* was the manner in which the tight-lipped narration of the alienated Adams was so much at variance with Hemingway's own garrulous personality. Those who didn't know him could be forgiven for imagining him to be a diffident and even morose young man, and this, of course, applied to future short story collections (if not novels) as well. But nothing could have been further from the truth.

The negative tone of the book affected Hemingway's parents, raised as they were in a generation that taught them never to wash their dirty linen in public - or, indeed, to admit it existed. There were wonderful things in the world, they pointed out to him, and perhaps he should go looking for them. Hemingway's answer was that he did, but he didn't always find such qualities in places he might have expected. Like the poet Wordsworth, he would find sermons under the stones rather than in churches, and beauty in the Greek tragedy of the corrida. He would also find diamonds in the quarry of his subconscious, and in those downbeat criminals and punch-drunk boxers who peopled his stories. They were a lost generation perhaps, but infinitely more interesting than those who, like his parents, professed to be members of a 'found' one. They were, in any case, the only game in town for him, and so many gritty antidotes to Oak Park, where his father lived a life of silent terror until the day he put a gun to his head and pulled the trigger, thus blowing the lid on the lie of his existence thus far.

His parents wished Ernest to be virile but not a braggart; extrovert but not rakish. It was okay to win a literary competition, but writers were just that bit too left of centre for Oak Park tastes. As he began to make his way in Paris and elsewhere, they felt entitled to feel they had created a monster. His father wanted him to go to college, but Ernest's college was the forest, the finca, the green hills of Africa.

When his father wrote to him telling him he disapproved of the sordidness of some of his stories, Hemingway replied by saying that in trying to grapple with life in all its parameters he had to describe not only the beautiful, but the bad and ugly as well, 'because if it is all beautiful you can't believe in it. Things aren't that way. It is only by showing both sides - 3 dimensions and if possible 4 - that you can write the way I want to.'

His *apologia* for all the bloodletting in his collection was interesting: 'I have been working for a precision of language and to get it at the start have had to treat of things where simple actions occurred. The simplest, and what I had seen the most of, was one form and another of killing.'

This wasn't the kind of thing his father wanted to hear, which meant that the book's existence was more a source of embarrassment to him than a cause for celebration. In a temper he decided to return all copies of the book which had been dispatched complimentarily to him.

Surprisingly enough, it was Grace rather than Clarence who wanted to keep a souvenir copy of her son's first book, as she thought. (She hadn't seen *in our time* or *Three Stories and Ten Poems*). Let's not forget that this was the women who, when Ernest was in seventh grade at school, protested to his English teacher that *The Call of the Wild* was far too violent a text to impose upon his tender mind. Little did she know what was to come.

Ernest, in fact, soon became a taboo subject in Oak Park. His father said he would prefer him to be dead than notorious. Even those stories of his which were serialised in magazines had to be smuggled into the Hemingway household by his siblings, and kept far from the gaze of his ogre-like mother.

She still continued to write to him, telling him condescendingly that she knew one day he would write a book that would appeal to his better instincts, but she was only egging him on to further explorations of the dark corners of the psyche with her intransigence. He knew she was only willing to love him on her terms, which was no kind of love at all, but as long as his father was alive he was willing to keep a separate peace with her, even if it was only cosmetic.

The book served warning to the American populace that Hemingway was here to stay, but was it ready for this kind of literature yet? Oak Park certainly wasn't. Nor was H.L. Mencken, who dismissed the book with this offhand broadside: 'The sort of brave, bold stuff that all atheistic young newspaper reporters write. Jesus Christ in lower case. A hanging, carnal love. And two disembowellings.' Shattering, perhaps, but there was more where that came from, and there wasn't a lot the H.L. Menckens of the world could do about it.

Suddenly, the lad with the 'supple look like a sleepy panther' was beginning to make waves; before too long he would outshine his colleagues for keeps, at least as far as commercial success was concerned.

Ernest Hemingway, for better or worse - and to some people it was both - had arrived.

The Sun Also Rising

Anybody as talented as Hemingway would have risen to the top of the literary tree *anyway,* but he had his path smoothed by the people he met in Paris, people who admired him as much for his magnetic personality as his lean, athletic style of writing. Chief among these was F. Scott Fitzgerald.

When Fitzgerald met Hemingway in 1925, he was an established author, having written *Gatsby* and also *The Beautiful and the Damned* and *This Side of Paradise*, whereas all Hemingway had to his credit were some offbeat stories published in minor magazines, and two limited edition - and rather flimsy - books. Such was his charisma, however, and his self-belief, that Fitzgerald almost felt himself to be the apprentice, and Hemingway the established scribe.

Just as Anderson gave Hemingway a letter of introduction to Fitzgerald, so Fitzgerald, in his turn, effectively gave him one to Maxwell Perkins, his Scribners editor. Hemingway, he told Perkins, was going to be The Next Big Thing. He was the business, the real McCoy, and it was only a matter of time before everybody would be talking about him. In fact it had already started.

This was a huge boon for a writer who had, as yet, little clout despite whatever potential resided in him. To have an established writer like Fitzgerald easing his path into the big time was more than he could ever have hoped for a year or so ago when he was crying as the rejection slips from prestigious magazines slipped through his letter box refusing yet another story that read like an anecdote.

Fitzgerald told Hemingway once that he was 'the first American I wanted to meet in Europe - and the last'. Such naked admiration embarrassed him more than anything else.

Fitzgerald got off on the wrong footing with him by being so obviously awed by him. Neither did he do himself any favours by passing out after a negligible amount of beer: a classic Hemingway no-no. Hemingway always had a protective older brother attitude to him, as he had to Joyce, but as time went on he felt Fitzgerald was selling his talent short for the fast buck. He also disparaged Fitzgerald's ill-disguised admiration of the trappings of wealth. He really did believe the rich were different from everyone else, quite apart from having more money; Hemingway, as that famous riposte attests to, clearly didn't.

'I always had a very stupid little boy feeling of superiority about Scott,' he told Perkins in 1939, 'like a tough little boy sneering at a delicate but talented little boy.'

His relationship to Scott's wife Zelda was somewhat more complex. If he had a tendency towards misogyny it was more than indulged by Zelda, a woman who, by all reports, did everything in her power to destroy her husband's creativity - not only by plying him with drink so that he wouldn't be able to attempt to write, but also by passing contemptuous remarks about the size of his penis, the ultimate spousal ignominy.

Zelda was a pampered southern belle who intrigued Scott for precisely these reasons, despite the price such qualities exacted. 'Each fault,' he would write of one of his (very similar) fictional creations, 'was knit up with a sort of passionate energy that transcended it.'

Like Hemingway she was a leader, her relationships with people characterised (and limited) by that fact. Like Hemingway too, she was unable to take criticism.

She felt Hemingway was a sham, whereas he thought she was crazy. Fitzgerald loved both of them and yet they hated each other. What was wrong? Maybe something as simple as the fact that both of them were used to being pampered and couldn't be at home with even the vaguest hint of dissatisfaction.

Hemingway saw Zelda as a controlling woman like his mother. For him, as well as being fanatically jealous of Scott, she was an 18-carat schizoid bitch who only seemed to be able to enjoy herself when others were suffering. In her husband she had an easy target because writers didn't come much more thin-skinned or impressionable than Scott.

Hemingway said he often wondered if Fitzgerald wouldn't have been the best writer the world ever had if he hadn't been married to someone that would make him waste everything. There had to be something wrong with a woman who believed, as she did, that Al Jolson was greater than Jesus.

Even as Hemingway accused Zelda of wanting Scott to drink to excess so it would curb his literary bent, so Zelda countered by saying that Hemingway was a bad influence on Scott because he led him into company where drinking sprees would start. Zelda, like Alice B. Toklas with Gertrude Stein, resented sharing her partner with Hemingway - perhaps because she knew he saw through her and might eventually poison Scott's attitude to her.

It didn't take Zelda long to castigate Hemingway for wearing, as she put it, false hair on his chest. (Max Eastman would level the same charge at him after the publication of *Death in this Afternoon*). Was he, as it were, 'found out' by Zelda this early in his life or was she merely trying to protect Scott from being dubbed effeminate in comparison to him? Or was she simply jealous of his success and pub popularity? Whatever her motives, the manner of her shooting from the hip in such forthright fashion seemed to pre-date much revisionist thinking about Hemingway. She showed an insight into his almost defensive espousal of virility. He was aghast, but the point still hit home. Zelda may have gone mad afterwards, but she was eminently sane when she spoke like this, whatever Ernest might have said to the contrary.

Another possible reason she hated him was because she was so similar to him. He ruled the marital roost as she did, and she couldn't take that.

The negative vibrations that passed between them, in any case, were manifest to anyone with half an eye. If Hemingway saw his father in Scott's vacillation, his mother was writ large in Zelda's role as metaphorical castrator of her husband. When she was visiting Hadley and Ernest once, she said to Hadley, 'I notice that in the Hemingway family you do what Ernest wants.' In the Fitzgerald family, Scott most definitely did what Zelda wanted. She couldn't live in Scott's shadow, no matter how famous he became, and she was amazed that Hadley seemed comfortable living in Hemingway's.

Hemingway saw Zelda as a preying mantis, a woman who was decidedly deadlier than the male. Zelda, in retaliation, accused her husband and Hemingway of having a homo-erotic relationship.

Hemingway had just finished his novel *The Torrents of Spring* when he met Fitzgerald. It was a satire of *Dark Laughter*, the latest book by Sherwood Anderson. Anderson had done Hemingway some favours already, but Hemingway was irked by being compared to the older man in his style of writing. *The Torrents of Spring* was an adieu not only to Anderson, but also to the young Hemingway. It was also the book which would terminate his relationship with Boni & Liveright, who published *In Our Time*, and pave the way for him to join Scribners with Fitzgerald.

Fitzgerald became Hemingway's intermediary with Scribners, and a man who took great delight in keeping Maxwell Perkins up to date with all his movements and motivations. Hemingway was hardly aware of this, but Fitzgerald direly wanted him aboard the good ship Scribners, which was probably one of the reasons he encouraged Perkins to publish *The Torrents of Spring* as a contract-breaker for his friend.

Hemingway dashed off *Torrents* in a week, but those seven days would buy him out of a contract with a publishing company he wanted to be shot of so that bigger doors would open for him.

The fact that he repaid Sherwood Anderson's generosity in giving him letters of introduction to anyone who was anyone in the Paris literary set of the twenties by lampooning his worst book, is one of the most indefensible acts he ever performed. He added insult to injury by writing to Anderson and saying there was 'nothing personal' in the activity. If it wasn't personal, what was it? And if he felt so strongly about the decline in Anderson's talent, was there not a more propitious and professional way to tell him?

Boni and Liveright had an option on Hemingway's first three books but after rejecting *The Torrents of Spring*, his second, they relinquished their option on the third, which played right into Hemingway's hands and left him free to go to Scribners.

Hemingway's anxiousness to get a book deal from Scribners could be traced back to the fact that Maxwell Perkins had actually accepted *In Our Time* for that publishing company at the same time as Horace Liveright had in 1925 but due to a glitch in the post he hadn't received the letter until he had committed himself to Liveright. He was now putting that glitch to rights, albeit in a somewhat underhand fashion.

When submitting *The Torrents of Spring to* Liveright, he tried to cover himself vis-a-vis Anderson by saying, 'In the golden age of the English novel Fielding wrote his satirical novels as an answer to the novels of Richardson. In this way *Joseph Andrews* was written as a parody on Richardson's *Pamela*. Now they are both classics'. This seemed to be a lame attempt at defending himself. Hemingway didn't for a moment imagine he would elevate *Dark Laughter* to the status of a classic by lampooning it. Still less did he expect Liveright to fall for his waffle - as he confessed to Fitzgerald when *Torrents* was rejected a few months later by Liveright, as he knew it would be.

Hemingway didn't like Horace Liveright personally anyway, and believed he had done little or nothing to promote *In Our Time* since it was published, so he felt he owed him nothing.

He said to Fitzgerald that he knew Liveright 'could not and would not' be able to publish the book, 'as it makes a bum out of their present ace and best-selling writer.' He did not, he added, 'have that in mind in any way when I wrote it'. This last comment one finds very difficult to believe.

His letter to Anderson in May 1926, in which he tried to justify his behaviour, is almost risible in its would-be rationalisations. Writers had to pull their punches, he averred and 'when a man like yourself, who can write great things, writes something that seems to me rotten, I ought to tell you so.' Fair enough, but did he have to publicise it to the nation in the form of an under-the-belt broadside? Especially in view of the favours Anderson had done for him in writing all those letters of introduction to Stein and Co? It all smacked of biting the hand that fed him, and his comment in the same letter, 'Outside of personal feelings, nothing that's any good can be hurt by satire' is irrelevant since he had just told Anderson that *Dark Laughter wasn't* any good.

Anderson took the lampoon on the chin, amazingly enough, even telling Hemingway he felt the publicity would do him (Anderson) good. If Hemingway had bitten the hand that fed him, Anderson was now feeling that same hand again with a gracious forgiveness.

The satire would have ironic reverberations for Hemingway, for after he became famous it would become an especial hobby of nitpicking students in every second university in America to satirise his style of writing in the same way as he was now doing to Anderson.

Perkins wasn't overly enthused about *The Torrents of Spring*, as Liveright guessed, but he knew he wouldn't get Hemingway without it so he was willing to take it on that basis, in the knowledge that *The Sun Also Rises* - the only book he had ever accepted without having seen - was following hard upon.

Perkins was conservative by nature, but willing to bend the Scribners rules to accommodate this precocious new talent who would, he felt, draw fresher blood to the company when they saw his work. He deemed Hemingway to be more incisive than Fitzgerald, more dangerous than James Jones and more punchy than Thomas Wolfe - the main three writers Scribners had on their books at this time.

A critic in *The New Republic* called the book Hemingway's 'declaration of independence' from Anderson, but was it really that? In a sense, he wasn't so much disavowing the debt he owed to

Anderson as demonstrating how much it preyed on his mind.

This is a one-joke book, but part of the joke reverberated on Hemingway himself, because in it he displayed elements of his own literary style so he was in a sense sending himself up as well as Anderson. Or at least serving warning to critics to look out for such lapses of his style in future works. He once told Aaron Hotchner that parodies were 'the last refuge of the frustrated writer'. The greater the work of literature, he held, the easier the parody. 'The step up from writing parodies,' he continued, 'is writing on the wall of the urinal'.

Imitation, in other words, is the sincerest form of flattery. These words were spoken not at the time *Torrents* was published, needless to say, but when Hemingway himself had become the butt of other more pungent broadsides than he himself had perpetrated with this book.

His parody of Anderson was as much motivated by frustration as fun. It was his way of telling the world he had crawled out from under Anderson's shadow - if, indeed, he had ever been under it in the first place. The satire was biting, but no less than Hemingway, the would-be guru of 'the one true sentence', felt he deserved.

Torrents wouldn't be remembered as one of Hemingway's more memorable books, but it was one he had to get out of his system. It was also a relief from the dourness many perceived in *In Our Time* - and a signal that he could limber himself up for larger volumes if and when the occasion demanded. It was also the book which began a lifetime contract with Scribners, a lifelong friendship with Maxwell Perkins - and a fourteen-year marriage with Pauline Pfeiffer.

Hemingway was drifting away from Hadley even as he was writing *Torrents*. There were signs that she was tiring of the frenetic pace at which they lived. She wanted a quieter life, and that was never going to be on the cards with this man.

Money was also starting to come his way with the Scribners contracts, which meant he was no longer playing second fiddle to her financially.

She had fulfilled a great function in exorcising the ghost of

Agnes, who had destroyed his confidence in himself, but now that he was established in Paris, and among a coterie of stylists who appreciated him not only for his work but his ebullient personality, the last thing he wanted was a woman to tie him down. Domesticity was death to him - as he demonstrated to his mother time and again - and after Bumby was born, Hadley started to look matronly. For the young man just crawling out of his literary chrysalis, it was time to move on.

Hemingway was also beginning to show a wandering eye for other women. Chief among these was Duff Twysden, a titled British lady with a fondness for drink, and someone who drew men around her like magnets. It's doubtful if he ever slept with her, but they flirted openly together as Hadley watched on helplessly during the Pamplona fiesta that would give him his first big book.

He had always been impressed by titled English ladies, and Duff Twysden had it over most of them in the sense that she also knew how to enjoy a good time. She could drink and cuss like the boys in the back room which was his favourite type of woman and the type he always needed to prevent there being any disharmony between his love life and his social one. He wasn't the typical chauvinist in the sense that he wanted one woman in the boudoir and another one in the pub. He preferred it when his women could go hunting and fishing with him, and then be compliant housewives back home *chez* Hemingway.

While he was waiting for *In Our Time* to be published in the summer of 1925, he decided to go to a fiesta in Pamplona with a group of acquaintances. The group consisted of his friend Bill Smith, the humorist Donald Ogden Stewart, Duff Twysden, Twysden's Scottish cousin Pat Guthrie and Jewish novelist Harold Loeb. And of course Hadley. The fiesta gave him not only a book but, ultimately, his fame.

To make the trip, finances being tight, he borrowed money for the transport and bullfights from Ogden Stewart. He set out with Hadley in late June, meeting up with Smith a week later. In Pamplona they were joined by Twysden, Guthrie and Loeb. Twysden and Loeb had just spent a weekend together, despite the fact that she was living with Guthrie. Such romantic musical chairs would be a feature of her life to come as well, and Hemingway was perhaps more awed about this than he let on.

Each of the people at the fiesta, including himself, featured in *The Sun Also Rises*. Bar Hadley. This was significant.

It's probably the closest Hemingway ever came to writing the kind of book Scott Fitzgerald specialised in. Life was a party, but with a dark subtext. The philosophy of the characters is 'Eat, drink and be miserable, for tomorrow we die.' The fact that it opens with a pair of epithets from the Bible and Gertrude Stein is a classic case of going, as one wag put it, from the sublime to the ridiculous.

Though it comes to us replete with a Biblical quote about life (and death) being bigger than its characters, it would probably have been a better book without these lofty overtones. The quotation, one imagines, is one that would have had little relevance for any of the characters in it, seeing as their whole orientation is towards the instant rather than any cosmic gameplan that may or may not exist.

The upbeat title, coupled as it is with the celebratory air of the Biblical echo, were probably conscious devices employed by Hemingway to deflect or offset charges of dourness that might be laid at its door. It did, after all, feature a bunch of characters who nosepicked their grievances pretty relentlessly for 200 pages.

The book is interesting because of its reversal of the traditional male/female roles, what with Lady Brett being the promiscuous one and Jake, in familiar Hemingway mode, imploding quietly at the edges. The irony is that his impotence has come courtesy of an act most men would have been proud to have performed in the war. Hemingway told Leicester that he had got the idea for Jake's predicament from a genito-urinary hospital ward in Italy where they put him after he was nicked in the scrotum by a piece of shrapnel. It was there that he saw 'all these poor bastards who had everything blown off.'

His dialogue has never been more naturalistic than here, with the exception of the early stories. There's an air of the sophomore student about it, but the prose moves so limpidly you can't quibble. The first draft, written in Valencia and Paris, only took forty-eight days, but the revisions - laboriously worked at in Austria and New York - tightened things up to an almost unrecognisable degree.

What we're served up is a cocktail of bartenders, prostitutes, matadors, lowlifes and gin-sodden pedants, but the tight-lipped banter is compulsive, edged as it is with a bleak dismay and fake gaiety.

Romero, the bullfighter, is the ostensible hero of the book in the sense that he's the only one who emerges from it with his full dignity intact. He is also, however, its most boring character. Ranting on about the proper dignity of the kill may have worked in *Death in the Afternoon* and *Green Hills of Africa* (many readers thought they didn't even in these books) but fiction should be about people rather then polemics, a point Hemingway would often make when he was discussing his two major war novels.

His original version of the book began with the words: 'This is a novel about a lady. Her name is Lady Ashley and when the story begins she is living in Paris and it is Spring'. Scott Fitzgerald prevailed upon him to delete the first chapter, which continues in this vein, and the book is a deal more effective for the omission. (Hemingway would have less respect for some of Fitzgerald's later suggestions.)

It's a book before its time in the sense that it features a crew of laidback anti-heroes the likes of which would become fairly common novelistic currency a couple of decades on when a quite different war would leave the Walking Wounded similarly aimless and bored.

It was a coming-of-age work for him, a watershed. Never again would he be 'just' a cub reporter who dabbled in the headier realms of fiction. No, he was now a card-carrying novelist who had written a book that wasn't only witty and incisive; it also acquired some cult status as a standard-bearer for a time. The world hadn't had Brando or Dean yet, but these rebels without causes would do for the time being.

The characters act as if they've somehow suffered at a much more profound level than other mere mortals but, being the gallant old boys that they are, or purport to be, they conceal their angst under so many carefully chosen *bon mot*s and oh-so-clever asides...at least while the wine is flowing and the bulls running and the love going good. They always seem to be on the verge of some revelatory pronouncement that doesn't quite make it to their lips. Instead they speak in monosyllabic grunts, with a hint of gallows humour. Their code precludes frankness just as it does breaking down under the weight of all that navel-gazing. Besides, you can always have another glass of absinthe to anaesthetise the pain. And maybe the finca will be swell.

He has captured four people during a vacuum in their lives, a kind of air pocket of the emotions. This is his favourite scenario because it allows him to champion the sensations of the now, to make his characters come at us without histories or the need for them, or no admission of their existence. Drink is the drug that brings oblivion and the party goes on endlessly, shot through with all those smart-alecky epithets that conceal the demons within. No wonder Scott Fitzgerald thought so much of it.

The fact that they're all numbed by the war in some form or another gives credibility to the search for instant gratification. The notion of death, as Samuel Johnson said, concentrates the mind wonderfully. If not into a solid philosophy of existence, as least a pragmatic working principle. As Jake puts it, pre-dating the edgy epistemology of Frederic Henry and any other Hemingway character you care to mention, 'Perhaps as you went along you did learn something. I did not care what it was all about. All I wanted to know was how to live in it. Maybe if you found out how to live in it you learned from that what it was all about.' The inside-out philosophy, in any case, is enough to be going on with for a motley crew of *soi disant* misfits.

The impossibility of a relationship developing between Brett and Jake is already becoming vintage Hemingway. In any book he will write afterwards we will see the dynamics of love and fulfilment summarily scuppered by acts of God and/or man, be such frustration the result of emasculation in the war, rabid incompatibility, mutual hatred, death, suicide or murder. The sweetest songs may be those that tell of saddest thought, but in Hemingway's nihilistic canon, even the valedictions are flat.

The irony, of course, is that Brett is tired of men who just want her for her body. The chemistry between herself and Jake is almost perfect. Another woman might have lived with his wound - the Maria of *For Whom the Bell Tolls*, perhaps, if not Catherine Barkley. (Another irony was biographical in nature. Jake couldn't express his attraction for Brett in a physical way, and neither could Hemingway for Duff Twysden - albeit for wildly different reasons.)

Hadley had been distressed that she herself was nowhere to be found in the book - a telling prelude to what was to come and an exemplification of the fact that she was drifting out of her husband's life. It's ironic that he wrote most lovingly of her only after he had left her. She would have been touched with the characterisation of Catherine Barkley and Maria, two heroines in whom she would definitely have seen herself, if she had still been married to him when *A Farewell to Arms* and *For Whom the Bell Tolls* were published. As she would have been by the literal depiction of her in *A Moveable Feast*. All of these books are like valentines to her. When they were together he wrote adoring missives to her, but his short stories, as we've seen already, show anything but devotion to the marital state.

Hadley was never a part of the hellraising that went on in Pamplona. She had an admirer in the bullfighter Cayetano Ordonez, to be sure, but it was platonic. As far as the drinking and repartee went, she was a silent observer more often than not, which probably explains why she didn't end up in the finished version of the book.

Hemingway had previously brought Twysden to the sawmill with him many times, and met her in cafes and bars either with Hadley or alone. He flirted openly with her, which often brought Hadley to the point of tears. He was oblivious to this, even when she excused herself from the company, leaving him to trip the light fantastic with his user-friendly alcoholic and good time gal.

Duff was very much in the Zelda Fitzgerald mould - a carefree woman who exuded an air of danger and was capricious both sexually and financially. A kind of *femme fatale* with girl-next-door overtones, she enjoyed Hemingway's interest in her, as he did hers in him, but neither of them felt comfortable about fulfilling it sexually because of Hadley. (He wasn't yet at the stage of his life where he could be unfaithful to a wife and still keep a clear conscience about it).

Twysden was like a queen bee, playing herself off against Loeb, with whom she had so recently spent a week, and Guthrie, who seemed to perform little more function for her than to fill in time. In as much as she could love anybody, she probably loved Guthrie...or did she simply need him? Loeb she picked up and dropped at will. She admitted being attracted to Hemingway but wouldn't do anything about it because of Hadley. This may have been true or it may have been a convenient way of not bruising his large ego by admitting she didn't want him to be her lover.

If Twysden had been as pushy as Pauline Pfeiffer would soon be as she sought a conduit into his heart, one suspects he might have been tempted to leave Hadley for her, or at least conduct a discreet affair with her. She was a social butterfly, and well able to whoop it up with the menfolk in her life as well as excel in acerbic repartee - all qualities revered by this *bon vivant* and all, unfortunately, lacking in Hadley. When he met Hadley first he told her they would conquer the world together, but now, suddenly, parts of that world were getting a little too close for comfort.

Hemingway, of course, envied Loeb's freedom to indulge himself with Duff; a freedom he himself would doubtless have had were it not for Hadley. This was an emasculation of a different type to Jake's, but no less searing. Neither can it have been easy for Duff. (One sometimes forgets that *The Sun Also Rises* is as much about Brett's incapacity to act out her sexual needs as it is about Jake's).

A more practical reason Hemingway stayed away from Twysden was because she was a dope addict, and he could hardly live with that - either financially or otherwise. It's unlikely he slept with Twysden, despite Hadley's suspicions. (Years later Mary would have similar suspicions about Adriana Ivancich, but here again it's doubtful if Hemingway's infatuation was consummated. Even Agnes von Kurowsky insisted their romance 'never got beyond the kissing stage').

One of the reasons Brett is such a captivating character is because she doesn't become romantically involved with Jake. The 'pillow talk' in Hemingway's books is frequently mushy, but things don't develop along these lines with this pair, with the result that the banter between them has an added edge. Familiarity breeds contempt in fiction as in life.

There's no real hero or heroine in the book and it's all the better for that. Brett is credible because she's neither angel nor bitch. She may have lost a lover in the war, but she's not wounded like other Hemingway heroines. She's more protagonist than victim.

Dashiell Hammett once said that Hemingway had 'never been able to write a woman', claiming 'he only puts them in books to admire them'. Or, he might have added, to have them admire *him.*

Women often act as spoilsports in his stories, as interlopers on male bonding sprees. Just as Aunt Sally was a killjoy for Huck Finn, and Hemingway's mother for his own early roistering, so did most of his female characters attempt to put the brakes on the male fun, either through jealousy or a pragmatic edge. Brett Ashley, who could party with the best (or worst) of them, is the notable exception to all this.

Whatever its faults, *The Sun Also Rises* remains Hemingway's most lively book, and the one least laden down with symbolism or pseudo-profound baggage. In *A Farewell To Arms* Frederic Henry tells us abstract words like honour and dignity mean little to him, but that doesn't detract from the fact that the book is still *about* these qualities. As are most of his books, in some form or another. *The Sun Also Rises,* however, is an early enough work not to be infected with its author's need for an all-encompassing hero like Frederic or Robert Jordan or Santiago or Colonel Cantwell to hover over the proceedings like an omniscient commentator. Jake Barnes may be detached, but his narrative voice meshes into the *mise-en-scene* infinitely better than his novelistic successors.

Hemingway always resisted the tag of 'lost generation' to describe Jake and his cronies. He preferred to see them as 'just a few drunks' who filled a book he wrote in six weeks. When critics wrote that he was obsessed with the amoralty of such a generation he responded, with righteous indignation, that it was the critics themselves who were obsessed with that particular breed, not he. They weren't totally lost, in any case - nor amoral either, having their own freewheeling definition of honour.

Morality, he once said, was what you felt good after, but maybe he should have rephrased that to read, 'Morality is what Hemingway feels good after', because, for all his free living, there were many strict guidelines he and his cohorts laid down about what constituted true and proper behaviour, and what was crude and indefensible. His ethical relativism was tainted with a plethora of esoteric dictates.

Even though he himself put in the reference to the Lost Generation in the Preface to the book, he always downplayed it afterwards, talking instead about the quote from Ecclesiastes that ran alongside it about the earth abiding forever. 'Nobody I knew at that time,' he would say afterwards, 'was wearing the silks of the Lost Generation or had even heard the label. We were a pretty solid mob. The characters in the book were tragic, but the real hero was was the earth.' This is all fine, but his tone appears defensive in retrospect. Surely his achievement was in creating characters who didn't *have* to be tragic, as in novels of the past. His beef was anti-heroes, or none at all. Nobody who ever read this book came away talking about the earth. They enjoyed the descriptive passages, but the controversies and the memories were of Jake and Brett and Robert Cohn and Mike.

He said he wrote it as tragedy rather than satire, but one wonders if it has the necessary depth for that. The underlying tenor is that life is jolly dreadful, chaps, but, hell, let's live for the moment old sport, even if we live to regret it something goddamned awful in the morning. In the end, it wasn't the earth that abideth forever, but Hemingway's doomed, wisecracking characters who epitomised the birth of cool.

The reviewer who said the book was an 'amazing narrative of English and American after-the-war strays runnings up and down France and Spain in wistful wildness' wasn't far off, but he didn't catch the existential undertow. Hemingway himself was amused by this trivialisation, which he alluded to in a letter to Maxwell Perkins in 1927.

The tangled skein of the book is more effective stylistically than the more firmly-focused later novels, where his self-conscious finesse tended to assert itself too stridently over the action. Here, on the contrary, the 'winner take nothing' subtext was so muted as to be almost invisible.

Jake's wound prevents him from being the typical Hemingway hero we will soon come to know (if not love) so well. It means he doesn't appear as a Hemingway clone so much as a part of the book's frenzied mosaic, and it's a better work of fiction for that. It's more accomplished structurally because less obvious, and Jake slots into that structure as a fittingly abstracted cypher.

The other characters in the book also seem to live their lives without appearing to be under the guiding hand of an intrusive author pulling the strings. They drink and cajole one another to desensitise themselves to their post-war angst. Bullfights serve a similar function for them, as does sex. The arch-enemy is thinking. This is to be avoided at all costs as the cult of sensation becomes their holy grail.

Though the book developed a certain cult status (and its fair share of Brett Ashley lookalikes) it was as much a satire of the expatriate subculture as a championing of same. Not for Ernest the rich dilettantes sipping coffee outside fashionable bistros as a kind of temporary experiment before they ran back to Daddy's lucrative business in the States. In fact he had always had a horror of such phoneys. That's why Jake is both character and commentator in his guise as Hemingway's alter ego. We don't get as many rambling internal monologues from him as we will from Frederic Henry and Robert Jordan in novels to come. That's one of the reasons many people still regard this as Hemingway's most assured work - or at least the one with the least amount of authorial pollution. The *carpe diem* philosophy is tinged with a bittersweet edge: this is its power and also its pathos. The fact that it doesn't quite become tragedy doesn't hurt the book; in fact it enhances it.

It eventually became a kind of lay Bible for the disaffected, whether he intended this or not. As with all his books, he felt he was just telling a story. But if the writing was good enough, as he also liked to say, readers brought things to it and, in effect, wrote much of the plot themselves. The secret was to throw out feelers which would tap into the collective unconscious. It was a two-way process, with the author merely a conduit for a barrage of mordant *données*.

Hemingway couldn't understand the critics who lambasted it because it featured people they deemed unsavoury. Surely, he mused, the pages of literary history were littered with such disreputable (anti) heroes all the way from the Bible to Homer to Henry Fielding.

John Dos Passos said the characters in the book were so well drawn 'you could recogise their faces on a passport photo', but he was less impressed by the overall tone. 'Instead of being the epic of the sun also rising on the lost generation,' he wrote, 'this novel strikes you as a cock and bull story about a lot of summer tourists getting drunk and making fools of themselves in a picturesque Iberian folk festival.' Surely this was to miss the point, though; the novel's *sine qua non* was its repudiation of anything grand or verbose. *The Sun Also Sets* might have been a better working title.

Conrad Aiken was closer to the point. The characters may have been unattractive, he said, but Hemingway's narration also made them dignified and tragic. Christopher Morley said it all reminded him more of Greenwich Village than the Left Bank of Paris. This was another astute observation, but so what? They were American expatriates, after all. Why should they sound like French people?

One critic dubbed it *Six Characters in Search of an Author - With Guns*. Robert Littell called it a *'succes de scandale* of a *roman a clef* floated on *vin ordinaire'* - which sounds more like a description of *Across the River and Into the Trees* in hindsight.

Other critics busied themselves trying to find out who exactly was who, as if to join the dots on Hemingway's interesting life abroad.

Sherlock Holmesing one's way through *The Sun Also Rises* can only get us so far. If Jake Barnes *is* Hemingway, or Robert Cohn *is* Harry Loeb, why did he write the book as a novel instead of a memoir? It's not cablese, not reportage. Contrary to what some reductive critics may believe, we can't 'crack' a text with a master key. Neither would it be very much fun if we could. The richness is in the implication and the imagination. There are always more questions than answers.

Other critics wondered aloud why Loeb came in for such a pasting as Robert Cohn. This was a vicious portrayal whatever way you looked at it and it had a long-lasting effect on its subject. Author Denis Brian interviewed Loeb in the early seventies and Loeb told him he was still hurting after Hemingway's derisory depiction of him in the book.

Loeb had rescued Hemingway's *In Our Time* from the slush pile at Boni and Liveright and was rewarded by being lampooned ferociously - in the same way as Sherwood Anderson's largesse had been rewarded by a literary sideswipe not long before. Maybe Hemingway resented the fact that he had accepted favours from these two men and found it necessary to deny the debt by an act of vicarious aggression. Or is this to be too Freudian about it?

Hemingway never seemed to be able to acknowledge a debt to anyone, however, when he was trying to make his mark. Scott Fitzgerald said he would always do a favour to the man a notch ahead of him on the ladder, but Robert Coates put it more ominously. 'If you gave him a helping hand,' he said, 'you were dead.' Alternatively, did Hemingway portray Loeb negatively as a result of anti-semitism? Or because he was jealous of his fling with Twysden? Or was he simply upset that Loeb was a better tennis player than he was?

Hemingway was woeful at tennis both because of his bad knee - the heritage of Fossalta - and his poor eyesight. Nevertheless, what he lacked in expertise he compensated for with his almost childish enthusiasm and delight over his (very occasional) good shots. Loeb was more amused than impressed by him.

Hemingway told Peter Viertel that he was anything but an anti-semite. If such a quality was present in his book, he argued, it was from his characters, not him. He merely compiled a document of the time and couldn't be held responsible for his characters views and expostulations. (Archibald MacLeish said the satire of Loeb was more anti-Loeb than anti-semite).

Loeb, in any case, was disgusted by Hemingway's portrayal of him, and sent out a message to say that he wished to shoot the author. Hemingway replied that he would be in Lipp's brasserie from two to four on Saturday and Sunday afternoons and everyone who wished to shoot him should come at that hour 'and for Christ's sake stop talking about it.'

Hadley tried to convince Loeb that he was a composite charac-ter but he still tortured himself all his life brooding over the satire of him. He was originally supposed to be the hero of the book, he claimed, before Hemingway fell out with him. He wasn't even sure why this happened. He surmised that it was probably because he went off with Twysden when he should have been oohing and aahing over the bulls, an unforgiveable aberration for a supposed friend of this author.

Hemingway himself said to Loeb that if Cohn *was* him, then Jake Barnes must be Hemingway, adding 'Do you think I had my prick shot off?' On the other hand, Hemingway was in a kind of 'moral chastity belt' (to use Scott Fitzgerald's phrase) as regards Twysden, so he may have found it necessary to get rid of this jealousy for Loeb's freedom by lampooning him. Hemingway always liked to win his women, and when he didn't he tended to think with his nervous system rather than his head. He evinced a similar reaction after Arnold Gingrich, his *Esquire* editor, married Jane Mason, a woman with whom he would have a long-lasting affair with in the thirties. It was different, of course, if he himself walked out. He never harboured any ill-will, for instance, towards Paul Mowrer, who would eventually marry Hadley after his marriage with her broke up. His relationships with Twysden and Mason were more complex, both of these women appearing to toy with him as Agnes did. He was attracted to both of them but felt manipulated by them as well, which meant that he was always going to be on the defensive no matter who they took up with afterwards. He always claimed Mason was keener on him than he was on her, but she insisted her feelings for him were merely platonic.

He had a kind of grudging respect for Gingrich, but regarded Mason's former husband Grant as little more than a 'wealthy twerp'. Both are parodied in *To Have and Have Not*, with Helene Bradley being cast as a wealthy woman who lusts after writers and cuckolds her husband with some *élan*.

All of this extraneous analysis, in any case, deflected from the main point: *The Sun Also Rises* was the most spontaneous book Hemingway would ever write. It had a sense of life going on rather than the feeling that events were being dragged towards pre-ordained conclusions.

Different generations have viewed it differently, of course, and it's tame now, like most of Hemingway's work, even the novels that were deemed too daring for Hollywood when films were made from them. In 1955 he actually described it as 'a tract against promiscuity', which was ironic. But then he tended to change his appraisal of his works with each passing decade - as did the revisionist critics. Such revisionism is still going on, as perforce it must with all good writing and most open-ended texts.

Shortly after the book was completed he broke with Hadley, just as he would break with Pauline after his next big book, *For Whom The Bell Tolls*. Marital stability and literary masterpieces were strange - and incompatible - bedfellows. It was always time to move on to the next frontier. Maybe men without women wrote better books. Or at least men without married women. Domesticity had an annoying habit of cramping his literary style.

When *The Sun Also Rises* hit the stands, suddenly the world seemed to be overcome with would-be rebel heroes acting disgruntled with life even though they were born with silver spoons in their mouths. These were the precursors of the pampered teenagers of the fifties - the original Me Generation - scratching their navels and mouthing quasi-philosophical one-liners through clenched teeth while ordering another daiquiri from the bar.

The book went on to sell 7,000 copies in the first two months, which gladdened his heart. Authorial status bought him the leverage (and wherewithal) to live the life of a man of action, which, in turn, fed into the material of future books. It wasn't long before Hemingway was as comfortable preaching about writing 'a damn good book' as he was about the best way to catch a marlin, or shoot quail. There was a way to write and a way to fight and he knew it and wanted to share it with the world...whether the world wished to know or not.

After *The Sun Also Rises* the struggling author who thought he was doing well even to get flimsy stories placed in magazines not so very long before became a trendsetter who shaped as well as mirrored the habits of a generation. The man who wrote *in our time* had suddenly become a prophet *of* his time.

His parents would hardly agree. Hemingway's father didn't drink, smoke, or swear, so it would have been difficult for him to sympathise with the characters presented here in any shape or form. From this point of view at least, he and his wife were birds of a feather.

After Grace finished the book, she enquired of her newly-famous son if he had other words in his vocabulary besides 'damn' and 'bitch'. She said that she hoped he would one day write a book about the noble things in life. But what was nobility, Ernest countered, except a word? And a meaningless one that that. 'Only the names of places had dignity' he would write in *A Farewell to Arms*. Oak Park certainly didn't have it.

'Honestly, Marce,' Grace fumed to Marcelline after reading it through to its conclusion, 'with the whole world full of beauty, why does he have to pick out thoughts and words from the gutter?' What she didn't realise was that many Hemingway heroes (or even anti-heroes) perceive chinks of heaven from precisely such gutters. And that *her* 'beauty', encased as it was within such vapid parameters, left him exceedingly cold.

Both of his parents were as underwhelmed by their son's celebrity status as they were by his books. Even if he was The Pied Piper of the disaffected, where could he lead them except into more blind alleys?

The public saw it differently, however. The original print run of *The Sun Also Rises* was 5,000 but it sold out in record time. It was reprinted seven times in the next ten months, leaving nobody in any doubt that Hemingway had totally eclipsed Scott Fitzgerald, his former Svengali in Scribners.

In more practical terms, the publication of the book meant he could virtually name his price for future works. Gone were the days of having precious inserts into *This Quarter* and *Transatlantic Review* - two magazines that may have done much for his critical standing, but little for his over-riding ambition of becoming a household name. The connection to Boni & Liveright was a step along the way, and one he was more than happy with at the time, but Scribners was like a dream come true.

The Sun Also Rises was made into a movie in 1957. Errol Flynn was one of the stars, but as Hemingway noted, any film with Flynn as its best actor was its own worst enemy. This was a trifle harsh, as Flynn turned in one of his best performances here - probably because he was playing a character pretty close to himself. Tyrone Power was also effective, his reserve suitable for the emasculated Jake. And Ava Gardner was born to play Lady Brett. Robert Evans was artificial as Romero but because this was an idealised character maybe that suited too.

Hemingway was unhappy with the film version, as well he might have been, but it wasn't as poor as some of the adaptations of his work. The war novels translated almost directly to celluloid, but different manoeuvres had to be employed for works like *The Killers* (which only featured five minutes of his actual dialogue). *The Snows of Kilimanjaro* had a large degree of internal monologue, as had *The Old Man and the Sea,* which wasn't exactly ideal fodder for a primarily visual medium.

The Sun Also Rises had a wealth of dialogue, which helped, but the subject matter was somewhat obtuse. Impotence wasn't exactly a conversation piece at this time. Neither did it make for erotic cinema. As Darryl F. Zanuck bluntly put it, 'How the hell can you make a story about a guy who can't get it up?'

The fact that Jake's doctor actually uses the word 'impotent' was in itself a milestone for 1957 cinema considering the manner in which the notorious Hays code had bowdlerised books up to this. Film critic Hollis Alpert summed it up when he said, 'One has the sense of an historical occasion.'

The original draft of the film version stipulated that the sun should come out from behind heavy clouds as Brett speaks her last lines in the movie, 'There must be an answer for us - somewhere'. Thankfully, such a finale was dispensed with, but Hollywood came dangerously close to it. In the book, as in most of Hemingway's works, we're only left with hints and guesses.

Such hints and guesses, however, gave him a window to a huge public who sympathised and empathised with them. Almost without warning, our young tyro was getting his wings and becoming a force to be reckoned with on the big literary stage.

Being a card-carrying novelist of standing after *The Sun Also Rises* gave Hemingway a good feeling about himself and what he was about.

It was perhaps what he had instead of God.

A Farewell to Hadley

Duff Twysden was the first serious threat to Hemingway's marriage. She was born Mary Smuthwaite, the daughter of a wineshop manager, which may have given her an early exposure to the alcohol she loved so much. She was divorced when Hemingway met her, and living with Pat Guthrie. She had an open relationship with him, both of them 'sleeping around' when the mood took. Guthrie also had homosexual tendencies and was a hopeless alcoholic. She was wild and manipulative herself, and had walked out on a child she had by her second husband. Clearly, she was a lady to be contended with, and for Hemingway an exciting antidote to Hadley, even if he couldn't respect her quite as much, or ever hope to engage in a lengthy relationship with her.

Duff, as author Peter Griffin put it, 'wore the scent of opium like a perfume'. Her recklessness and liberal attitude to sex was also a refreshing antidote to Hadley, who was becoming more 'married' with each passing year, especially after the arrival of Bumby.

Hadley needn't have worried that Hemingway's flirtation with Twysden, upsetting as it must have been to watch, would result in a fullblown love affair. They were poles apart in their characters, and Twysden seemed to be more flattered by his attentions than fascinated by him. Neither would he have been entranced with the idea of marrying somebody as flighty as this. Despite his hellraising - or maybe because of it - he liked his wives to have their heads well screwed on.

Hadley turned a blind eye to their dalliance and never asked him if he slept with her. This was wise as Hemingway wasn't a man who liked to be reminded of his moral confusion, particularly when he was still sleeping with the woman he was in the process of falling out of love with.

But in the summer of 1926 she watched him flirting openly with someone in much the same way as he had done with Twysden so recently - and this time there were decidedly more ominous overtones. Her name was Pauline Pfeiffer and she would become the second Mrs Hemingway.

Like Hadley, Pauline came from St. Louis. And, as was also the case with Hadley, Hemingway was introduced to her by Kate Smith. When he met her, she was in the company of her sister Jinny and he took to the latter more. Pauline, for her part, saw Hemingway as being scruffy and uncouth.

She was a fashion reporter for *Vanity Fair*. Intelligent as well as debonair, she might have been Scott Fitzgerald's Daisy Buchanan come to life and Hemingway was obviously attracted to her. She came into his life exactly at the time when he needed a new injection of vigour.

Pauline looked every inch the quintessential flapper girl with her bobbed hair and jaunty manner. With her chic demeanour she made you look; with her intelligence and facility for repartee she made you listen. Hadley saw this and it worried her, but her husband had been smitten before by the likes of Duff Twysden and it had passed off. Hopefully this would too.

It didn't, though.

Pauline wasn't beautiful in a chocolate box sense, but she was glitzy and compact, and she exuded vitality. Hadley was more composed and serene, which might have been fine a few years back, but now it smacked of domesticity for a man who wanted a woman who was more hands-on as far as his career was concerned. Hadley was tiring of travel but the last thing Hemingway wanted to do was settle down. He needed a woman to carry him on to his next phase.

Pauline won another brownie point when she encouraged him to publish *The Torrents of Spring*. Hadley, gentle soul that she was, believed it was under the belt, but Pauline, who was made of sterner stuff, felt anyone was fair game. She was more cavalier about the book, seeing it merely as a gentle satire. If Hemingway needed a final reason to spurn Hadley for Pauline this was it.

Hadley had never thought much of Hemingway's flair for comedy, so *Torrents* was never going to be her favourite book. Pauline also knew how to flatter her future husband, and flattery got you just about anywhere with this writer.

Pauline was also more brisk, and a more likely candidate to accompany him on safari than the retiring Hadley. Her advice on his writing - *Torrents* nothwithstanding - would also be more clued-in. When he met Hadley he was promising; when he met Pauline he was already famous. It's as unlikely to assume Pauline would have married a merely 'promising' Ernest Hemingway as it is to speculate that a famous Hemingway would have sought out such a gentle soul as Hadley to care for him.

Hadley was starting to not want to do things with Hemingway by now. She was slowing down, either due to age or tiredness. The way was open for a more vibrant woman, a pilot fish, to make her play for him. Hemingway had enlivened Hadley's personality, becoming her Svengali for life as she had become his for his writing, but the vitality seemed to come only with his name on it. She drank and went ski-ing only because he was doing these things, and she admired his books for that reason too: because the man she loved wrote them. Left to her own devices she would probably have been a more stay-at-home type. This is why Sara and Gerald Murphy, the couple introduced to her by John Dos Passos, were right to suggest she was 'miscast' as his wife. She was. But only because the 'new' Hemingway was starting to become fond of the finer things of life - the good wines, the best food, the most prestigious resorts. He needed a woman who wouldn't wear last year's wardrobe.

Hadley was an ideal wife for an insecure man who needed love and affection; Pauline an ideal one for a man on the cusp of major success. If Hadley was a crutch, Pauline was a lamp pointing the way to further glory. There's an old saying that a man owes his success to his first wife and his second wife to his success: it would seem to apply here. Which isn't to imply that Pauline married him *for* that success - but it didn't hurt.

She wasn't only like Hadley in that she came from St. Louis and was some years older than him; she too had a trust fund and was well connected, being the daughter of an affluent Arkansas landowner.

Hemingway was an established author when he met Pauline, but wasn't earning enough to support himself in the manner in which he would have liked, so her financial standing wasn't to be sniffed at. Book royalties were fine, but they had a habit of being unpredictable, and easily whittled away by African safaris and the like. Pauline's comfortable financial status was attractive to Hemingway after all the years scrimping in his cold water lodgings in Paris. All in all, she seemed to fit into his recently re-invented image of himself like a hand in a glove.

It's interesting to note that many of the women central to the early years of his life exerted financial power over him, all the way from his mother through Hadley and Pauline. (Small wonder, then, that his *Kilimanjaro* alter ego focuses so much on it.)

A more salient point was that in Pauline he had a woman who was willing to forfeit her own career to tend his. Neither would she - like Hadley - let children get in the way of his craft.

The common rumour of the time was that Pauline came to Europe to find a husband. Perhaps, but Hemingway didn't exactly have the right credentials. For one thing he was already married, for another he wasn't Catholic. He also drank to excess, dressed scruffily - at least by the Pfeiffer standards - and he lived on the wrong side of the Seine. On the other hand, he was handsome, exciting, and on the way to being a top author.

Hemingway once claimed that Pauline stole him from Hadley; that she made him love her, as it were. This was either a very clever piece of rationalisation for a move he felt guilty about or a very poor reflection on his new wife - or both. He also blamed the Murphys for encouraging him to leave Hadley.

He was never a man you could call self-piteous, but he did his damnedest in *A Moveable Feast* to offlay the responsibility for his desertion of Hadley on to the shoulders of Pauline, Dos Passos and the Murphys. 'Under the charm of these rich,' he wrote persuasively 'I was as trusting and as stupid as a bird dog who wants to go with any man with a gun.' The canine Hemingway wagged his tail with pleasure and plunged into what he called 'the fiesta concept of life' with these people, living the good life with them and sleeping with one of them, the one who would eventually become his second wife. But was anybody holding his arm and forcing him to do this? It was a very insidious picture he painted, disavowing any complicity on his part at all. One might imagine we were reading about a teenager rather than a very forceful man in his mid-twenties.

The point is that he left Hadley because he wanted to. Maybe he didn't want to leave her in quite these circumstances, or quite so soon, but it would have happened with or without the Murphys, and with or without Pauline. She was merely the exemplification of his growing dissatisfaction with Hadley, even if he would deny this in his middle years, when marital devotion seemed suddenly preferable to the *frisson* of the ski slopes, or the boudoir.

Their relationship began platonically. Pauline liked to lie in the bed with Hadley and Hemingway in her pyjamas without any sexual overtones. She also liked to go skinny-dipping with them, free spirit that she was. Neither was the sexiness of her figure lost on Hemingway, contrasted as it was with Hadley's growing frumpiness since Bumby. Pauline watched and waited, plotting her move like a military campaign. Sooner or later, she knew Hemingway wouldn't be able to resist her, but she pretended to be as interested in Hadley as she was in him. Hadley was too trusting to suspect an ulterior motive even when it was staring her in the face.

Pauline often told Hadley she loved her more than Hemingway, as if to ward off suspicion of her trying to wangle her way into his affections. The situation between the three of them amounted to a *menage-a-trois* without the sex. Hadley feared the worst for a long time but felt if she ignored it, it might go away.

When Pauline started to accompany them on ski trips to Schruns, however, Hadley became worried. She knew she was no match for her in the charm stakes so she decided to sit it out, hoping all her husband needed was some temporary *divertissement*. In some ways Pauline even took the pressure off her to 'perform'. Reserved by nature, she could retreat into the background while the younger couple had their high jinks.

Hadley couldn't understand what it was that Pauline had which she hadn't. Was it her sex appeal? She had seen her naked, she informed her husband, and didn't notice anything exceptional. Hemingway himself couldn't even put it into words.

Pauline herself felt her greatest asset was her practicality. She regarded both Hemingway and Hadley as rather hopeless romantics. What Hemingway needed to advance his career, she felt, was a wife who could also double as a kind of business manager or PR person. She felt up to the task of handling both roles.

Hemingway himself didn't even think Pauline was beautiful. It was her personality and sexual magnetism he fell in love with. And her vitality. Hadley didn't have her *Vogue* wardrobe either - though this was more Hemingway's fault than her own. (He was too busy bringing her on holidays and buying her paintings like Miro's 'The Farm' to be able to afford a proper wardrobe for her).

Hadley was doubly fearful of the threat Pauline posed because of her awareness of the way Hemingway could so easily be lured off-track in matters of the heart. He was always quick to respond to a woman's advances even if he wasn't in the least interested in her romantically. If he *was,* as was the case with Pauline, it became that much more difficult to say 'Hands off - I'm married.'

If the decision was left to Hemingway, he would have strung both Hadley and Pauline along together indefinitely - not exactly playing them off against one another but refusing to acknowledge his growing attraction to Pauline because he didn't want to give Hadley up. It was true what he said to his parents in a letter he wrote to them after Pauline blew the situation open: he was simply in love with two women at the one time.

His physical courage was never in question, but he lacked the moral gumption to square up to Hadley and tell her exactly how much he had fallen for Pauline. He preferred to keep the two relationships going simultaneously until events conspired towards some resolution. It was the messy - and spineless - way to do it.

Hemingway, in fact, probably never even *understood* the difference between moral and physical courage. After William Faulkner accused him of lacking courage in the forties (meaning he didn't take enough chances as a writer) he completely misunderstood his meaning and retaliated by getting Buck Lanham to send Faulkner a testimonial to his bravery in the war.

Pauline was also well aware of his tendency towards vacillation. She knew full well he was capable of casting her in the mould of 'the other woman' until such time as his infatuation with her had spun itself out. With this in mind, she eventually did all in her power to advertise the situation between Hemingway and herself to Hadley, hoping to accelerate a dramatic resolution.

She had played her cards carefully until she brought matters to such a pass. She was well aware of the importance of keeping the affair a secret in the early stages, all too well aware that the very illicit nature of their meetings was half the thrill for Hemingway, if not for herself. The ultimatum had to be timed until it was too late for Hemingway to avoid it, or want to run away from it - which was, in fact, what happened. Hadley eventually asked Pauline's sister Jinny if she thought Pauline was falling in love with her husband. Jinny replied, 'I think they are very fond of each other', which was all Hadley needed to know where she stood.

Jinny's comment, Hadley felt, was like an announcement that their marriage was over. When she went back to the sawmill,

Hemingway was alone and she confronted him with the situation. He didn't want to know about it, fending off her accusations. 'Why can't we go on the way we are?' he said meekly, trying to straddle both women in duplicitous fashion. Hadley might well have gone along with this state of affairs hoping it would burn itself out, but now that it was out in the open, Pauline seized the moment, realising Hemingway was well capable of vacillating and maybe staying with Hadley unless she acted fast. She expressed a wish to meet Hadley, but Hadley demurred, fearing she would be no match for her in a showdown.

But there was no turning back now. Pauline had succeeded in getting the situation out in the open through Jinny and it was only a matter of time before she would have her man one way or another.

The woman who had overseen *In Our Time*, *The Torrents of Spring* and the first draft of *The Sun Also Rises* - not to mention all the stories where he cut his literary teeth - was soon to be out of his life for good. Her 'parfait, gentil knight' - as she had dubbed him after reading Chaucer's Prologue to *The Canterbury Tales* - was suddenly turning into the villain of the piece.

He would never be as happy as he had been with Hadley, however. He was, as John Dos Passos put it, suddenly 'an expatriate from the Garden of Eden'.

Not only did he never stop loving Hadley; his love for her grew with time even though they were apart. This was due to the fact that the women he met - and married - afterwards could never hope to emulate her purity and selflessness. Also, distance (and time) lent a certain amount of enchantment to his memory of the years they spent together. (By the time he came to write *A Moveable Feast* at the end of his life, she had become almost a fantasy figure).

Hadley remained philosophical about Hemingway leaving her right up until her death. She never bad-mouthed him as his other wives would, insisting that he had always treated her like a perfect gentle-man. Their relationship just ran its course; it was as simple as that.

She showed her love for him much more by letting him go away from her without rancour than she did even during the heady days of their famous epistolary courtship. She must have thought their feelings for one another would last forever then, as must he. To have a love that meant as much as life itself whisked away in an instant is a stern test of character, but Hadley withstood the storm and got on with her life. Hemingway was touched by this, as well he might have been. It would stand in sharp contrast to the behaviour of future wives when these marriages, in their turn, would go sour. The cantankerousness of Pauline, and later on Martha Gellhorn, made him appreciate Hadley for what she was. (He would never forget her refinement, and kept in touch with her right until the end of his life, phoning her mere weeks before he killed himself for help on the composition of *A Moveable Feast*, the book in which he idealised her in the same way he had done during their halcyon years, as if no time had elapsed at all, and nothing had gone bad.)

After Hemingway's parents heard the rumours of his impending divorce they wrote to him saying they sincerely hoped that such gossip wasn't true. The irony was that their own marriage was hardly ideal. (Neither of them, for example, knew the other had written to him, which was in itself a comment on their poor communication with one another).

Divorce had always been a dirty word in Oak Park. Even if married couples abhorred one another they stuck together for the sake of respectability. It was the same with any other problem. The whited sepulchres of this arch neighbourhood concealed a multitude, and now the son of one of its most respected denizens was casting a pall on that tradition - first with his 'dirty' books and now with his marital split.

His father wrote to him saying he rejoiced in his talents and success, but qualified the praise by telling him he prayed for him 'that you may in some way reclaim your dear Hadley and Bumby'. He exhorted him to 'put on the armour of God and shun evil companions', and ended with the old chestnut: 'Remember - What doth it profit a man if he gain the whole world and lose his own soul'.

Hemingway wrote back a conscientious letter saying the split was amicable and that he loved both women but had to do what he was doing nonetheless. To close friends however, he would phrase it all more bluntly. When they asked him why he was leaving Hadley, he said: 'Because I am a son of a bitch'. Had he said this to his mother, he would have been giving her yet another stick to beat him with.

Hadley had made it a precondition of the divorce that he would spend a hundred days away from Pauline. What she was really doing was hoping against hope that within that time frame he would realise he really loved her more than Pauline and come back. Alas, it didn't happen that way, the device only serving to throw Hemingway and Pauline closer together. The forbidden fruit had always been a great balm to a relationship, all the way from *Romeo & Juliet*. Nonetheless, Hemingway, a man who was infinitely more prone to loneliness than one would imagine, didn't think he'd last the pace and confided to Pauline that suicide might be the only option for him.

Separated from Pauline, he wrote dramatically: 'You see Pfife I think that when two people love each other terribly much and need each other in every way and then go away from each other it works almost as bad as an abortion.'

Three months into the proposed hundred days Hadley realised the jig was up and freed her distraught husband from his enforced isolation. 'I might have been the Emperor Tiberius,' she remarked afterwards, all too well aware that the velvet glove would probably have been a more beneficial approach to the crisis than the iron fist.

After the divorce papers were finalised she told Marcelline: 'If I'd had any sense at all I'd have let him go with Pauline and burn himself out and then we could have begun again.' Possibly, but one doubts the marriage would have lasted much longer anyway. There would have been another Pauline Pfeiffer if this one didn't work out, and another one after that again. He was like a man with a mission, and his wife was just one part of the plan.

When she wrote to tell him that the three months separation

clause (what he would call The Hundred Days War) was officially off, he became so excited and full of good will that he replied by informing her he was giving her all the monies he would earn from *The Sun Also Rises*, and also making a will that would make Bumby the chief beneficiary of any income he ever received from his books.

The son of a bitch, it seemed, still had some redeeming qualities. But without Hadley, as he well knew, there probably wouldn't have been a book in the first place.

The gesture was really one of relief rather than bounty: he was buying his way out of the marriage in the same way some said he had bought his way into it, courtesy of Hadley's Trust Fund. Now they were quits.

What made Hemingway even more guilty about it all was Hadley's dignified attitude. If she swore at him or hit him it would have made it all marginally easier, but she bore the situation with true stoical fortitude - almost like a Hemingway code-heroine, in fact.

Bumby often remarked in years to come that it was a blessing in disguise that Hemingway divorced her when he did, because she was still an attractive and desirable woman in 1928, and the marriage was fated to end sometime anyway, considering they were both going in different directions fast even by the mid-twenties.

In order to marry Pauline, who was a Catholic, Hemingway effectively had to state that his marriage to Hadley, a non-believer, had been invalid, which was somewhat ironic considering this was arguably the only one of his wives whom he really loved. He also claimed that he had been baptised by a priest as he lay wounded in Italy during the war, which was always going to be difficult to prove or disprove. Knowing Hemingway as we do now, of course, there's every chance it was another of his colourful (but for now very convenient) tall tales.

If this was the case, however, why did he marry Hadley in a Methodist church two years later? It's likely he was anointed in 1918 but allowed the ritual to take place more from fear that he would die than any more religious conviction.

His reasons for converting to Catholicism seemed to be based more on expedience, and fascination with Catholicism's cultural appendages, than anything more theological or orthodox. He was aligning himself to what Nick Adams had called a 'fake ideal' to get out of a dead marriage, moral idealism already being a thing of the past.

From another point of view, Catholicism appealed to the romantic in him. It was a colourful religion, and it also had its share of poets, alcoholics and beautiful dreamers: three of Hemingway's favourite kinds of people.

Pauline saw his conversion a different way. 'The outlet of confession will be very good for him,' she noted.

The literary set of Paris was devastated at the news that he was splitting from Hadley for once and for all. They looked like the happiest married couple (if not the *only* happily married couple) in the bohemian brigade. Ford Madox Ford, Ezra Pound, Gertrude Stein and Scott Fitzgerald all had unusual and/or trouble-strewn relationships, but Hemingway and Hadley looked for all the world like an idyllic pair. They were usually surrounded by couples who flaunted their promiscuity and had 'open' marriages, which made their own all the more unusual. (Though Hemingway himself once told Bill Smith that if he wasn't in love with the woman he married, he'd sleep with whoever he wished to 'without entanglements')

Hemingway gave Hadley the gift of self-belief and self-reliance, but no sooner had she mastered these gifts than he left her. Another woman would have been embittered by this turn of events, but with Hadley the glass was always half full. She appreciated what he had done for her and accepted the fact that their relationship had burned itself out. She recovered from the divorce much better than Pauline would fourteen years on, getting her life together while she yet had a life to live.

Even though he deserted Hadley, he still insisted on seeing her after Pauline went back to the States. When he did, she told him she had fallen in love with Paul Mowrer, the man she would eventually marry. Ironically enough, Mowrer was already married with two children. Hemingway approved of him and was pleased at this. He cabled Pauline in their familiar code and said 'Harrison happy'. 'Harrison' was Hadley. He had taken the name from her former piano teacher, a man she had once fancied. In this instance it had a certain wry significance.

Hadley didn't 'steal' Paul from his wife in the way that Pauline 'stole' Ernest from her, as his marriage was dead for many years now. He had merely stayed with his wife for the sake of their children.

Hadley told her friend Alice Sokoloff towards the end of her life that she wasn't in love with Mowrer when she first met him, but that the love 'grew and grew and grew' as they did things together. Mowrer invited Hemingway to dinner one night after he heard he was having problems with Hadley and asked him if it was true that the marriage was over. Hemingway told him it was, but didn't know the reason why he was asking.

Mowrer was the foreign editor of *The Chicago Daily News* and the first recipient of the Pulitzer Prize for foreign correspondence. He was a lover of poetry and the outdoors, but there any comparison with Hadley's previous husband ended.

Hadley and Mowrer had an immediate rapport and enjoyed many happy, tranquil years together. Being Mrs Paul Mowrer didn't have quite the same buzz as being Mrs Ernest Hemingway, but Hadley was past needing that kind of adrenalin now; maybe she never had.

Their marriage was seen by many to be an anti-climax, but it had an austere charm for Hadley that was almost a pleasant antidote from the alliance with Hemingway, which was like living over the San Andreas fault. Bumby claimed that she would have died young had she stayed married to him, such was the pace of their life.

Mowrer and Hemingway never fell out, and Hemingway always referred to him fondly in his letters, but sometimes Hadley had to check herself if she reminisced too poignantly about the Paris years with her old husband for fear of alienating her new one. (After she published her memoirs in 1973, she gave a lecture about her life to a group of college students and one of them said to her, 'Wasn't it an awful letdown living with Paul Mowrer after Hemingway?' She was too upset by the question to reply to it, but the reality of the situation was that she fared much better in the romantic lottery than Hemingway himself, who went on to have three problematic marriages after Hadley, neither of which quite captured the magic he had with her. 'We always loved each other,' she would tell Jack, 'we just couldn't live together.')

Hemingway wrote to Scott Fitzgerald in October to say Hadley was divorcing him - itself a misleading phrase - but that he would refrain 'from any half-turnings on of the gas or slitting of the wrists with sterilised razor blades'. The self-pitying tone is tinged with humour, as well it might have been. He, after all, was the one who had called the shots. He was getting what he wanted, despite the momentary pain.

Fitzgerald asked Hadley rather tactlessly one night, 'Are you always going to live under Ernest's shadow?', but nothing could have been farther than the truth. She was only under his shadow as long as he loved her. When the love went away she dusted herself down, got on with her life and became her own woman. She was never one for torturing herself nurturing dead dreams.

The fact that Hemingway was bequeathing all received and future royalties from *The Sun Also Rises* to Hadley meant that he was, as he put it, 'poorer than any time since I was fourteen, with an earning capacity of what stories I sell to Scribners'. Generosity, however, was a way of assuaging his guilt over Pauline. 'The only thing in life I've ever had any luck being decent about is money,' he said 'so I'm very splendid and punctilious about that'. He was giving Hadley the twelve pieces of silver, in other words; he would clothe her in mourning as 'Pfife' waited patiently to share his bed on a permanent basis.

He was an author with Scribners; he had his new woman and he had fame. But would he be able to exploit them to the full or was he going to carry a sense of paradise lost with him? Would marriage fix everything or botch it up completely? It wasn't like trying on a new suit of clothes and discarding the old one. Hadley cast a long shadow and would continue to do so, long before things 'went to hell' with Pauline.

He had spent most of his young life thus far dreaming of a big book that would make him rich and famous. Now that it was here, ironically, he couldn't celebrate it as he might have wished. Hadley was gone, and Bumby too, and with them all his old routines. Neither had he the money from the book. He loved Pauline, but maybe not quite as much as when theirs was a forbidden love, and staying with Hadley still an option. This was a more business-like liaison than the one with Hadley, and no longer would he be very poor and very happy in a tiny Paris dwelling. From here on in he was a successful writer rather than an heir apparent and that created its own challenge. He would have to justify the title in a new guise, and with a degree of moral guilt Pauline could only partially assuage.

He added insult to injury one night when he walked into a bar with Pauline and spotted Hadley across the way. In a drunken stupor he started to tell her that their marriage was a null affair because it hadn't been performed by a priest, whereupon Hadley exclaimed astutely, 'If that's the case, then Bumby is mine alone.' Hemingway responded to this (legitimate) assertion by telling her he wanted Bumby to become a Catholic as well, but Hadley dug in her heels, telling him Bumby was an Episcopalian and an Episcopalian he woud stay, at least until he was eighteen, when he could be 'as many Catholics as he wants'.

Hemingway's official denial of the viability of his marriage to Hadley in the eyes of the church in effect made Bumby illegitimate. It galled her that he used her Protestant religion as a way of nullifying his marriage to her vis-a-vis the Catholic church so he could marry

Pauline. (Years later, Pauline would also witness him pulling a similar stunt when he used her inability to procreate as a way out of that marriage.)

He gave A.E. Hotchner a different reason altogether why Catholicism was such an attractive religion to him. After divorcing Hadley, he told Hotchner, he found it difficult to make love to Pauline. To try and alleviate the problem, he went to doctors, and even a mystic. The latter man advised him to fasten electrodes to his hands and feet, but this didn't work either. Pauline finally suggested prayer. He went to a church two blocks away and then back to bed with her and the pair of them 'made love like we invented it.'

Afterwards he told Leicester, 'We never had any trouble again', adding gamely, 'That's when I became a Catholic.'

Fame and Misfortune

Hemingway divorced Hadley in 1927. He published another collection of stories later in the same year. The title said it all: *Men Without Women.*

The New York Herald Tribune said his talent had contracted instead of expanded with the book, a sentiment repeated by other critics who were already tiring of his expectable scenarios.

'He discards details with a magnificent lavishness,' wrote Dorothy Parker after she read the book. 'He keeps his words to their short path.' Not everyone was as impressed.

Virginia Woolf's critique of the book was harsh, but vividly insightful. Hemingway's characters, she opined, 'are the people one may have seen showing off at some cafe, talking a rapid, high-pitched slang because slang is the speech of the herd.' They seemed to be at their ease, she said, 'yet if we look at them a little from the shadow (they're) not at their ease at all...So it would seem that the thing that is faked is character. Mr Hemingway leans against the flanks of that particular bull after the horns have passed.'

He's cruder here than he has been before - about homosexuality, about castration, about violence in general...and about his own family background.

The book was published in October. Two months later it had sold a record 13,000 copies. It's a collection which is distinguished more by its shorter stories than the long-winded ones like 'The Undefeated' and 'Fifty Grand'. 'In Another Country' was one of Hemingway's own favourites and it's not difficult to see why.

Set against the backdrop of his physiotherapy sessions at the Ospedale Maggiore after being wounded in the war, the main emphasis of the story isn't himself but another war veteran, a major who has just lost his wife. It's here that it acquires its poignant status. Nobody should have anything in their life that they cannot afford to lose, the major announces, in true Hemingway spirit. Becoming dependent on anything means we're open to being hurt, and in the lottery of life that usually means one day we *will* be. These are the kinds of stakes we play for, in war and peace alike. The major's wife dies just as Catherine Barkley did, leaving a lost and bitter man behind.

'In the fall,' he writes, 'the war was always there, but we did not go to it any more.' It's a sentence that begs many questions. What war, for instance? And where is 'there'? Who, for that matter, is 'we'. And what does 'any more' mean? Sentences like this, stripped of anything but the essential, whet the appetite for more. It's a language that's pruned almost to nothing but is still stylised.

Hemingway isn't so much shrinking language here as extending its possibilities. All those supposedly flat sentences aren't really flat. They're always pregnant with meaning; there's something beyond them enclosed in them. Each time a reader read them he could intuit new subtexts and new innuendoes. You knew that he meant more than he said, and also that he was luring you into adopting some stance. He didn't state what this was, but left enough hints for you to conjure up your own parameters.

The 'go to it' phrase also suggests the war is an event, a kind of circus. In a sense, we're back in the traumatised world of Krebs from 'Soldier's Home'. In fact what's related here is probably truer to the reality of Hemingway's war wounds than what was written in the earlier work. His character here has been given medals simply because he's an American. He had been wounded in the war, 'but we all knew that being wounded, after all, was really an accident.'

The most famous story here is *The Killers*. An ostensibly straightforward parable about an ex-heavyweight boxer awaiting the arrival of two hitmen from Chicago, Robert Frost called it 'the world's greatest short story.' This was somewhat generous: there isn't *that* much beneath the surface as in much of his other work.

Even though it only runs for thirteen pages, *The Killers* became a full-length film: apt testament to the richness inherent in even the slightest of Hemingway's tableaus. The idea of a man with nowhere to run is appetising, delivered as it is in this hard-boiled lingua. Hemingway refuses to ink in the details of his plight, and we end as wisely as we began.

Much the same could be said of 'Hills Like White Elephants', another scenario that's stripped to the bone. We're presented with a nondescript man and his girlfriend as they sit together outside a railway station in the Ebro valley. He tries to persuade her to have an abortion against her wishes, though couching his wishes in such delicate terms that you have to read the story at least twice to realise what a bastard he is. They're both frustrated in different ways. Her reluctance to 'let the air in' makes him nag at her like the drip-drip of a tap until she finally explodes with 'Will you please please please please please please please stop talking?'

The couple drink beer and bicker as they wait for the Madrid Express to take them to that city for her abortion, but nowhere is this fact mentioned. We get it all by innuendo, a fact that anybody familiar with Hemingway's patois will be expecting. Rarely has his repetition been as impressive as here, however, in capturing the nagging of the male character.

In a conversation that dangles tensely, we see him exploiting his girlfriend verbally just as he has physically. They converse in fits and starts with muted theatricality as he studiously avoids tackling the issue head on. The beer and the hills act as temporary distractions but we always return to the main (unstated) point at issue.

This is one of Hemingway's most simple and yet reverberative stories, no more than a fragment really, delivered in the lean, frugal style that made him famous.

The idea of having 'it' done - the word occurs about a dozen times, like a drumbeat - is something that disturbs the woman deeply, the man less so. The emptiness of their relationship is captured in their monosyllabic exchanges, and when the woman says 'I feel fine,' at the end of the story, we know she's anything but that. One is reminded of

Mrs Elliot feeling 'quite happy' at the end of 'Mr and Mrs Elliot'. Hemingway wrote it while on honeymoon with Pauline, perhaps as a wry coda to his marriage to Hadley, a marriage that came unstuck largely due to the manner in which Bumby had come between them.

'The good parts of a book,' he said once, 'may be only something a writer is lucky enough to overhear, or it may be the wreck of his whole damn life.' Hemingway put the latter element into many of his books, but in 'Hills Like White Elephants' we feel we're eavesdropping on a private conversation, which lends the story a lot of credibility.

He always insisted he made it up, which is probably true. Its source, in any case, is neither here nor there. What's important is that he has captured two people's characters in a cameo without really telling us anything about them. The dialogue, again, is the main narrator.

'Now I Lay Me', Scott Fitzgerald's favourite story from the collection, was probably the one his mother could never forgive, considering the manner in which he came out of the closet so forcibly about her in it. We're presented with her burning all his father's beloved tools and arrowheads: one of the few times Hemingway chose a real-life incident with which to amplify his feelings of scepticism about the long term viability of the marital state. The scepticism itself, however, is fairly ubiquitous. (Hemingway's disenchantment with male-female relationships can be located in any number of stories, from 'Hills Like White Elephants' through 'Cat in the Rain' to 'Cross Country Snow', 'A Canary For One', 'Homage to Switzerland' and so on. None of these features a happily married couple - or even a happily dating one.)

In the same way as Hemingway thought he would silence those who accused him of copying Anderson with *The Torrents of Spring*, so he tried to addle those who accused him of copying Ring Lardner by spoofing him in his story 'Fifty Grand'. The Lardner label haunted him through most of his early writing career. Indeed, in his teens he was dubbed 'our Ring Lardner Junior' by *Trapeze,* one of the magazines he wrote for. The point is that Lardner was a comic writer, and Hemingway someone who *began* with comedy and then went into the grisly innards of the psyche. It's a bit like comparing Bob Hope to Woody Allen.

This wasn't one of Hemingway's greater short story collections, but it outsold *Tender is the Night,* which can't have made Scott Fitzgerald too proud. It didn't have the surprises of its predecessor, but *In Our Time* was always going to be a hard act to follow. Readers were already beginning to secondguess the precocious author with the incantatory undulations and snapshot snippets.

Reviews of the book ranged from those who saw Hemingway as the pioneering voice of a new age to those who disparaged his 'sordid little catastrophes' as the work of a nihilist bore.

He himself had mixed feelings when critics called the stories nothing more than reportage. On the one hand he was flattered because it was high testament to their veracity considering he made them up, but on the other, if readers believed these critics, and many did, it reduced him to the level of a journalist posing as a fiction writer.

After he was accused of being a mere documenter of facts rather than an imaginative writer upon the publication of *In Our Time,* he commented to Scott Fitzgerald, 'God. what a life I must have had'. Years later he would say that all good books were alike in the sense that they were 'truer than if they had really happened'. Life, in other words, is unbelievable, but it's the duty of fiction to have a higher value. Truth may be stranger than fiction, as the old saw goes, but fiction must be purer and more refined.

Hemingway was also working on *A Farewell to Arms* at this time, but the writing of that book was halted by the most devastating news he could have received from Oak Park: his father had committed suicide.

The man who had spent all his life saving other people's had now taken his own. It was that absurd - and that sudden. If he had contemplated it before he had never voiced such thoughts to any living being. What a private hell he must have endured during his last years, Ernest mused, when those he was living with trivialised his health and financial concerns, and misinterpreted his erratic behaviour patterns. But it was too late for soulsearching or fingerpointing now. Now all they could do was bury him. And - if they were lucky - forget the sins of the past.

He was numbed when he heard the news but maybe it wasn't totally unexpected. On his last visit home he noticed his father wasn't the man he used to be. Not only was he suffering from hyper-tension, but also diabetes, insomnia, angina, blinding headaches and high blood pressure. There were also a horde of very pressing financial problems from which he felt he couldn't extricate himself. In 1925 he invested his life savings in some Florida real estate which depreciated in value, making it difficult for him to meet the Oak Park mortgage now that his medical practice, the main source of revenue in the past, was slackening off.

After his own father had died in 1926, he wrote to Ernest saying that he had slipped away with no pain, adding: 'The day before he had written several letters *and paid up all his bills'*. (The italics are mine). So one must never underestimate the importance of finances for him.

Apart from the fact that Clarence's medical practice was dwindling, Grace was also losing some of her musical pupils to the more sophisticated academies that were springing up in the area. All in all it was a bleak scenario what with the dead Florida property and a family still not fully raised. His wife also had extravagant tastes, and seemed blissfully unaware of any crisis. Maybe he felt that by killing himself his family would have been able to get by on his life insurance policy.

At the time he died he had made plans to retire to Florida, where he would have been a virtual neighbour of Ernest's in Key West. He intended to practice medicine there. It would also be a way of being close to the Florida land they owned, to see could he escape from that bum deal with something salvaged. But now that could never be.

Clarence's judgement in property was about as well-advised as his choice of wife. The bottom fell out of the Florida land rush almost as soon as his signature was dry on the purchase document. If he had gotten out early when he sniffed disaster he might have been able to cut his losses but he hung on through 1927 and 1928 hoping the tide would turn. It didn't - and neither did a couple of hurricanes in Florida help. The dream seemed blighted, like most other things about his later life. The man who had been a habitual worrier now had good reason to be concerned. It was looking increasingly unlikely that he would be able to move close to his famous son and sit out his last years fishing the Gulf Stream with him. He was bitched from the start.

According to Marcelline, Clarence almost totally changed his personality in his last year, becoming increasingly agitated for little or no reason and retiring to his room like a recluse. He kept everything under lock and key - including his clothes closet - and communicated only vaguely with his wife and children. Concern about money, health and his dwindling practice made him a mental wreck. The only thing that sustained him was the prospect of moving to Florida. 'Gracie will paint her pictures and I'll grow oranges,' he told everyone. But maybe he knew deep down that it was never going to happen.

When Nick Adams asks his father why the indian killed himself in 'Indian Camp', he replies, 'I don't know. Nick. He couldn't stand things, I guess'. And now the physician had done himself in - not with a cut-throat razor, but rather his father's Civil War pistol. Was it his domination by Grace or a morbid fear of bankruptcy that caused it? Not long before he pulled the trigger he had asked his brother George for a loan to help him out of the financial crisis that started after the Florida property slumped, but it was refused.

When he told George of his financial problems, George told him to sell off the Florida lots, but he said he couldn't, that they were an investment for his family. It was a classic confrontation between a romantic and a realist, with neither giving way.

George's reaction to Clarence was: You got yourself into this mess, get yourself out of it. At the funeral, George tried his best to paper over that particular crack, stressing the fact that Clarence's financial affairs were in order on the day he died. This was a lie, but one he had to tell to preserve his social standing in Oak Park, and stave off any possible broadsides from Ernest or his siblings.

Hemingway must have had a residue of guilt too. Only the previous September his father had written to him asking him if he would accompany him on a trip to the Smoky Mountains in North Carolina. Ernest replied that he was too busy with his book, and Bumby as well, to entertain the idea. Clarence wrote back saying he understood his predicament.

On the morning of December 6, Clarence woke with a pain in his foot. He feared it might be gangrene, the result of his neglected diabetes, having once had a patient who lost a leg that way. He mentioned it to Grace, but only casually. Afterwards he did his daily calls. When he came home he told Grace he was going to lie down until lunchtime. He made his way slowly upstairs, hanging onto the banister railing. A short time later Leicester, who was home from school with a cold, heard a shot. He would never forget the sound it made. When he ran into his father's room, he saw him sprawled over the bed, a Smith & Wesson revolver in his hand. It was a clean, fatal shot; a traumatised doctor's alternative to surgery and/or bankruptcy.

Hemingway often changed his theories about why his father killed himself. Under the influence of drink he would tell people 'the All-American bitch' was responsible, but in 1929 he said in a letter to Grace that his Uncle George had 'done more than anyone to kill Dad'. Blaming his father's death solely on his mother, while understandable considering his own experiences with that woman, fell into the great Hemingway tradition of 'Whatever you don't fully understand, blame it on a woman.'

When he got the news, he must have felt a momentary pang that it wasn't his mother who put the pistol to her temple. His father, after all, was 'the only one I ever gave a damn about'. Also, if the old man was *really* that concerned about money, Ernest could have helped him out very soon considering the fact that the soon-to-be-published *A Farewell to Arms* would make him very wealthy indeed.

He told A.E. Hotchner that it took him twenty years to learn to face up to the suicide. What bothered him most was the fact that he had written him a letter enclosing a cheque for a debt his father was worried about, and it arrived the very day of the suicide. Hemingway believed that if his father had opened the letter he wouldn't have pulled the trigger.

He would have had more respect for his father if he killed himself from depression than if he did so out of fear of his wife. The former would have been the kind of philosophical gloom he himself would succumb to some thirty years on, but the latter was the true mark of a *clochard*.

When journalist Robert Manning asked Hemingway towards the end of his life if he thought his father showed courage in killing himself, he said, 'No. It's everybody's right, but there's a certain amount of egotism in it and a certain disregard of others.' He failed to expound further, changing the topic as if it was a sore point, as indeed it was.

In both *For Whom the Bell Tolls* and *Green Hills of Africa* Hemingway refers to his father as a coward for killing himself. His excessive anger at him for doing so possibly hints at a fear that he too could see himself one day going down this turbulent road. Indeed, he had often talked about suicide as an escape-hatch from his problems, even as early as when his marriage with Hadley was breaking up and he was forced to spend time away from Pauline before the divorce was finalised. By condemning his father as a coward, he was, in a sense, pre-emptying the criticism of those who would accuse him in the same vein in 1961. Had he really preconceived the manner of his death this early? One can but surmise.

At the funeral he said to Madelaine, half in jest (or was it?) 'I'll probably go the same way'. Even in his Paris notebooks he speculated about various ways of killing oneself. In fact he spent so much time flirting with the idea of suicide - if not the possibility of it - the manner of his father's passing must have posed, as Archibald MacLeish noted 'a personal threat'.

In retrospect it's possible to see the suicide almost as a dress rehearsal for his own one. They had similar personalities, both being hyper-tense, and towards the end of their lives, each suffered badly from high blood pressure, diabetes and near-paranoid financial concerns.

He also told Marcelline at the funeral that his father would burn in hell for all eternity for this 'mortal sin'. It was a comment that was uncharacteristic of him, and maybe he said it to give a jolt to his old rival, or as a kind of reaction to his father's comment not so long ago about him being in danger of losing his own soul after deciding to leave Hadley.

His father was a product of his generation, conservative and parochial in his way but a decent soul nonetheless, trying to do the best for his children according to his lights, no matter how much life ground him down. He made the ultimate sacrifice in killing himself so that his insurance policy could see them out of the financial straits he couldn't live with. Was this the damning sin Hemingway would charge him with, or a stab at a kind of tacky martyrdom?

Whatever it was, the upshot was that Ernest was now the 'man of the house' (Leicester was still in school). It would be a new experience for Grace to have to take orders from the young man she had once branded as being a sponger before kicking him out of Windemere. He was a man of means now, and not someone likely to let her of the hook for the sins of the past. He slotted himself into the new role like one to the manner born, which was a bitter pill for his mother to swallow. She might have been able to bully him as an adolescent, but hardly now. The boot was on the other foot and he who paid the piper was calling the tune.

Suddenly, playing cello for a woman he despised when he really wanted to be in the woods with his father seemed like a scene from another life. The balance of power had shifted to the erstwhile rebel for once and for all, and Pressure Under Grace was very definitely a thing of the past.

There were many financial problems to be sorted out, however. His mother's assets comprised the summer cottages on Walloon Lake - which Ernest had been turfed out of all those years ago - the dead Florida property, the home residence in Oak Park which still had an outstanding mortgage, and an insurance policy worth $25,000. It wasn't the scenario she had envisaged as a young woman intent on conquering the world. Nor did she envisage being answerable to the person who had once been a liability to her, and someone she had walked on. It was a far cry from Madison Square Gardens to being advised to get rid of the Florida property and take in boarders, but that was how matters stood as viewed by Hemingway *fills*.

It must have been sweet revenge for him to be able to talk to the All-American bitch man-to-man for once. It was like a metaphorical vindication of his father - but coming just that little bit too late to do the old man any good.

The irony was choice. Grace had delighted in the role of Maternal Banker when she told her son he had overdrawn on his emotional bank account when he was twenty-one; now, seven years later, he had the opportunity to tell her she had overdrawn on her *actual* one.

Suddenly, it seemed a long time since those robins sang their sweet songs on July 21 1899.

'Never threaten me with what to do,' she wrote to him after he told her to sell off the Florida property, 'Your father tried that once when we were married first and he lived to regret it.' Maybe he did, but his son wouldn't. It was presumptuous of Grace to imagine she could still bargain gamely with a man who, apart from being on the brink of world fame, was the one who now held the purse-strings.

His reply to her was crisp. 'I am a very different man from my father,' he wrote, 'and I never threaten anyone. I only make promises. If I say that if you do not do certain sound things I will no longer contribute to your support it means factually and exactly that.' The scoreline between the two old enemies was now one-all. She would never write him an aggressive letter again, and any time she visited him it would be with her tail between her legs. In practical terms, the old bitch had lost her teeth.

Even though he despised her, he still set up a trust fund for her with $30, 000 of his own money and $20, 000 of Hadley's. In return for his generosity Grace asked him if there was anything he wanted. He told her he would like to own Windemere Cottage on Lake Walloon, and she promptly deeded it over to him, hoping he would bring his sons back to it some day so they could experience the same childhood memories as he did. (This never transpired, however. Not only did Hemingway not wish to write about Oak Park; the idea of spending time back there again turned his stomach. He subsequently gave Windemere to Madelaine on the understanding that it should never be sold, and that it should eventually go to his godchild Ernest Hemingway Mainland.)

Before he went away, he asked her to send him the gun his father had used to kill himself. In retrospect such a request is significantly morbid. It was also one he repeatedly denied, preferring to tell friends that she had actually sent it to him unsolicited. It had been seized by the coroner's office but was released after much bureaucratic paper-filling. When Hemingway received it he threw it into a lake in a kind of ritualistic cleansing.

The practical details of the funeral took Hemingway's mind off the tragedy somewhat. So did his work. By now he was seven months into his new novel, just as Pauline was seven months pregnant with his second child. Each would be a traumatic birth in its way.

Writing had always carried him through the depressed periods of his life. It had helped him through the divorce with Hadley and now it would do the same with his father. Indeed, it was because he was so immersed in *A Farewell to Arms* that he had to turn down his father's invitation to join him for a trip to the mountains.

He effectively wrote the book anywhere he could hang his hat - Wyoming, Key West, Kansas, and so on. The theory was that shifting locations so haphazardly would entice the muse to visit more readily. It was an impressionistic work that showed the influence of both Joyce and Stein in the stream-of-consciousness passages, but which also had his wilfully bumpy stop-go idiom - the latter perhaps more suitable to his subject matter. The style was almost a conscious repudiation of the 'cablese' that had characterised him heretofore. This had been fine for the stories, but he was going for the bigger stage now. It was time to trade in spareness for the epic sweep.

The title of the book was ambiguous, carrying an inset message that this wasn't only a renunciation of war but also, more autobiographically, of Hadley too. The farewell isn't only to Catherine Barkley, but her real-life inspiration.

He started it, as he started everything he wrote, as a short story (its first paragraph, indeed, is similar to the opening sentences of 'In Another Country') and it grew osmotically from there. Hemingway's stories had created such a rumpus, publishers kept pushing him for something whereby he would flex his literary muscles on a larger canvas, but he didn't see it happening like that. The fact that it did was as much a surprise to him as anyone else. (He even started *For Whom the Bell Tolls* as a story, which is hard to believe when you look at it now.) If his novels have urgency - and few would deny they have - it's for this reason. Such urgency gave them a sharpness that kept one's eye from wandering, and a tightness of construction that made every word count.

Another reason he wrote the book was because most of his Paris friends had written books about the war, and 'like the last girl on the block who hasn't been married, I felt my time to write a war book had come.' Already we see the competitive urge, the sense of writing as an activity like boxing where nobody remembered the guy who came second. 'I was an awful dope when I went to the war,' he confessed afterwards, 'I can remember just thinking that we were the home team and the Austrians were the visiting team.' It was like a game of baseball...and getting shelled by a mortar Hemingway's self-styled version of a home run.

It was also, of course, a love story, and even if Catherine was one-dimensional and compliant, he still saw it as his *Romeo & Juliet*. (*For Whom the Bell Tolls*, eleven years later, would be his *War & Peace* - and *The Old Man and the Sea* his *Moby Dick*.)

He wasn't at Caporetto (he was actually a cub reporter in Kansas at the time) but so faithfully did he record that retreat that the fascist government banned the novel from publication in Italy until after World War Two. 'All good books,' he would tell A.E. Hotchner in 1954, 'have one thing in common - they are truer than if they had really happened, and after you've read one of them you will feel that all that happened, happened to you and then it belongs to you forever: the happiness and unhappiness, good and evil, ecstasy and sorrow, the food, wine, beds, people and the weather.' It is the duty of fiction to be believable, novelist John McGahern once told me 'because life isn't believable.' Hemingway would have gone along with that.

He once told a group of would-be scribes: 'If you invent successfully it is more true than if you try to remember it. A big lie is more plausible than the truth. People who write fiction, if they had not taken it up, might have become very successful liars.'

This was one of the few war novels to be read as much by women as men. Hemingway alchemised a harmless little affair with a flighty nurse into a work that became a benchmark for his age, and one of the most epochal anti-war statements of modern times, albeit couched in a love story.

The opening paragraph is probably the most praised piece of Hemingway's whole canon. Not without reason, though one can take or leave those critics who read symbols of death through pregnancy into it. It remains a piece of beautifully hypnotic prose, a meticulous re-creation of a scene. This is largely due to the word 'and' being used, as Hemingway would later say, 'over and over the way Mr Johann Sebastian Bach used a note in music when he was emitting counter-point.' He had never been the music scholar his mother wanted him to be, but she would have been pleased at this analogy, even if her ear for limpid prose let her down.

The writing disimproves later, however, with Frederic and Catherine tending to speak in that kind of formalised diction that suggests the pair of them are on a first date together rather than in the throes of passion. This will also be a problem with the scenes between Robert Jordan and Maria in *For Whom the Bell Tolls*, in stark contrast to his proficiency with dialogue in the stories, where less is very definitely more.

Joyce was right when he said there was much more to Hemingway's style than people realised. If it looked easy, such an effect was only achieved after multiple re-writes. The same held true of the laconic language stripped of superfluity. He wrote to his sister Carol in 1929 apropos her own writing: 'Never use slang except in dialogue and then only when unavoidable. I am guilty of using 'swell', but only in dialogue, not as an adjective to replace the word you should use. All slang goes sour in a short time. I only use swear words that have lasted at least a thousand years for fear of getting stuff that will be simply timely and then go sour.' This is also why Hemingway chose the big themes of love, war, honour, integrity, death and the world of nature - the old verities that go on forever.

A Farewell to Arms has the first exemplification of what will become Hemingway's trademark nihilism: 'The world breaks every one and afterwards many are strong at the broken places. But those that will not break it kills. It kills the very good and the very gentle and the very brave impartially. If you are none of these you can be sure it will kill you too but there will be no special hurry.' The last line is beautifully sardonic, a magnanimous concession from the cruel fates that hover over his characters dispensing their rough justice and wanton slaughter.

Catherine has to die because it's not really in the Hemingway ethos to have people who love each other live happily ever after. Robert Jordan too will die in a future book, as will Colonel Cantwell. The only people who live are those who are unhappy...and not always these either.

Hemingway's creative powers were always activated by the sense of an ending: either the ache of regret, the pang of separation or the dying of love. Or dying *period*. Remorse was also a catalyst, or suffering that went back into the past. He liked to present us with characters whose histories only became an issue as his plots unfolded. But when such histories did unfold, they usually came with a residue of pain. This applied both to his male and female characters. The famous Hemingway 'code' dictated that such pain be borne quietly and with dignity. It was apparent not in what his characters said as what they didn't say. Or maybe in their tone of voice, or a non-committal aside.

He would always alchemise such pain. He said writers should welcome tragedy 'because serious writers have to be hurt really terrible before they can write seriously.' (Maybe it's precisely *because* Hemingway's characters - and indeed Hemingway himself - led lives of such heightened sensations that they had to desensitise themselves when things went wrong.)

An air of ominousness, in any case, hangs over the book as a whole. It's apparent in the rain, in the impending violence, in the retreating armies. So the world breaks everyone, and afterwards many are strong at the broken places. Frederic Henry certainly is. And he has many of them. As he leaves the hospital finally and walks back to the hotel in the rain, we're looking at a man who has cauterised all need out of himself. He is attacking life on its own brutal terms. If you don't care, you can't be hurt. So will he learn not caring. As will Hemingway.

As Frederic makes his final exit we remember him telling us

some chapters before that abstract words like glory and honour and courage were meaningless beside the human tragedies that unfolded daily in the rigours of war. 'There were many words that you could not stand to hear and finally only the names of places had dignity.' Or maybe the name of your dead wife...

The original ending tied up the characters' fates in neat ribbons, but Hemingway re-worked it to give it a more direct and literal edge. (He would do the same to *For Whom the Bell Tolls* years later for the same reason: to give more impact to that book's dying fall. It gave him a chance to recap on his own war experience, embellishing or subduing it as the mood took, in the same way as he tinkered around with the Agnes affair until it became the emotional fulcrum of the book.

Henry is a character even more traumatised than Jake Barnes but equally stoical about it, realising through clenched teeth that winners take nothing in a war. And losers even less. Hemingway delivers this message in diction that stuns us with its nonchalance. Once again it's left to us to fill in the spaces of Henry's emotional deadness. Having lost the war of the head he also loses that of the heart. Catherine in fact, is the lucky one to have got out of life.

'The more things in life that we love,' Henry reflects, 'the more things there are to die.' The best survival tactic is to burn the need out of oneself, as Hemingway did with Agnes. She didn't die, like Catherine, but she still left him, forcing him to come to terms with her absence in the only way he knows how. Catherine's death may even be seen as Hemingway vicariously 'punishing' Agnes for jilting him. According to Marcelline, Agnes' rejection of him was the real spring-board behind *A Farewell to Arms*. Were it not for his heartbreak, she contended, that book might never have been written.

Hemingway claimed he re-wrote the ending a staggering thirty-eight times. He was still searching for that 'one true sentence' and it didn't matter what lengths he had to go to in order to find it. His son, Patrick, asked him to edit a short story he had written one day, and after he got it back he said to his father, 'But Papa, you only changed one word'. His answer was perhaps predictable: 'I know, but if it's the *right* word, that's a lot.'

This was all very well, but there were certain problems involved in the book's overall credibility. The character of Catherine, for instance, was too idealised. Even as she lies dying at the end of the book, she thinks only of Frederic. 'Don't worry,' she says, and 'Poor darling'. Heroines don't come more angelic than this.

Catherine has frequently been condemned by critics as being unconvincing because of her submissiveness, as has the Maria of *For Whom the Bell Tolls*, but the irony is that these two women are modelled on Hadley, a real person who epitomised this very quality. They're also suffering from traumas in their past, as she was. The meek and wounded heroine is a staple in Hemingway, as is the strong, wounded hero. It is interesting that these staples are based on fact and yet often look implausible, whereas some of his weirder characters, created out of the furnace of his imagination, seem more credible by far.

We mustn't, however, synonomise Catherine with Agnes. His 'affair' with her didn't go further than 'brief hand-holding under cover of her taking his temperature,' according to Henry Villard, another hospital patient of that time. But Hemingway was always able to make legends out of trivia, and that's what happened in the odyssey from Agnes to Catherine. It also happened in his ultra-vivid evocation of the Caporetto retreat in the same book, despite his not having been there. In fact it's eminently possible that if he *had* been at Caporetto, and *had* consummated his fling with Agnes, *A Farewell to Arms* would have been a lesser book.

Agnes was always embarrassed by the fact that people mistook her for Catherine Barkley, seeing herself coming off badly in the comparison. 'I wasn't that type of girl,' she insisted, referring to the fact that Catherine was sexually free with Frederic Henry, unlike herself with Hemingway. Just as Hemingway romanticised himself in the macho character of Henry (she liked to remind people that

Hemingway never actually fired a shot in the war) so he exaggerated the intimacy between an injured Red Cross volunteer and a feckless nurse in a Italian hospital in 1918. Catherine, she claimed, was his wish fulfilment; the woman he wanted Agnes to be.

His own character, she said, wasn't anything like Henry's. He came into the hospital unspoiled, but as a result of all the attention he received, ended up becoming pampered and boorish. In this she saw the seeds of the man he would soon become, the self-serving mythmaker of the fifties. Fossalta, to be sure, had a lot to answer for.

Hemingway was spurred by his rejection of Agnes to write a fantasy of what he wanted to happen, and used his experiences with Hadley and Pauline to help him along his way. Catherine was a composite characterisation in the same way as Harold Loeb was in *The Sun Also Rises*, even if Loeb had too much tunnel vision (if not self-immersion) to see it as such. Agnes and Pauline weren't quite so persecuted looking for themselves in Catherine Barkley.

Catherine's Scottishness comes from Duff Twysden, her immediate circumstances from Agnes and her life-and-death crisis in childbirth from Pauline, so one mustn't be too facile in claiming she 'is' Agnes.

Pauline didn't die, but she was warned if she got pregnant again she could be in danger of doing so. Hemingway amassed all these diverse strains into a character, and situation, that had all the stuff of grand passions acted out against the backdrop of bullets and bravery.

A Farewell to Arms is a hyped up version of *All Quiet on the Western Front*. Having said that, however, the publication of that equally famous book denied Hemingway the right to call himself the only novelist who went behind the trenches and entered into the belly of the beast that was war, or wrote about it from the inside out.

All Quiet on the Western Front, in fact, was the only book that could challenge it on the best seller list. Not even the crash of the stock market in 1929 affected sales. The promise he had shown in *The Sun Also Rises* was suddenly transformed into a blockbuster which would sell to those who might have seen the previous book as too eclectic.

Shortly after it appeared on the shelves Dos Passos said to him, 'Do you realise you're the king of the fiction racket?' If he didn't, it would soon be an unavoidable mantle for him. As would the mantle of the writer as fodder for university dons. The latter role caused him even more grief with the passage of time. (After he heard a critic was lecturing on *A Farewell to Arms* in 1929 - his first exposure to the Hemingway litcrit industry, perhaps - he told Maxwell Perkins, 'God, it would be fine to walk in and ask a few questions and then say 'Shit, sir, I do believe you are mistaken'.)

When *A Farewell to Arms* was made into a film with Gary Cooper in 1932, the studio issued a publicity puff of Hemingway focusing on his wartime achievements and his pugilistic prowess. Hemingway delivered a counterpunch in the form of a letter to Max Perkins wherein he said that the only reason he went to Italy during the war was because there was less chance of dying there than there would have been in France. He also denigrated his talent as a boxer, which must have come as a surprise to those who had watched him consciously building up a belligerent persona over the years. Now that it was established, however, he was free to play with it as he would, and chip away at his own legend.

The irony was that if anyone else but himself had suggested he had gone to Italy so as to avoid being killed in France, they would have received either a solicitor's letter or a punch in the jaw. The publicity machine, he seemed to suggest, had outlived its usefulness. He had evolved from an adolescent firebrand into a genial man of letters who needed celluloid accolades like he needed a hole in the head.

The film version wasn't just bad, it was preposterous. The reason Gary Cooper deserted, Hemingway claimed, was because his girlfriend wouldn't write him any letters!

It wasn't long before he completely disowned the film. In a letter to Oak Park he opined jocosely that it wouldn't be long before they had Catherine giving birth to the American flag and re-naming the movie 'The Star Spangled Banner'. Well they didn't quite go that far, but one gets his drift. Hollywood had sanitised war in the same way as Oak Park sanitised life itself: by turning its face away from tragedy and pretending it didn't exist. (He also abhorred the re-make starring Rock Hudson, walking out of this after half an hour. A further irony lay in the fact that Hudson was a closet homosexual).

David O. Selznick produced the re-make but wasn't looking forward to adapting a Hemingway novel after the stories he had heard about his reactions to previous films of his books. He hoped Hemingway would like the picture, he said, but added that this was unlikely because, as he put it, 'If a character goes from Cafe A to Cafe B instead of Cafe B to Cafe A, or if a boat heads north instead of south, Hemingway is upset.' This was to simplify his grievances out of all proportion. It was, in fact, typical Hollywood.

Hemingway could never understand why anyone would go out to buy his book after seeing a film this melodramatic and trite. Somebody ought to have explained to him that it was well-nigh impossible to under-estimate public taste. Besides, even if people picked up *A Farewell to Arms* for the wrong reasons, there was still a reasonable chance they'd continue reading it for the right ones.

On first appraisal Hemingway's work looks like any film-maker's dream because of its crispness and the clarity of the dialogue, but if we look a little deeper we become aware that the subtlety of his locutions may be better suited to the page than the stage. Aldous Huxley was aware of this fact when he turned down the challenge of adapting one of his novels for the screen with these wise words: 'What Hemingway has to say is in the white spaces between the lines'. Such a comment would have pleased him mightily; it was the iceberg theory come home to roost.

In his next book, a study of bullfighting, Hemingway had no Jake Barnes or Frederic Henry to hide behind, so he decided to invent a new character, one called Ernest Hemingway, to impart his manifesto.   Such a character irked as many readers as it entertained, but *Death in the Afternoon* is a book which has weathered well with time, despite its author's genial, long-winded quirkiness.   It's an invaluable reference book that perhaps tells us more about Hemingway than its subject, but beneath what Anthony Burgess called 'the foliage of nonsense, the bar-room metaphysics and the pompous *longueurs*', there's a beautiful book trying to get out.   It was churlish - if understandable - for Max Eastman to dub it *Bull in the Afternoon*, as he did, or to accuse its author of having false hair on his chest as he wrote it.

The book has the kind of gently hectoring tone Hemingway would adopt all his life on practically every subject he would decide to tackle, from the best place to have a meal in Montmartre to how many leopards you had to kill to reach safari-heaven.   This was Papa being Papa in print for the first time, bullying us with words as he would bully literary enemies with his fists, or political ones with a double-gauge shotgun.   Just as he knew the best writers to learn from and the best way to hunt and make love, so he also knew everything worth knowing about the finca and its convoluted parabolas.   He was yet only twenty-nine, but already speaking to us like the paternalistic seer of the later works.

His friend John Dos Passos said *Death in the Afternoon* was 'absolutely the best thing' on bullfighting, but he was less impressed where 'old Hem straps on the long white beard' and pontificates.   It was a fair point, and Hemingway took it in good faith, whittling down the text as a result of it...but not enough.

In many ways, bullfighting is just a springboard for Hemingway here, allowing him to sound off on anything he wishes under this broad rubric.   And that's the way he wanted it.   He was never an ideal debater, his mind too rich to confine itself to any one topic for too long. He needed a licence to ramble - or waffle.   Points were better scored in context rather than from a debater's podium.

Even from Page One, with all those 'trues' and 'trulys' we know he means business. The bullfight ritual was an ideal metaphor for him to express his grace-under-pressure thesis. The fact that it was a duel to the death crystallised everything he felt about man's basic struggle against the world of nature. Here was a microcosm of all our lives written in bald terms on the grit of a circular arena with a studded costume and a red cape. The bull charged and the bullfighter evaded the charge or fell prey to it. He had nowhere to run and nobody to make excuses to. He didn't pretend to be anything he wasn't, like those of us in other walks of life. The only creature he attempted to deceive was the bull itself, through a mixture of style and guile. At the end of two hours either the bullfighter was left standing or the bull.

There was no more to it than that, no more except the elegance of the veronica, or bringing the bull to its knees. Some people condemned it all as being barbaric, saying it wasn't a fight at all because the bull had no chance, but Hemingway disagreed. For him it was theatre and a true exemplification of gallantry. As he watched the bulls being killed - or, occasionally, killing - he felt the Shakespearean emotions of pity and fear. He became both elated and sad at the spectacle. He saw killing as a christian sin but a pagan virtue: and his primary loyalty always lay with pagans.

'This is not being written as an apology for bullfights,' he wrote in one part of the book, but that's precisely what it was. And for all his fine writing and persuasive argumentation, if you hadn't been an *aficionado* before reading it, you would hardly be after doing so. Basically it preached to the already converted.

Bullfighting, for Hemingway, was the last vestige of paganism left in the world, which was why he was immediately drawn into it. It was paganism with a balletic overlay, however: the epitomic struggle of man and beast, a test of courage and artistry...and death in the heat of the afternoon sun.

The bullfight isn't sport, he says, but tragedy. It means danger for the bullfighter but certain death for the animal. He writes about brave bulls and cowardly bulls, about graceful toreros and manipulative ones, about people who 'show their contempt for death on a hot day in their own town square.' There is absolutely nothing for them to gain, he tells us, except the inner satisfaction of having been in the ring with the bull. But like being in Paris in the twenties, it is a thing that, once you have done it, it stays with you forever.

The 'minor aspects' of the contest, he writes, 'are not important except as they relate to the whole', thus absolving himself of the problem of how to deal with the agony of the horses, or the gratuitous bloodletting that troubled John Q. Public. What the torero seeks is honesty, he argues. Not tricked emotion but the purity of the execution.

What we were being served up here was a kind of mystical totalitarianism, the gospel according to Ernest Miller Wemedge, a form of literary guerrilla warfare where the reader was sat in his seat and invited to touch the hem of his pedagogue's garment whether he liked it or not. Bullfighting wasn't just a question of putting spears into the necks of dumb brutes, we were reliably informed; it was a spectator sport of sub-Homeric proportions, a cathartic ritual where one had to kill cleanly and beautifully without subterfuge or a failure of nerve. And the language our garrulous author would employ to transmit this message would also be without subterfuge. Throughout it all he makes a strong case for bullfighting as an artistic spectacle, but a letter he wrote to his friend Bill Horne in 1923 probably better exemplifies his true reasons for patronising the finca. 'It's just like having a ringside seat at the war,' he said, 'with nothing going to happen to you.'

Bullfighting for him was like a staged war where the soldiers were dressed not in uniforms but suits of lights - and where they could, at least within limits, set their own terms. They could kill and/or be killed with more dignity than the average battlefield permitted, and to that extent could be expected to embrace their fate with open arms, whatever way it panned out. No guts meant no glory, but if they went in close above the horns and still avoided a *cornada*, a kind of immortality was theirs.

To a non-convert this might appear to be a gratuitous panegyric to slaughter but for Hemingway bullfighting was about confronting yourself at a moment of truth. The death of the bull, if indeed it occurred, was just a necessary evil - not the overall point of the exercise.

Hemingway published another short story collection the next year called *Winner Take Nothing*. It was transcribed in the same lean style as before, the tight-lipped stories providing a cumulative effect like so many kicks in the groin.

In 'Fathers and Sons' he touches upon his father's suicide for the first time in his literary career - but not the last. In 'The Mother of a Queen' he takes another sly sideswipe at his mother by writing about a man who stops paying the rent on his mother's grave, thus causing her remains to be dumped on a public bone-heap. She also features in the 'The Light of the World' in thinly-disguised form. If we wish, we can interpret the story as Hemingway's whinge about having to send a monthly cheque to a woman he abhorred - in coded metaphor. But maybe this is to go a bridge too far. 'Capital of the World' is transcribed in almost the same tight-lipped argot as 'Hills Like White Elephants' but lacks its edge.

Winner Take Nothing had him on his familiar thematic hobbyhorses of death, decay, corruption, alienation, despair, condemnation, but here they seemed to lack an overlay of credibility. What we were seeing was Hemingway writing Hemingway. The stories didn't *gain* from these themes. If anything, they were hurt by them. It was all beginning to be a bit *déjà vu*. The shocking wasn't as coruscating as it used to be. Not only were the characters numbed now, but the readers as well. Our author, glutted with fame and an easy mode of transcription, was approaching auto-pilot mode.

With one notable exception, it must be emphasised. Because in 'A Clean, Well-Lighted Place' we witness perhaps his most darkly beautiful story, a bittersweet paean to anyone the world over who ever had trouble making it through the night, for whatever reason. It's a delicate descent into the lean grey wolves of the subconscious, delivered with his customary insouciance. All the desperado poets and lonely souls need a light for the night. Finally, at sun-up, they will go to sleep. Or maybe not. You can rub plaster over the wound of your depression, but clean, well-lighted places are only there for a while, and afterwards there's your own mind to be negotiated, without waiters or bodegas or youth or brandy or nieces. You can attempt suicide, perhaps, and afterward be cut down, but what dignity is there in that?

The cafe provides the old man with a brief respite from his inner demons, but when it closes, these demons return with a vengeance. When one of the waiters asks a colleague what his problem is, he gets the answer 'Nothing'. In actual fact nothing *is* his problem. Or, more specifically, *nada*.

Pier Francesco Pasolini called this story 'a Magna Carta of nihilism': he wasn't exaggerating. It is also, however - like every nihilistic story Hemingway wrote - intensely poetic in its way. Rarely has there been a more piquant dirge to nothingness.

Is it possible that the old waiter in the story is Hemingway himself? Let us remember he too needed clean, well-lighted places after his wounding at Fossalta.

And Oak Park's lousiest Catholic would be no stranger to a prayer that began 'Our nada who art in heaven'.

White Hunter, Black Heart

Hemingway was on safari in Africa from December 1933 to February 1934. It bequeathed him one mediocre book and two stunning short stories.

A new phase of his life had begun. Bored with writers, if not the actual craft of writing itself, he needed a new injection of vigour and excitement to fuel his muse, and he would find that in his friend and mentor Philip Percival on safari in deepest Africa. The failed bullfighter would now seek out a different type of quarry in an activity which, while neither graceful nor a spectator sport, had its own macho code and set of coordinates for those who liked to test their *cojones* on a daily basis.

The mediocre book was *Green Hills of Africa*. He claimed that his main ambition here was to write a book that, as well as being a journalistic treatise, could also cut it as a work of the imagination. In a sense, this was the rock it persished on.

Edmund Wilson said of it, 'Almost the only thing we learn about the animals is that Hemingway wants to kill them.' Truly, we had learned much more about bulls from *Death in the Afternoon,* but maybe it was churlish to deny him his indulgence. It was never meant to be straightforward documentary. He had always blurred the lines between fiction and journalism in the same way as his spiritual godson Norman Mailer would do in another era. It might be more beneficial to read this book alongside the great safari stories - *The Snows of Kilimanjaro* and *The Short, Happy Life of Francis Macomber* - than in isolation.

Green Hills of Africa tried to do for that country what *Death in the Afternoon* did for Spain so many years before, but Hemingway didn't seem to know his safaris as profoundly as he did his corridas. He ranted on about killing cleanly and well in somewhat the same manner, but there was a depth and structure missing from this book that was in its predecessor, and a rather cavalier attitude to violence that seemed to undermine the respect he purported to show for his beasts of prey.

Here, as in *Death in the Afternoon*, we witnessed him nailing his iceberg theory firmly in its coffin as he declaimed on every issue that crossed his mind with garrulous excess. It's as if all that tight-lipped narration needed an outlet. And then some.

The central irony about this book is that it's most effective when Hemingway diverts from his main theme to entertain us on peripheral issues like literature and whatnot. The safari is a useful umbrella for him, but there's too much of it...and too much of it is dull.

The wittiest review I ever read of this book was penned by one Granville Hicks, who wrote about the kinds of things it told us. 'Hemingway got up very early in the morning,' Hicks writes, 'and went out and chased a lion or a rhinoceros or a kudu, and he either shot him or he didn't, and if he did, someone named Karl shot a bigger one. So that evening they all got a little tight. This went on for a month, and finally they found themselves beside the Sea of Galilee, drinking, and Karl made a good crack about not walking on the water because it had been done once, and Hemingway said he would write a book so that P.O.M. (Poor Old Mama, i.e. Mrs Hemingway) could remember what Mr P.J. (their guide) looked like. And so we have *Green Hills of Africa*.' This isn't exactly the kind of thing to enthrall a Hemingway fan upon reading it, but one has to admit it's deserved. He has been self-indulgent before, but here he evinces more than one trait of the Pub Bore.

To find the rich product of Hemingway's 1933 safari experience we have, to turn to *The Snows of Kilimanjaro* and *The Short Happy Life of Francis Macomber*, two stories about men who feel they've sold out to their wives' richness and power. The two men manage to reclaim some semblance of dignity by the end of the stories, even if they have to die to do so. The females of these stories, the rich bitches who hover over them, remain more stagnant. As mentioned before,

Hemingway found it difficult to create a female character who wasn't either an angel or a bitch - except perhaps for Brett Ashley, his most three-dimensional female creation, if not his only one. Nevertheless, the dynamic of each story propels it forward with such gusto that one hardly notices. Macomber becomes brave even if it's too late, and Harry reaches the catharsis of self-knowledge even as his disease eats into him - a metaphor for the manner in which Hemingway's own life has become rotten to the core since he became famous.

The Snows of Kilimanjaro isn't so much a misogynistic treatise as a broadside against Walden - or, if you like, Hemingway himself - who scapegoats his expedient wife for his own literary compromises. It's modelled on Tolstoy's short story 'The Death of Ivan Ilych' both thematically and stylistically, but Hemingway has grafted on a neo-modern slant that gives it its acerbic bite. In fact he's packed enough material into this story to fill three full novels.

Harry lies dying of gangrene, which Hemingway's own father feared he was about to contract on the day he killed himself. His wife Helen is modelled on Pauline, whom Hemingway was having problems with by now. She shows little concern for him as they argue beside a mimosa tree and await the arrival of the plane that will airlift him to a hospital and his reprieve from a lonely and painful death in the wilderness. 'She was a fine woman, marvellous really', Harry says to himself sarcastically, the real truth being that she's a grade-A bitch who has witnessed his descent into physical and artistic destruction without batting an eyelid.

Harry himself doesn't even blame his wife. 'If it had not been she,' he surmises, 'it would have been another.'

'I'm getting bored with dying as everything else,' he says, and the relationship between himself and Helen is so bad, you believe it.

Kilimanjaro get its main power from the intensity of Harry's pained reminiscences and impending death coupled with the banality of his exchanges with his wife. Sentences like 'Death had come and rested its head on the foot of the cot and he could smell its breath' sit

151

alongside smalltalk about whiskey soda, creating the jarring effect. 'The marvellous thing is that it's painless,' he says in the brilliant, blackly comic first sentence, 'That's how you know when it starts.' From here on in, the downward spiral is blatant and tortuous. 'So this was the way it ended,' he says in T.S Eliot mode, 'bickering over a drink.' Not with a bang but with a whimper. Being badgered by a tetchy wife as the life drains from his dead head.

She's 'awfully sorry' about the odour, but other than that, they might as well be playing bowls on the lawn. For Harry it's a 'pleasant surrender' to the inevitable because he has been dead for many years inside himself anyway. He has too much fat on the soul, his only saving grace being that he knows it.

He experiences some kind of compromised catharsis before the story ends, and so does the main character in *The Short, Happy Life of Francis Macomber*. Both stories are written in a laconic fashion which only barely conceals the silent desperation of the characters. Both also feature their author at the height of his creative powers. Indeed, *The Snows of Kilimanjaro* ranks up there with *The Old Man and the Sea* as arguably the greatest long short story Hemingway every wrote. In the view of this writer, it excels it.

Macomber experiences his moment of truth in a gallant act - like a bullfighter going in over the horns. It may be too late to save his marriage, or his life, but he's still, as it were, 'undefeated' in Hemingway's understanding. He has learned what it is to taste fear and like it.

The issue of whether his wife Margot did or didn't intend to shoot him at the end is another issue entirely.

Just as Samuel Beckett once said that he didn't know who or what Godot was, and if he did he would have said so, Hemingway claimed he wasn't quite sure if Margot Macomber shot her husband deliberately or not. 'I could find out if I asked myself,' he allowed, 'because I invented it. The only hint I could give you is that it is my belief that the incidence of husbands shot accidentally by wives who are bitches and really work at it is very low'. On another occasion he said that Margot hated her husband because he was a coward, 'but when he gets his guts back she fears him so much she has to kill him.' Maybe only Margot Macomber herself could solve the conundrum.

His confusion about Margot's motives is reminiscent of a comment he made to Martha when he was writing *For Whom the Bell Tolls*. 'I think that son of a bitch Pablo is going to steal the dynamite exploder,' he said to her one day. When she replied, 'Don't you know?' he merely exploded into laughter.

Macomber is a man who loses both his nerve and his wife, the latter loss being partially if not totally caused by the former. He gets back his nerve, but doesn't live to reap the cathartic benefits.

Both stories were filmed in years to come, with equally disastrous results as far as their author was concerned.

Hollywood's bowdlerisation of *The Snows of Kilimanjaro* (dubbed 'The Snows of Zanuck' by an outraged Hemingway) was fairly typical of the manner in which film-makers had savaged his books over the years, and would continue to do so. Zanuck had made 'one minor alteration' to his story, Hemingway told Leicester wryly, in letting his hero live. To him, this would be like letting Hamlet or Lear waltz into the sunset whistling Dixie. 'Now all we need,' he went on, 'is to have some Hollywood gag writer take that poor bloody Colonel Cantwell of *Across the River and Into the Trees* out of the back of that Buick and let him hike back to Venice down the middle of the Grand Canal and into Harry's bar dry-shod. They'll probably call it *Across the Selznick and into the Zanuck.*'

He said to Ava Gardner in pained tones after he watched the movie version, 'The only good things about it were you and the hyena'. She didn't have the heart to tell him the latter was a dubbed human voice.

The bland, treacly ending of the film, in which the planes really do rescue Harry rather than just in a dream, was typical Hollywood sanitisation, and reminiscent of the proposed finale of *The Sun Also*

Rises where the sun was supposed to light up the screen during the final tentative exchange between Jake and Brett.

The Macomber story was also filmed in years to come - as *The Macomber Affair* - with predictably commercialistic overtones. The blurb said things like 'Gregory Peck Makes That Hemingway Kind of Love To Joan Bennett.' For those who could have been forgiven for asking what, exactly, was the Hemingway kind of love, we were subsequently informed that it was 'Love like the lash of a whip'. He took all this in his stride, adopting a take-the-money-and-run attitude, but it can't have done his morale any good to see his work trivialised like this. Not that he expected anything different from Hollywood.

In *Kilimanjaro,* he writes very well of a writer who can't write. It can be read, as Carlos Baker noted, as an exemplification of Hemingway's fear that he too would die without having realised his potential, having sold out to, if not money, a life of action and hell-raising that cut in on his craft.

We may also read it as a frank *exposé* of how things had gone to hell with Pauline, as is evidenced by his dalliance with Jane Mason, which lasted on and off from 1931 to 1936.

Hemingway himself denied that the plot was autobiographical, pedalling the story - which may have been an apocryphal one to cover him from being seen as a thinly-disguised Harry - that it concerned what 'might' have happened to him if he had given in to a rich woman who offered to pay for an expensive African safari for him. This was probably Mason.

He met her the same way he met Marlene Dietrich: on the *Ile de France*. The year was 1931 and Pauline was seven months pregnant with Gregory. When Hemingway's wives were pregnant he always seemed more likely to stray and this time was no exception. He was smitten with her from the off and she reciprocated in kind.

Mason, who was bored with her husband, accompanied Hemingway on the fishing trips that bored Pauline, but their liaison went much farther than that, even if he remained discreet with her on

The Pilar while others were present.

She seemed to be almost another Duff Twysden to him. Like Zelda Fitzgerald she enjoyed the finer things of life, and, also like Zelda, she had a distinctly unstable temperament and grew bored easily, being prone to increasingly frequent bouts of depression. Hemingway would have found her too hot to handle as a wife but he enjoyed dallying with her as Pauline looked the other way - as he had once dallied with Pauline while Hadley pretended not to notice.

His relationship with Mason was tempestuous, both of them being loose cannons, and prone to unpredictable highs and lows. She was beautiful but also hard, like Helene Bradley in *To Have and Have Not*. Hemingway generally liked his women to be more compliant than this, but she exerted a strong sexual power over him - at least until she had a nervous breakdown and he moved on. 'She fell for me,' he punned after she had attempted suicide by jumping from a balcony in 1933. Such a cheap shot left nobody in any doubt about his feelings for her by now - or rather his lack of them.

She subsequently married Arnold Gingrich, which caused all sorts of complications when Hemingway presented Gingrich with *To Have and Have Not,* which features a character based on Mason in a none-too-flattering light.

This is a book that's slick and professional, but so bereft of human interest it leaves you with nothing. Harry Morgan - the owner of a cabin cruiser temporarily working in Havana as a fishing guide - is one of the few forgettable anti-heroes Hemingway created. This, I feel, isn't because he doesn't have a compassionate streak buried inside him but rather because his creator fails to capture it properly.

The character of Morgan falls apart largely because Hemingway places such a large socialist burden on him as the novel goes on. He will place a similar burden on Robert Jordan in a couple of years in *For Whom the Bell Tolls,* but because Jordan is such a fully fleshed-out character, the socio-political overtones won't jar so much. Expecting Morgan to be a peg upon which he could hang a thesis would be risky enough in a finely-crafted book, but in a shoddy one like this it only compounds the throwaway nature of the whole enterprise.

In almost every critical appraisal of this book I've read, the 'Love is all the dirty tricks you taught me' speech (delivered by Helen Gordon to her husband) is quoted, which must say something to us about the dearth of literary virtuosity in the remainder of the book. It's a fabulously written passage, and vividly symptomatic of the dead wood of their relationship as well as the overall bleakness of the novel, but the over-reliance on it as a thematic reference-point only serves to highlight the banality of what comes before and after it.

His characters here, as Edgar Johnson observed, 'are indeed the hollow men, wandering in despair or jerking galvanically through the mist of Hades, a grey world of doom'. In other words - what else is new? But there's a lack of resonance in the dementia that points to later lapses in Hemingway's work. It's as if he's losing his grip - or maybe his interest - in his pet themes and styles. Or did the book reflect the 'yellow sere' into which his life had sunk at this point, where writing provided only vague relief from a soullessness brought on by the unfulfilling life he was living? If this is so, whether he realised it or not, he might have been getting his muse in training for his next 'big book'. (*For Whom the Bell Tolls* will seem as if written by an entirely different author, buoyed on by infinitely more resonant concerns.)

Not only is *To Have and Have Not* a stylistic mess: it doesn't even have the unifying thread of a character one can feel for, or with. Hemingway might have got away with Harry Morgan in one of his stories, but over this length he fails to generate enough fellow feeling to make readers identify with his plight.

Hemingway himself said, with a slight hint of tongue in cheek, that it was 'teenage work devoted to adultery, sodomy, masturbation, rape, mayhem, mass murder, frigidity, alcoholism, prostitution, impotency, anarchy, rum-running, Chink-smuggling, nymphomania and abortion.' The message, that 'a man alone ain't got no bloody, fucking chance', is much balder than we usually get from Hemingway. Why is he not playing his hands close to his chest any more ?

Though the book is gritty and unconscionably hardbitten, it still remains one of the few novels Hemingway wrote that doesn't have his indelible authorial stamp on it. There's a richness noticeably absent from the narration, and nothing between the spaces except silence. If this is written according to the dictates of his famous iceberg theory of literature which suggests that six-sevenths of a book's meaning should be kept under the metaphorical water, here's one iceberg that has *nothing* beneath the water - and not much above it either.

Interestingly enough, it's the only book he ever wrote set in America. Asked why he had never written about his home country before, he replied flatly, 'Because nothing ever happens there'. John Dos Passos, who spent seven years working on his masterpiece *U.S.A.*, might have smiled at this putdown.

Hemingway had been bad before this book and he would be bad after it, but he had rarely been as boring as here. Even though the dialogue was slick, it was difficult to keep the motivation going to continue turning pages.

There's a sameness in the narration of the book which wars against it acquiring any real reader involvement, or empathy with the characters. It's as if it was written in fits and starts by a severely disgruntled man. His darkness was always suggestive before, but here it's merely dim. He also shows far too much of himself as the author.

Hemingway cobbled it together disingenuously from two previously published stories ('One Trip Across' and 'The Tradesman's Return') and it betrays such jagged origins. 'Since he was a boy,' one of Morgan's companions says of him, 'he never had no pity for nobody. But he never had no pity for himself either.' And neither do we, the readers, have pity. Either for Morgan or anybody else on display here. Whether Harry is killing or being killed, the reader feels the same sense of *sang froideur*.

To Have and Have Not was more successful as a movie than a book, thanks largely to the presence of Humphrey Bogart and Lauren Bacall in the starring roles, and an in-your-face script from William Faulkner. The film's most memorable line, however, 'You know how to whistle, don't you? You just put your lips together and blow', came from the film's director, Howard Hawks.

Hawks is alleged to have secured the film rights by claiming he could make a movie out of Hemingway's worst story. This was one of the few slices of abuse about his work that Hemingway took on the chin.

The book may have been directionless and eminently forgettable, but the fact that it was filmed three times has to say something to us about its dramatic possibilities on screen. Indeed, it's probably the case that the purer the book, the less chance it has of having an authentic translation to celluloid. This one was blunt and harsh, which gave Hollywood much to work with. It's interesting too that the first movie version was the only example of a Hemingway work which gave Hollywood a new star. Lauren Bacall was an unknown before this role; after it she was a household name, and on the way to becoming Humphrey Bogart's new wife. Despite the huge age gap between them - he was old enough to be her father - she would rescue him from a life of alcohol, frustration and violence with Mayo Methot. (Hemingway was also a man who loved younger women by this stage of his life. He would have his own Bacall in Adriana Ivancich in a few years time).

He was pleased with the movie version, more pleased in fact then with any Hollywood adaptation of his work since *The Killers*. He was always more difficult to please with the major novels, of course. *To Have and Have Not* was never going to be one of his favourite books, so anything was a bonus. His main grievance in this instance was financial. He had sold the rights for a paltry $10,000 to help tide him over the writing of *For Whom the Bell Tolls*. It was little more than pocket money for him, and insult was added to injury when the two subsequent film versions (*The Breaking Point* and *The Gun*

Runners) netted him not a cent.

Hemingway was having as many personal as creative problems at this stage of his life, the juice having been long gone from his relationship with Pauline. Jane Mason had been an accident waiting to happen, and so also was the pretty young journalist from *Collier's* magazine who would soon steal his heart - if not his soul.

When Martha Gellhorn walked into Sloppy Joe's bar in December 1936 with her mother and brother, Hemingway was knocked off his feet.

For one thing, she was more physically fetching than Pauline. A blue-eyed blonde with, as Hemingway put it, 'legs that went all the way up to her shoulders', she had an immediate attractiveness to him. She was also a published author with a best-selling collection of stories (*The Trouble I've Seen*) under her belt. One journalist even compared her economy of language to his own frugality.

Hemingway was dressed in Basque shorts and a grubby T-shirt when he met her. He had no shoes on him and the shorts were held up by a piece of rope. He must have looked like a bulky version of Santiago to her, but when she heard his name was Hemingway - like most young college girls of her generation, *The Sun Also Rises* had been a kind of Bible to her - the fact that he was both hygienically and sartorially challenged mattered not a whit.

As was the case with Hadley, Martha had more than a little in common with Hemingway. Just as Hemingway's father had been an obstetrician, so was hers. And her mother, like Hemingway's, was a suffragette. Both Hemingway and Martha were also composers of verse, short stories and fiction - albeit with widly varying degrees of success. Another quality they shared in common was a charm and persuasiveness that had drawn people to them all their lives. And - a related trait, no doubt - a desire to be the centre of attraction. They both also shared a fairly frantic *wanderlust,* Martha hating her native St. Louis ('If anyone is going to sit in that dump of a city, let them stew in their own juice' she once said) almost as much as Hemingway did

Oak Park.

There were comparisons with Hadley herself too. Both women had attended Bryn Mawr college, and Hemingway met them both shortly after they had lost a parent. Martha's father had even attended to Hadley as a patient at one stage in St. Louis.

In an amazing geographical coincidence, not only were Hadley and Martha from St. Louis, but also Pauline. Hemingway quipped to Hadley in 1939 in a letter, 'If one is perpetually doomed to marry people from St. Louis, it's best to marry them from the very best families.'

They found they had even more in common with one another when the discussion between them turned from literature to politics. When an enervated Martha informed him that she was interested in going to Spain to campaign against the Fascists, Pauline might as well have looked for a door marked 'Exit'.

She knew this herself too. When people spoke of Spain in years to come, she would cry out: 'Don't mention Spain to me. That war lost me the man I loved.'

'We just knew that Spain was the place to stop Fascism,' Martha would later announce. 'This was it. It was one of those moments in history when there was absolutely no doubt.'

Pauline, by now, had reached her sell-by date for Hemingway in the same way as Hadley had in 1926, having become the classic ball and chain figure who couldn't share her husband's thirst for adventure anymore. She watched him falling for Martha as Hadley had watched him falling for her, equally unable to do anything about it. Hemingway himself, though, was less tortured by what was happening then he had been in the similar circumstances of a decade before.

His guilt complex over leaving Hadley lasted right through the marriage with Pauline, perhaps even resulting in a wish to punish her - be it conscious or subconscious - by leaving her. She had, after all, taken him away from the one woman he would ever truly love.

He was fascinated by Martha, but in a different way than he had

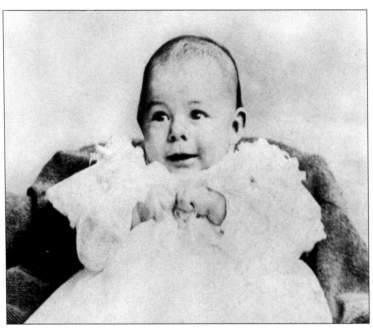

Hemingway in his christening robe at 3 months old

The famous *Summer Girl* photograph from 1901

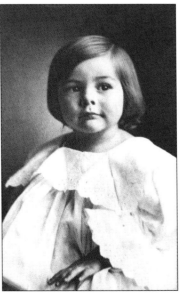

Could anyone foretell this boy would grow up to be a hunter?

Ernest and Grace in 1903

A devilishly handsome young Hemingway with his football team
(Seated front left)

Portrait of the artist as a young man

With Agnes Von Kurowsky, the prototype for
Catherine Barkley in *A Farewell to Arms*

Father and son reconcile their differences, 1919

Showing off a day's catch at 21

The young suitor with Hadley
during a visit to St. Louis in March 1921

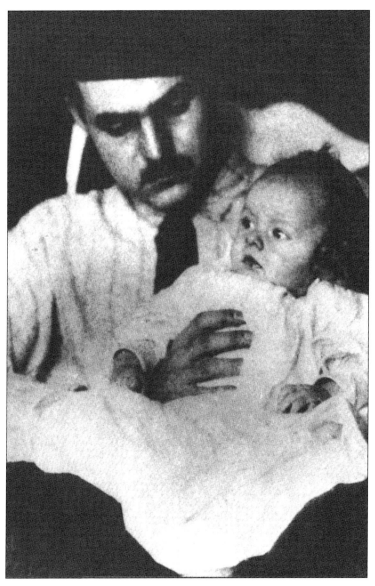

Bumby sits on his father's lap in their
Notre Dame de Champs home in 1924

Ernest and Hadley play happy families in Schruns, 1926

The Pamplona ensemble of 1925:
Hemingway, Duff Twysden, Hadley and friends

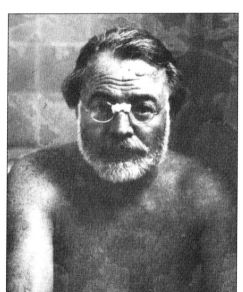

A querulous Hemingway
gazes at the camera from
his bathtub after one of
his many accidents

With Pauline on the beach at San Sebastian, 1927

King of the jungle

With fishing friend in
Key West, 1929

Displaying some trophy heads in
Africa in 1933 after a safari

The gaucho dozes on board
The Pilar with tommy gun
and liquid refreshment

In his over-used
undersized suit in Paris

Checking a map in France,
circa D-Day

In contemplative mood
in Normandy
in September 1944

Examining captured German
military equipment with
close friend Buck Lanham
around the same time

The lost and forlorn author reads a press cutting
towards the end of his life in a hotel bedroom in Malaga

been by Hadley and Pauline, two women who were willing to do his bidding and become Mrs Hemingway - unlike the Grace Hall of a generation before.

Martha was the last in a long line of lovers Hemingway entertained during the bad years of his marriage to Pauline, the most obvious of which was Jane Mason. Martha wasn't as beautiful as Mason, but neither did she have that woman's emotional instability. She set her cap at Hemingway much the way Pauline did when he was married to Hadley, inveigling her way into a friendship with husband and wife as a means of eventually up-ending the marriage. Hemingway, however, as was the case when Pauline appeared on the scene when he was married to Hadley, was more than willing to be diverted.

It's arguable that Martha married him as a career move as well as being hooked by his charisma. He himself had got many a leg-up from established authors when he was starting out, but the last thing he wanted was somebody using him for the same purpose. Especially his wife...

Buck Lanham said she was 'a bitch from start to finish, and every other member of my staff who met her - and most did - thought so too.' Right from the outset she looked to be going for the Main Chance.

Winston Guest, who helped Hemingway locate enemy submarines during World War Two, also claimed Martha was a 'tough, mercenary bitch' who married Hemingway solely to advance her literary career. Gellhorn debunked this theory as rubbish, saying that she was already established as a writer before she met Hemingway and that he gave her little if any financial backing for her journalistic work. Indeed, the very volume of her military assignments in themselves proved both her earning power and her refusal to freeload on the Hemingway bandwagon. She was also adamant that she would never call herself 'Martha Hemingway' on any of her books or articles.

Hemingway showed her a draft version of *To Have and Have*

Not shortly after they met and she was impressed. He was dizzy with her beauty and she with his animal magnetism. They were also both fired up with the Spanish situation. Hemingway wanted to cover it for NANA, the North American Newpaper Alliance, and Martha for *Collier's*. But they could mix business with pleasure...

The Spanish Civil War, as Jose Luis Castillo-Puche put it, was for Hemingway 'an embodiment of every aspect of the myth of the bullfight, from the worship of virility to blood communion to a sort of hymn of the bridegroom at a nuptial feast.' He went to Spain in 1937 with Martha, who was now his mistress, to get a hands-on impression of the Fascist takeover.

NANA paid him a dollar per word for his correspondence: a journalistic precedent. Neither were they bothered by the fact that his columns would tell the world more about himself then about the Civil War. He was being employed as a kind of middlebrow pundit who would give the view from the ground: a worm's eye appraisal of the convoluted warring factions. The political unrest provided him with exactly what he needed to galvanise him emotionally and artistically.

The Hemingway who went to Italy in 1918 was still there to be tapped. He was more famous now, and maybe his reflexes were that much slower, but he was still hungry for action, especially when there was a cause at stake. 'My sympathies are always for exploited working people,' he said, 'even if I drink with the landlords.' He fraternised with generals, but his heart was with the foot-soldiers. Or, as he put it himself, 'I mix with shits, nor lose the common touch.'

The war, in fact, was about to adrenalise him in almost exactly the same way as World War One had done nineteen years before. In 1918 he seemed destined for a life of loafing before the Piave gave him a conduit for his energies; now the guerillas of the Spanish foothills were doing likewise. Life in Key West, as in Oak Park, was making him fat and smug. It was time to get fire in his belly again; time to smell fear.

The fear would also, hopefully, awaken his creative juices. Just as World War One propelled him to write his first major novel, so would this one - along with Ms Gellhorn - inspire him to write his last major one.

'Ernest needs a new woman for each big book,' Scott Fitzgerald commented after Pauline took him from Hadley when he was writing *A Farewell to Arms.* It seemed to be true too. Hadley wetnursed him through *The Sun Also Rises,* as did Pauline through *A Farewell to Arms,* and now Martha was on hand to put him through his paces for his largest undertaking thus far.

The Civil War purified him as it purified Robert Jordan, the hero of the novel, by hooking him up to an ideal that was bigger than himself. The idea of losing himself in a cause was replicated in the style of the book as well. His previous two novels were narrated in the first person, but now he opted for the third. First person narration, he said, 'was a cinch'; the other mode of delivery called for more of a professional approach. (The book was originally written in the first person, incidentally).

For Whom the Bell Tolls is a political novel, but it's an adventure story before everything else. This is its dynamic. The love scences are forced, with Hemingway on unsure ground as he's making the earth move for Maria and Robert Jordan under their sleeping bag. He's much more comfortable when writing of blowing bridges.

The political naivety of the book is more than cancelled out by its dramatic potency. The humanist in Hemingway may have hated what war did to people, but the adventurer in him thrived on it, and out of this mix came most of its adrenalin, creating a tension between old-fashioned adventure and a philosophical edge.

Neither Jordan nor any of the other characters seem to see life through their own eyes as much as Hemingway's: their perceptions too are filtered through his omnipotent glare, made all the more obvious for his attempts at concealment. Clearly, the persona behind the stories is long a thing of the past, but this is still a wonderful book because of its central dynamic. The issue of whether it captures Spain, or even

Spain at a particular time of its history, is beside the point. What it does is give us a glimpse into a tiny segment of it, filtered through the prism of his romantic idealism and contrapuntal roguishness.

On the surface this is a simple tale of the lives, loves and tragic fates of a motley crew of Castilian peasants operating behind the Fascist lines during the war that acted as a kind of dress rehearsal for World War Two, but this is merely the scaffolding within which Hemingway weaves his mesmerising prose-poetry and would-be apocalyptic ruminations.

Life is microscoped into seventy hours, and Jordan tries to live as many years in that time. This is only possible, he allows, if 'your life has been full up to the time that the seventy hours start and that you have reached a certain age.'

If the war in *A Farewell To Arms* is a game, here it's a religion. Fighting in it Jordan gets the emotion that he was expected to feel when he was making his First Communion but didn't.

The Loyalists fully expected him to be on their side in the war, as did the Communists, but Hemingway baulked at the idea of nailing his colours to any political mast. All he would concede was that he was anti-Fascist. Such dialectics, in any case, aren't the life-blood of the book; the human struggle is, and the *badinage,* and the adventure, and the love affair with Maria, and the cool passion of the narration.

He told Malcolm Cowley that it wasn't just the Civil War he put into it, but 'everything I had learned about Spain for eighteen years.' There were problems with the book, however.

Hemingway's abstract diction ('I have a boredom in the mountains', and so on) may appear to replicate peasant idioms, but the reality is that such phraseology is more a product of his imagination than the real way Castilians (who, incidentally, shun abstractions) speak.

The peasant formalism of the book fails because it's too erudite, his own voice coming through the expostulations. Maria's early willingness to share Jordan's bed is also inconsistent with her shyness, particularly considering her past sexual experiences. Hemingway knew Spain better than it knew itself, but sometimes in his fiction he tended to gild the lily in a way he resisted in his journalistic work.

The book also has a structural problem. More a mosaic of set-pieces than a well-rounded novel, it doesn't so much fail to cohere as never even attempt to. Hemingway the short story writer is much in evidence here, notwithstanding the huge size of the book. Each chapter seems to be a self-contained entity, and even though the characters that people these chapters are credible, they don't really develop. He dangles them like marionettes, and none moreso than Robert Jordan, a character so politically naive and romantically one-dimensional that he was tailor-made for the movie version. Like his literary precursors he's quietly profound, but over 400-plus pages his internal monologues about life, love, idealism and death tend to rankle. They read like Frederic Henry carted off to the Iberian peninsula and decked out in peasant garb, having traded in his army uniform for a beret.

The stylised expletives grate over time, as does the salty banter. Much more potent is Jordan's heart beating against the pine needle floor of the forest. There's too much mock-mystical philosophising with Jordan and the guerillas, giving the book a contrived edge. You always feel Hemingway is pulling his magician's strings over your head, unlike in the stories where you yourself are invited to write the plot, or at least embellish it. 'All bad writers are in love with the epic,' he said once, but maybe some great writers are too - to their detriment. The great beauty of this book is in its simplicity. When he gets too rarefied he loses us in the attendant self-indulgence.

One can only take so many sentences like 'Go and obscenity in the milk of thy cowardice' or 'I think this of the killing must be a very great sin.' Of course he would continue to employ this kind of sub-Homeric diction in *The Old Man and the Sea*, but more sparingly and with more of a concentrated effect resulting from it. When the language is used as an end in itself it's dull, but if it points towards the ominousness of the whole operation it becomes pregnant and highly charged. In general, though, whatever merits this possesses as a novel, and it possesses many, you can't help feeling it would have been a more effective book if there was less space between the covers.

Often you don't get the sense of real people conversing so much as theatrical personages in a pageant. For all Hemingway's earthy directness, you don't really smell their sweat. The style is too arch for that.

The description of love-making with Maria owes more than a little to Gertrude Stein: 'For him it was a dark passage which led to nowhere, then to nowhere, then again to nowhere, once again to nowhere.' If we saw this kind of purple prose in a Mills & Boon book we could be forgiven for emitting a loud guffaw. Hemingway just about gets away with it here because of the context.

The intensity of the love scenes in both *For Whom the Bell Tolls* and *A Farewell to Arms* results from the fact that we're aware that time is short for the lovers because death is hovering near. Frederic Henry can't die because he's the narrator, so it must be Catherine who draws the short straw, but Robert Jordan is doomed almost from the moment Pilar reads his palm. For both men, the price they pay for love is death.

Maria is perhaps too obvious a symbol of purity, and her dialogue with Jordan, which ranges from the formalised to the maudlin, doesn't do the book any favours. It's infinitely more effective in its air of hushed tension and its tragic sensibility - undercut, as ever, by a fair dollop of gallows humour. Clive James said Hemingway treated the war as if it were a bullfight, which is somewhat unfair, but considering the fact that he treated bullfights like Greek tragedies maybe it's not stretching a point too far after all.

The phrase 'Did the earth move' entered the language after the book was published and has been used as a stick to beat it with since. Not totally unfairly, one hastens to add, though taken out of context it appears more risible still. Almost as risible, in fact, as Gary Cooper making love to Maria in the film version with his coat on. Or as risible as Ingrid Bergman who, as Hemingway himself remarked 'looked more like Elizabeth Arden out of Abercrombie and Fitch than a peasant rebel.'

Maria never threatens to be a realistic creation. The fact that she creeps into a stranger's sleeping bag soon after being gang-raped by the Fascists is as hard to take as the fact that she doesn't even know how to kiss. Hemingway has tried to make her into a diamond in the rough, an earth-angel, and also to be an intrinsic element in the guerilla movement. The finished product reminds one of the *spéirbhean* of ancient Irish lore. She's two parts Hadley to one part Martha Gellhorn, just as Catherine Barkley was three parts Hadley to one part Pauline and one part Agnes. This is the occupational hazard of all composite characters. If the sources are wildly divergent, the finished product tries to marry too many incongruous threads. (She bears many physical resemblances to Martha, but was light years away from her in temperament. For Hemingway, Maria was like a Martha wish fulfilment: compliant as well as beautiful).

Edmund Wilson, always a cogent critic of Hemingway's work, put his finger on it when he said that the relationship between Jordan and Maria had 'none of the give and take that goes on between real men and women' with the result that it resembled 'the all-too-perfect felicity of a youthful erotic dream.'

Hemingway loved Spain with a passion, but sometimes, one feels, he imagines he knows it better than he does, with the result that his dialogue and descriptions ring false. An obvious example of the former is when Robert Jordan calls Maria 'rabbit' as a pet name. He ought to have known that 'rabbit' in Spanish is a crude term for a woman's vagina.

A more likely possibility is that he knew full well what 'rabbit' meant in Spanish, and was having fun sneaking the expletive past Maxwell Perkins - a familiar hobby. Even if this is true, it detracts from the purity of the book.

These were details, however, and relatively unimportant when we consider the sheer magnitude of the undertaking. Many critics felt he didn't have such a novel in him at this time of his career, having seen him spread his talents into so many diverse fields in the thirties. Hemingway himself was even surprised at the things that came out of him as he sat at his typewriter, occasionally imagining he wasn't writing the book at all, but that it was being given to him by some external force.

When he finally completed it he felt as exhausted and exhilarated as if he had fought in the war all over again. The blowing of the bridge in particular adrenalised him. After describing this he found he couldn't kill his hero, having lived in his company for seventeen months like a real life friend. He did write two final chapters to the book after the bridge had been blown, having always, as he put it, a tendency to want everything 'completely knit up and stowed away ship-shape', but thought better of it and ended the book as it began, with Jordan on the floor of the pine needle forest. It was a decision that was as right as cutting the first chapter from *The Sun Also Rises* all those years before, or the last one from *A Farewell to Arms* for similar reasons. The book, he told Arnold Gingrich, didn't only cost him a year and a half of his life, but also a marriage. But that was still a small price to pay for what he - and posterity - would see as his finest literary achievement.

In *A Farewell to Arms* he had operated on a fairly vast spatio-temporal canvas, but here he's almost claustrophobic in his approach. To this extent, *For Whom the Bell Tolls* is his most mature work to date, and the book in which he finally attains the mantle of novelist par excellence. (Not many authors can write 400-plus pages on a seventy-two-hour period with such elegance and intensity.)

After six months the book had sold a half a million copies. It was the best-selling novel in the U.S. since *Gone With The Wind*. By now he knew he had arrived at the forefront of American letters for keeps. And that this was the book that would give him to posterity, for good or ill. Yes, many bad writers were in love with the epic, but if you wrote truly, and blended it with lyrical riches and not a little psychological insight, maybe you were entitled to paint in large brushstrokes on any kind of canvas you wished.

The book spelt the end of a creative burst that lasted on and off from the early twenties. After it his genius would be fitful, and his effects over-emphasised. The fact that he virtually gave up writing stories after this time also meant that the old discipline he used to swear by was gone. He even started to break his own rules: a very significant phenomenon as he slid down the slippery slope to near-obscurity. Edmund Wilson gave the book the best review of all when he said, 'The big game hunter, the waterside superman, the Hotel Florida Stalinist, with their constrained and fevered attitudes, have evaporated like the fantasies of alcohol. Hemingway the artist is with us again; and it is like having an old friend back.'

Not everybody was satisfied, however. Scott Fitzgerald, who saw its publication as dramatising the by now agonising discrepancy between Hemingway's rapidfire success and his own impending rendezvous with Lady Obscurity, said it was a 'thoroughly superficial book', with 'all the profundity of *Rebecca*'. Hemingway, he claimed, whether out of jealousy or insight we can't be sure, was finished as a writer and had gone to Spain in a frantic attempt to source new fictive material.

Hemingway sent Scott a copy as a kind of olive branch (or was he merely gloating in his success?), inscribing it 'To Scott with affection and esteem'. This was ironic considering he had little affection for his old adversary by now, and even less esteem. Fitzgerald scribbled back a note of gratitude, saying 'I envy you like hell and there is no irony in this...I envy you the time it will give you to do what you want.'

The final qualification is interesting. It suggests he felt it was indeed a potboiler, a book that was like an index-linked pension for the globetrotter with those expensive tastes. He also said the book was 'better than anybody else writing could do', but privately he told his live-in love Sheilah Graham, 'It's not up to his usual standards. He wrote it for the movies', adding, in a comment that seemed to come from that madly diseased heart, 'Hemingway has become a pompous bore.'

The critic Arturo Barea said the book wasn't so much Spain as Hemingway, but surely this was to misunderstand its intent. It was fiction, after all, rather than social history. Barea, as John Teunissen commented, 'might very well have written a review of *Moby Dick* called 'Not Whaling but Melville'. And yet one can see Barea's point considering Hemingway himself touted the book as being the ultimate Spanish tract.

What we really get here isn't Spain *or* Hemingway, but a narrow corner of that country and its culture filtered through Hemingway's heady presuppositions and stylistic extravagances. In the same sense, *Green Hills of Africa* was more Hemingway than hunting, and *Death in the Afternoon* more Hemingway than bullfighting. But so what?

Stephen Spender said it more succinctly. Having Hemingway in Spain, he opined, was 'like letting Edgar Allen Poe into a small cellar containing one mad cat'.

Hemingway sold *For Whom the Bell Tolls* to Hollywood for $100,000 and it was also a Book-of-the-Month selection, which netted him a further $50,000. 'Rather a long cry from his poor rooms over the sawmill in Paris,' grunted a long-suffering Fitzgerald. And indeed it was. But they had all, as Sam Goldwyn might have said, passed a lot of water since then.

Fitzgerald was amused that it was a Book-of-the-Month selection, and also that the movie rights had been sold. 'Do you remember,' he wrote sardonically to Zelda, 'how superior he used to be about sales?' Yes, but that was a long time ago, and in another country. It was also when he was writing for low circulation magazines which had a lot of prestige about them, but paid very little money.

And then there was the inevitable movie. It may have been the biggest money he ever earned for the least amount of work, but it still sickened him to see David Selznick go Hollywood on it, exploiting every slice of melodrama he could lay his hands on, as Hemingway always knew he would. He even predicted the film would begin with an explosion, and it did.

Hemingway was instrumental in getting Ingrid Bergman cast in the role of Maria. She suited the idealised nature of the character as he had described her, even if she jarred with the rest of the guerillas.

Many critics had chortled over the earth moving under the sleeping bag in the novel. With the glamorous Bergman on celluloid they had even more fuel for their misgivings about Hemingway's authenticity. 'Miss Bergman', wrote one disgruntled critic,'weeps convincingly, but after nine months in a mountain cave looks as if she had just been voted the prettiest polo player in Pennsylvania.' If Hemingway had problems with Hollywood's tendency to sanitise his work, in this instance he had little reason to carp as he had not only approved Bergman for the role, but created in Maria one of his most artificial characters. Maybe a different Bergman behind the camera - Ingmar that is - would have been a better choice to zoom in on his foreboding subtext.

Hemingway divorced Pauline just two weeks after *For Whom the Bell Tolls* was published. Such a decision was a watershed in his life and career. It was the first time he had ever been solely dependent on his own financial resources. Maybe he sniffed the possibility of huge royalties from his treasured novel thus making his leaving of her less financially risky.

Everytime he broke with a wife, he always had another wife-to-be on hand to paper over the emotional cracks. The romance with Pauline was up and running when he left Hadley, as was the one with Martha when he ditched Pauline.

Hadley forgave him for leaving her, but Pauline wasn't quite so understanding. She hated him so much by the end of the thirties that she even refused to comment on draft versions of *For Whom the Bell*

Tolls. Hemingway saw this as a pity because, as he put it, she was 'the best damn critic' of any of his wives. He seemed less concerned about her marital alientation than the deprivation of her judgement. Though she turned sour on him, he blamed himself to some degree for this - a large admission from a man not usually given to self-castigation.

He tried to rationalise his guilt at leaving her by telling himself it was no less than she deserved for taking him away from Hadley. Her pain was reparation for her sin on that occasion. Exactly how he himself should be punished he didn't consider. Presumably there was one law for deserting husbands and another for cuckolding jezebels.

He also accused her of being a 'whore' without any justification whatsoever. Maybe he used such outpourings as ballast to shore against the ruins of his guilt over his second marital desertion thus far. She had become cold towards him even before he met Martha, but that was nothing compared to her behaviour when he told her he was leaving her. He had been so spoiled by Hadley's dignity fourteen years before that he was ill-prepared for this. It was, in a sense, the oldest story in the book. The price you paid for glitz.

Many of his problems with Pauline, he claimed, had a sexual root. In fact he once told Gregory that it was as a result of Pauline's difficult birth with him (it was another Caesarean section) that their marriage had broken up. This didn't say much for the depth of the relationship. Or, indeed, his familiarity with the rhythm method.

After Pauline had her second child she was warned that another pregnancy could kill her. The church banned contraception, which created understandable tension between them. He was willing to embrace the Catholic religion in order to marry Pauline, but wasn't overly impressed when, in further accordance with its principles, she refused to practise birth control.

A nominal Catholic most of his life, he found a convenient reason to divorce her when it was established that she could never safely get pregnant again after her problems giving birth. The idea of having sex without the possibility of procreation was anathema to the church and enabled the self-confessed 'lousy Catholic' to quote scripture for his purpose. That wasn't the way he would put it, however. He preferred to say 'Things went to hell' with Pauline in the same way as he had said things went to hell with Hadley after he fell out of love with *her*. Things also 'went to hell' in Oak Park after many years of being 'cockeyed happy'. In fact everything seemed to go to hell with Hemingway after a time. Even Hemingway. (Pauline once said to Mary Welsh, who would become the fourth Mrs Hemingway. 'If I hadn't been such a bloody fool to be a practising Catholic, I wouldn't have lost him.' She didn't elaborate but Mary concluded she was referring to *coitus interruptus*).

Pauline played financial hardball with him when they divorced, despite the fact that she was well off. This annoyed him intensely. It was a new experience for him, a far cry from the Hadley divorce where his generosity with *The Sun Also Rises* royalties was so appreciated. Years later she told Hadley she hated Hemingway with a vengeance for what he had done to her. Hadley said she could understand her feelings but she still had a soft spot for the old rascal. As he had for her.

Pauline, predictably, got custody of Patrick and Gregory, but they visited Martha often in years to come, and indeed were quite attracted physically to her as well.

One suspects Hemingway respected Martha less than any of his other wives, however. He created a Gellhorn clone in his only play *The Fifth Column* having his central character Philip Rawlings say at one stage about her 'I want to make an absolute colossal mistake'(by marrying her). Dorothy Bridges is a one-dimensional version of Martha, but even here we can see the recipe for disaster the liaison between herself and Rawlings (and, by extension, Gellhorn and Hemingway) will turn out to be.

Scott Fitzgerald commented, 'It will be odd to think of Ernest married to a really attractive woman. I think the pattern will be somewhat different than with his Pygmalion-like creations.' Fitzgerald is clearly referring to Hadley and Pauline here, but surely these two wives created Hemingway just as he did them. Pauline, particularly, was a self-made woman. Hemingway gave Hadley confidence in herself and a new vista on life, but he always said there would have been no novels without her.

The marriage to Martha was really one of mutual convenience. They both seemed more obsessed with politics and writing then they were with each other, even if they didn't see it this way at the time. It's also unlikely that Hemingway's physical attraction to Martha was reciprocated - unless fame acted as an aphrodisiac for her.

Whatever, they seem to have spent more of their honeymoon at the typewriter than in the boudoir, each covering the Sino-Japanese war on a tour of the Orient that was more business than pleasure.

Divorce was suddenly becoming a habit with him. But little did he realise that he was about to hook up with a relentless firebrand. She was as far removed from Pauline as Pauline was from Hadley. They would splutter along for seven years as husband and wife before the inevitable emotional meltdown that would finally give them both the mutual release they craved.

Great Scott

Scott Fitzgerald was arguably the man who did more for Hemingway's career than anybody else he ever met. He was also, as previously mentioned, the man he treated most shabbily in return for services rendered.

Fitzgerald first became alerted to Hemingway's talent as the result of an Edmund Wilson article in *The Dial*. It inspired him to seek the young man out. When they met, his expectations were more than justified. Hemingway was sitting at the counter in Dingo's bar with Duff Twysden and Harold Loeb when he came in, and was more intrigued than impressed by him.

Fitzgerald had just published *The Great Gatsby* and was clearly very chuffed with the endeavour. He spoke coyly of the book, which gave Hemingway some pause. He suspected it would be good, but Fitzgerald spoiled it for him with his precious attitude. One feels he would have had more respect for it if he came to it without preconceptions. As it was, he had heard too many flattering reports about it. Hemingway would later tell Fitzgerald he felt the novel wasn't all it was trumped up to be, and praised too lavishly in contrast to some of his other books, which showed their charms less obviously.

Fitzgerald was immediately attracted to Hemingway's brash charisma. He talked tough, but exhibited an affable core. Things went well until Fitzgerald, having imbibed one too many glasses of champagne, proceeded to ask Hemingway if he had slept with Hadley before marrying her. He then passed out and had to be brought home in a taxi.

He was as dazzled by the man as the writer. Not for the first time would this happen in Hemingway's life. Fitzgerald had told Maxwell Perkins that he was 'the real thing.' He certainly acted like it, charming Fitzgerald with his wry oneliners and naked ambition.

It wasn't long before Fitzgerald told him to stop selling his treasured stories to 'cuckoo' magazines for peanuts when he could be working for Scribners, his own publishers. Maybe Hemingway was more impressed by Fitzgerald from an opportunist perspective than he was by him as a man or a writer - though he did respect *The Great Gatsby* for its bittersweet edge. He also had a soft spot for Fitzgerald. This isn't as apparent from *A Moveable Feast* as it is from the letters. Let's remember that this book was written mainly at the end of Hemingway's life when he had changed his attitude to Fitzgerald. In later years he tended to focus on his artistic bankruptcy, but for the first year after they met, and intermittently afterwards, they were like soul-brothers. As was the case with Hadley, they carried on a kind of epistolary bonding, a Good Old Boy network with adolescent quips and vulgar banter. This was before Hemingway outstripped Fitzgerald in almost every department of his writing, when he became a hare to Fitzgerald's tortoise.

There are those who still claim that Fitzgerald was a superior writer to Hemingway, and also the most under-rated of the twenties Paris coterie. Many others feel he could never fully realise his talent because he was too anxious to make an impression.

Fitzgerald loved youth and money too much and was his own worst enemy in the way he managed his affairs. He drank to excess, married a woman who shortcircuited his creative powers, and in general lived a life that was always on the borders of self-destruction.

Fitzgerald wanted to fight in wars like Hemingway just as James Joyce wanted to hunt lions with him, but Nora Barnacle and Zelda Sayre knew their men better. Not only would their respective spouses not be suited to this kind of life, they knew; deep down they didn't even want it. When Nora said to her husband that Hemingway could shoot the lions and then he could smell them she was, in effect, underlining his frustration about the fact that he was 'only' a suburban writer. When Fitzgerald told Hemingway he would like to have fought in the First World War Hemingway informed him promptly that he would probably have been shot for cowardice.

Fitzgerald may not have exactly impressed Hemingway by passing out under the effect of drink on their first meeting, but he did impress him with his reverential attitude to his work. He told him he wrote simply and beautifully without authorial intrusion. His work, he opined somewhat bombastically under the circumstances, was on a par with 'Let there be light'. This was obviously music to the young Hemingway's ears. He was less impressed when Fitzgerald went on to say that he himself was quite happy writing high-paying stories for glossy downmarket magazines to help tide him over financially when his novels weren't selling as well as they might have been. As far as Hemingway was concerned, going down this road was a kamikaze act that could only have one eventual outcome: total capitulation to market forces and a summary denunciation of whatever talent one had been given. Fitzgerald was less apprehensive about the situation, seeing the 'magazine stuff' simply as a stopgap to make way for something better.

Hemingway felt Fitzgerald sold out his talent, whereas Fitzgerald felt Hemingway exploited his in all the wrong ways. One man stood at the bottom of the totem pole desperately trying to grab on to it while the other was perched at the top surveying the surrounding scenery. But neither was working properly on it - at least as far as Fitzgerald was concerned. Hemingway would have disputed the latter point.

Hemingway wrote to Fitzgerald many times afterwards to tell him how talented he was, but the very fact that he felt he had to do that says it all about how Fitzgerald was feeling about his writing. Fitzgerald, for his part, poured so much effort into commenting on Hemingway's work over the years one could have been forgiven for thinking that he cared more about it than his own compositions. He played the role of the tortured loser almost masochistically. It was like an old pair of shoes he could put on and take off. It was intensified by Hemingway's ever-growing success but also tangential to it.

Hemingway believed he almost took pride in 'his shamelessness of defeat'. It was like wearing a badge of dishonour. At the end of his days, according to his sometime friend, 'he judged a paragraph by how much money it made him and ditched his juice into that channel because it gave him instant satisfaction.'

He also said he went from youth to senility without negotiating the customary intermediary period of manhood. A cruel character portrait but an engrossing one nonetheless. 'He would quit at the drop of a hat,' he said, 'and even borrow someone else's hat to drop.'

Hemingway wrote to Fitzgerald in 1929, basically telling him to pull himself together and stop moaning about his creative problems. He wanted him to stay away from writing all those ridiculous stories and get stuck into a novel. The latter activity might not have paid as much, but it would pay enough to get by. (This was to ignore the lavish extravagance of life with Zelda. It took them approximately $30,000 a year to live, and Fitzgerald was only averaging a sixth of that from book royalties.)

When people criticised Fitzgerald's writing he panicked, running to the aforementioned magazines with his stories instead of addressing the problems they raised and trying to iron them out for his next major work. Hemingway said he had the sloppy Irishman's love of failure. As well as his love of failure, he felt what destroyed him was the strain of trying to out-write himself.

'I never had any respect for him,' he wrote in *A Moveable Feast*. 'expect for his lovely, golden, wasted talent'. In a letter to Max Perkins he said he was 'a rummy and a liar and dishonest about money with the in-bred talent of a dishonest and easily frightened angel.' He accused Fitzgerald, as he would subsequently accuse Peter Viertel, of 'whoring', i.e. selling their talent short for the twelve pieces of silver Hollywood offered. He used the stories to bale him out of financial difficulties in his youth, and at the end of his short, unhappy life he was using Hollywood for precisely the same purpose.

There was, after all, a wife to be kept in the height of fashion. Clarence Hemingway would have known the feeling.

Integrity in a writer, Hemingway told Fitzgerald, was like virginity in a woman; once sacrificed, it could never be won back. Fitzgerald begged to disagree, feeling he could straddle both furrows with equanimity, serving God when he was flush and Mammon when strapped for cash to supplement his extravagant lifestyle.

Hemingway hated Fitzgerald for writing to pre-ordained formulas. This wasn't only ethically and aesthetically suspect, but even self-destructive from an expedient point of view. 'All Scott ever got out of writing,' he claimed once, 'was a few bottles of whiskey and a few hotel rooms'. This was to understate the case by some margin, but his point holds good. Short-circuiting your talent for the easy money, in his book, was a one-way ticket to Palookaville, and Fitzgerald was the epitomic test case for that theory. As he told Arnold Samuelson: 'If you start writing phoney stuff for the pulps, chances are you'll never learn how to write anything else. I've known a lot of pulp writers who thought they'd keep on until they'd saved enough money to live on and then write good stuff, but it never works.' He claimed he himself was offered $25,000 for *A Farewell to Arms* by a publisher he didn't respect at a time he was broke but resisted the temptation to take it. (Maybe so, but before his life was over Hemingway was writing material suspiciously close to pulp for astronomical fees.)

Fitzgerald's *Tender is the Night* was published in 1934 to lukewarm reviews. It's main problem was that it was a twenties book being released onto a thirties market. Somebody should have told Fitzgerald to put the Jazz Age champagne on ice. He seemed to have forgotten that the Depression was over. A book like *The Sun Also Rises*, which asked some of the hard questions, might have been more preferable, but he was over-conscious of apeing Hemingway.

Fitzgerald was often tempted to imitate his mentor's rhythms. As his own talent waxed and waned, he sometimes found himself mimicking Hemingway's cadences when he ran into literary cul-de-sacs. In the end he had to stop reading him for fear of replicating his style by a process of infiltration. Choosing Hemingway (who had an antithetical approach to Fitzgerald both on writing and life), as a yardstick by which he measured his own achievements was always going to be unfair to both writers - and finally detrimental to one of them.

Fitzgerald underwent his famous 'crack-up' between 1935 and 1937, years which saw his talent buried under a mound of shoddy hack work and booze. He had become the property of the Sunday supplements by now, a man who couldn't hold his champagne or his talent. The bad habits he fell into had tarnished him irrevocably. Zelda also resented the fact that he wrote better than she did. She wouldn't play second fiddle to him, preferring to drag him down to her own level.

He admitted he was cracking up in 1936, but said that Hemingway was too. The difference between them was simply that 'his inclination is towards megalomania and mine toward melancholy.'

Both of them were drinking to excess at this point, but with one essential difference: Hemingway was able to work off his hangovers in athletic exploits. Fitzgerald, on the contrary, spent his mornings after the night before undergoing bouts of self-loathing.

After a while his soul-searching as to where it all went wrong became as boring to himself as to his auditors. 'He was a failure both as a success and as a failure' was the way Michael Romanoff put it. In a real dark night of the soul, Fitzgerald wrote once, it is three o'clock in the morning all day long. And now he seemed to have reached that particular pass himself.

Both Scott and Zelda, Hemingway said, fed off 'the festival conception of life'. They were both wired to the moon in their respective fashions. Not for them the dull discipline of a dawn rise to get a paragraph right: they were too busy tripping the light fantastic - and passing out on people's lawns.

The Princeton educator Christian Gauss compared Hemingway to an infra-red heater while Fitzgerald, he said, was more akin to an ultra-violet one. Fitzgerald felt he came off worse in the comparison.

As the years went on he would develop something of a paranoid sense whenever he was mentioned in the same breath as his former idol. Some of this was understandable considering the enormity of Hemingway's popularity and his own increasing marginalisation by the reading public, but much of it was also excessive. As Hemingway's literary powers grew, Fitzgerald felt his own niche at the cutting edge of Literature That Mattered severely threatened. He saw Hemingway writing the kinds of books he wanted to but couldn't, and by the late thirties he was selling his quixotic talent out for a few dollars more. Even as Hemingway flexed his muscles for his biggest undertaking to date, *From Whom the Bell Tolls.*

In the early years of their relationship, Hemingway was much more inclined to take Fitzgerald's advice about his writing, deleting unnecessary material in order to get the best out of the pared-down style, but after he became famous he seemed to say, 'What's good enough for the public is good enough for me, old sport.'

In all the years of their friendship, Fitzgerald was aware of who was kingpin and who riding shotgun. He knew, for instance, that any criticism of a Hemingway book had to be prefaced with lavish praise. And he knew better than to publish a book in any year Hemingway was publishing one. These were the unwritten laws governing their relationship and Fitzgerald was more than willing to accept them. Others wouldn't be so scrupulous.

In 1930 Hemingway had 'arrived' and Fitzgerald was already beginning his decline. He earned the princely sum of $31 in book royalties in 1929, in contrast to Hemingway, who made $30,000 in that year from *A Farewell to Arms* alone. Fitzgerald's former awe was by now turning to something approaching rabid envy. He would never be mean-minded about another's success but he wouldn't have been human if the swing in fortune didn't affect him. A couple of years later their turbulent relationship was as good as over.

'Ernest, he said, 'has made all my writing unnecessary. I talk with the authority of failure. We can never sit across the same table again.' If they couldn't, this was more due to his siege mentality than any overbearing qualities on Hemingway's part. He always wanted Fitzgerald to gee himself up for one last concerted effort for which posterity might remember him, but the more he descended into literary prostitution, the more Hemingway lost the last vestiges of respect for him.

Towards the end of his life Fitzgerald became like a fallen angel, wallowing in his failure to convert his early talent into work that would last. Hemingway told him his tragedy was that the stories he wrote supported him financially, which was a good point; they were the easy way of avoiding novel-writing.

In 1936, the year he entered his fifth decade, his books sold a total of seventy-two copies, which said it all. He was working on *The Last Tycoon* by now, a mish-mash of a book about Irving Thalberg, another *wunderkind* like himself and another Beautiful Dreamer who was running out of time. It remained unfinished at the time of his death - like so many of Fitzgerald's other projects.

Hemingway and Fitzgerald only met four times in the thirties and not at all after that. By the time Fitzgerald died in 1940 there was an almost total lack of communication between them. According as Hemingway became famous, Fitzgerald's criticism of his work seemed to fall on deaf ears. Hemingway agreed with his comments on the early draft of *The Sun Also Rises* and also listened when he advised him to cut the opening of his story 'Fifty Grand', but as the years went on he listened less and less to his old friend. Fitzgerald now had a double humiliation to undergo; not only was his own writing career going down the toilet, but even his editorial comments were being ignored.

Which isn't to suggest Fitzgerald's advice was always laudable; the changes he mooted for the final chapter of *A Farewell to Arms*, for instance, were nothing short of ludicrous.

Zelda, in Hemingway's view, was as responsible for Fitzgerald's death as Grace was for his father's. Scott didn't shoot himself, but he might as well have because he was committing slow suicide for many years before he finally died. Neither did Hemingway's mother pull the trigger that killed his father, but she messed his head around so much he felt there was no other recourse for him. Is this misogyny on Hemingway's part or accurate psychological insight? The jury is still out on that one.

Fitzgerald would have been better off to divorce Zelda before she went mad but he clung onto the ideal of marriage as he clung onto all the other Jazz Age superlatives. With the same tragic results.

Her insanity was probably related to her obsessive desire to be as successful a writer as her husband. Whatever the cause, it was the last nail in the coffin of his idealism. He began to have affairs after her decaying psychological state was diagnosed, and to drink even more heavily. He had been tippling since his teens, but success - and then failure - caused the habit to go out of all control. As Sheilah Graham put it, 'He needed the liquor to give him the illusion of his old brilliance, and to help him forget that he had lost it.'

Hemingway believed he died inside himself in his early thirties, and his creative powers followed suit a few years later, which meant that by the time he shuffled off the mortal coil in 1940 there really wasn't an awful lot of him left anyway. The reason Hollywood hadn't hurt him, he believed, was because he was long past being hurt when he went there.

Studio work provided the easy money to support his lavish lifestyle but it was killing him just like the gin was. Novels were his lifeblood, but they took time. The money from them was also uncertain. Like Ireland's Brendan Behan, who would die at roughly the same age as Fitzgerald, he was notorious for drinking his royalties. As he laboured at *The Last Tycoon,* his final, unfinished book, Sheilah Graham tried to persuade Arnold Gingrich to combine an advance to him with some of her own savings so that he wouldn't have to 'go' Hollywood again. She didn't care if the book sold or not, merely that he fulfilled himself by completing it.

Fitzgerald wrote too much too fast - and for the wrong outlets. He earned his money from the wrong editors and spent it on the wrong things. He abused his talent relatively early in life - *The Saturday Evening Post* hardly being a barometer of divine inspiration - and overvalued both youth and money at the expense of more lasting values. For this point of view Hemingway found it difficult to feel sorry for his predicament as he entered his forties.

On the odd occasion that they met, Fitzgerald also tended to embarrass Hemingway with his drunken rants and boringly laddish behaviour. Corridas and safaris were much more relaxing than this. Loth to give Fitzgerald his address, he preferred to meet him in the neutral territory of cafes and bars. It was in these places he prayed that his old friend wouldn't become obstreperous.

It's probably fair to say that Fitzgerald's artistic and personal disintegration can be plotted on a graph that also displays Hemingway's resounding success. Hemingway's gain was Fitzgerald's loss not only because Fitzgerald was the catalyst behind it, but also because he felt - mistakenly - that both of them laid claim to the same novelistic terrain. He failed to see that time would be kind to his own work even if present readers weren't. The likes of Monroe Stahr may not have been able to cut it with Robert Jordan, but he still had his place in the literary pantheon. Posterity might even say a higher place.

By the time he died, Fitzgerald was eaten up with self-loathing and ill-concealed resentment of his old friend's celebrity status. Because Hemingway's books sold so well, he took this to mean that they were that much superior to his own. Indeed, commercial success had tended to be his gauge for quality going right back to his own early writing days.

The fact that he failed to build on his early promise accelerated his descent into a miasma of booze and pills, but then he had never needed too much encouragement to over-indulge in such habits at any stage of his life. The irony was that alcohol inspired him for short bursts of creativity even if it couldn't sustain them. It kicked him into first gear and then promptly hurled him back into neutral, or reverse. He was all too well aware of the eventual downward spiral, but as time went on he became too addicted to do anything about it. Just as his relationship with Graham seemed to parallel the negative curve of his life - he always saw her as a kind of bargain basement Zelda, despite that lady's multiple faults - the alcohol also fed into his dramatic lack of self-esteem. Zelda was having more obvious crises in psychiatric institutions by now but the prospect of his own reputation going to seed filled Scott with an even more immense, if less obvious, dread.

He became famous too soon, and when his talent began to slip, he needed more and more booze to fill the empty spaces and to tell him it would all come right again. If Hemingway drank to reward himself for work well done, Fitzgerald did so for work that *would* be well done. It was like an IOU he wrote to himself, but which he failed to deliver on more and more as he fell into bad habits and the writing became a pale imitation of past glories.

Success was like a bucking bronco to him. He was able to milk it for a time, but then the diminishing returns set in while he was still yet a relatively young man. 'There are no second acts in American lives,' he said famously, and how true it was for him. All he could do was reminisce about 'the good gone times when still we believed in summer hotels and the philosophies of popular songs'. Or claw at screenwriting, not his natural avocation by a long chalk, for fast (if not easy) money.

Approximately a year before he died, Fitzgerald woke up one morning unable to move. He had had a cocktail of gin and sleeping pills the night before - as ever. His doctor told him he was playing with fire, that the temporary paralysis was God tapping him on the shoulder, giving him a gentle warning before the real one. 'What would you do if you were paralysed?' the doctor asked him. 'I'd blow my brains out,' he answered, *à la* Hemingway. 'Yes , but who's going to hold the gun?' the doctor enquired.

One of the original Bratpackers, he and Zelda lived a life of gay abandon at a time when the Depression was cutting deep into the collective American gut. No matter how much dustbowl poverty there was, they could always find one more party to attend, one more wild all-night escapade to negotiate.

He gave the Jazz Age its name, but he burned himself out almost as quickly as it did. When he died Zelda was in a sanatorium and his books were out of print. And he was broke.

A week or so before his fatal heart attack Graham showed him an article in a trade paper which described a Hollywood intellectual as 'a fugitive from the Scott Fitzgerald era'. 'You see, she said to him admiringly, 'you are an era'. It was a left-handed compliment, however. What the reference meant was that he was a has-been, an anachronism. He was forgotten but not gone.

He was so intrinsically a creature of his environment that he almost had to assume its socio-economic parameters within his own life. If the Jazz Age had excited him, so would the Depression drag him down. By the end of the twenties the party was over for him, and though he staggered on for another decade with some vestiges of the old magic he was really just playing out a ghostly version of his fantasies with Graham.

In an article in the *London Magazine* in 1964, Julian MacLaren Ross wrote that Fitzgerald outlived his meteoric fame as the chronicler of the Jazz Age and died too early to become a legend in his own lifetime. The first part of this statement is obviously true, but hardly the last. Considering the fact that his books were out of print when he was forty-four, he could hardly be deemed the stuff of legend even if he tottered on into his nineties.

The heart attack that killed him in 1940, in fact, was probably the most merciful thing that ever happened to him. It finally freed his tortured spirit from those frenzied moorings.

For a man as quintessentially different from Hemingway, his overall message to his readers was really the same in essence: idealists are punished, life is dreadfully cruel - and time eventually crushes us all. As he put it himself, 'Show me a hero and I'll write you a tragedy'. He was a hero himself of sorts, a kind of shopsoiled Monroe Stahr. The last novelistic tycoon, if you like, but one doomed to premature destruction. Both beautiful and damned for the same heartbreaking reason.

After he died, ironically, his books came back into vogue, the gritty realism of socially conscious thirties novels suddenly seeming more outdated than his own fanciful escapism. But this was too late for a man who was worth a total of $706 on the day of his death.

The effeminate, angelic prince was gone, all those years of swilling bootleg champagne and 4 a.m. gin finally taking their toll. The irony was that he had hardly drunk at all in the last year of his life; maybe withdrawal was too much to ask his body to take.

He could never achieve contentment this side of paradise, but maybe the lovable Irish drunk could broker some kind of a deal with his creator, courtesy of a body of work in which he was always the main protagonist in some shape or form, the pathetic but still life-enhancing keeper of an ever-dimming flame.

A Decade of Distaste

The forties weren't one of Hemingway's better decades, either personally or creatively. It was as if *For Whom The Bell Tolls* burned him out. He became suspiciously like a character he might have railed against in his fiction ten years before: a man who enjoyed the fruits of his success to the extent of exploiting his celebrity status. He enjoyed it when strangers called him Papa on the street (even if he didn't admit this), and basked in the aura of being America's best-known writer, if not the world's. He endorsed products, fed gossip columnists hot soundbites for their tabloid columns, became involved in pub brawls, pontificated on trivial matters...and in general seemed content to let his work play second fiddle to his life.

It was a decade that would see of many of his friends pass away. Apart from Fitzgerald, James Joyce died in 1941 from a perforated ulcer and Hemingway took the news badly. He hadn't seen too much of 'Poor, blind Jimmy' over the years but they had a mutual respect for one another's (wildly different) output and also a lively line in banter whenever they decided to get drunk together.

Gertrude Stein died in 1946, which didn't cause him to shed many tears, and Maxwell Perkins the year after. Perkins had always been as much of a friend and mentor as a professional colleague, and Hemingway was devastated at the news. He had written more letters to Perkins than anybody else over the years, and through them we can see the depth of his feeling for him as a man and an editor.

In the mid-forties, in any case, we can see a different kind of Hemingway emerging. We see a man who is more sure of himself than he was in the twenties and thirties, even though he has no right to be. A man who has become ensnared by the celebrity status he craved without admitting it. A man who has lost something of his old discipline and replaced it with bluff and swagger. A man, in short, who's starting to become guilty of all the qualities he pilloried in others when he was pure, idealistic and unknown.

After he was hit by fame, the fact poured into his writing and bounced back off it onto his own revamped identity. His fans set standards for him that he had to live up - or down - to. There was hell (and heaven) raising both on and off the printed page and a character called Ernest Hemingway, who might never have appeared inside a book cover under that name, was born. As Morley Callaghan put it: 'His imaginative work had such a literal touch that a whole generation came came to believe he was only telling what he himself had seen happen, or what had actually happened to him. His readers made him his own hero.'

For *Life* magazine he endorsed such items as beer and Parker pens for exorbitant sums. The idea of a writer being a personality in itself was new to the advertising world, but Hemingway had always made hot copy, no matter what guise he took on. Here he looked only too willing to embroider his legend.

He finally became not only larger than his work, but larger than life as well. Lillian Ross said people found his lack of pomposity a deterrent against being taken seriously as a writer, but this is something he would have enjoyed. He didn't have time for those who felt writers should be precluded from living life to the nth degree.

In time he became almost a prisoner of his legend. The more famous he became, the wilder were the tales about him. It was widely reported that he ran away from home to become a hobo, and also that he was a professional boxer and bullfighter. His war wounds were magnified out of all proportion, as was his poverty in Paris and the number of jungle trophies he bagged. Any story would suffice to sell a newspaper and when truth conflicted with the legend, the legend was printed. Casual readers of his life story as evidenced by the tabloid press could have been forgiven for imagining that he won the war against Hitler almost single-handedly. The reality of the situation was that he wasn't even an official soldier.

His war wound, as Malcolm Bradbury said, was the most famous since Philoctotes, his sleepless nights the best-known since those of Lady Macbeth. Everything he did, or said, was writ large on the face of popular culture. But the price for this was huge, and eventually he ran out of money to pay it.

In brief: the media built him up, and then took it upon itself to tear him down again with equal zeal. 'Excellence', as John McCaffrey put it, 'always excites envy, and public excellence excites gossip, which is the public expression of envy. Hemingway was the gossip columnist's delight, but the intense malice with which some of the critics unconsciously exploited his acts would suggest they had the sensational value of Wordsworth's illegitimate child, or Byron's love for his sister, or Frank Harris' copulation with *anyone.*' No wonder Hemingway loved the paparazzi. He would have even loved them more if he had lived a few decades longer, when they probably would have decamped outside the Finca Vigia with long range lens trained on his boudoir.

He was described as a bully and a coward, promiscuous and impotent, effusive and taciturn, mirthful and manic, extravagant and a tightwad. What matter that the epithets were contradictory? He was famous, the thinking went, therefore it was open season on him. That was the price you paid for being a celebrity - particularly such a vocal one as he was.

The other contradiction concerned his past. Had he really run away from home and earned his living by boxing? Or was it true that he was a failed footballer, a mediocre student, the cello-playing son of a domineering mother and a father who lacked the gumption to put her in her place?

He didn't wish to address such issues in public, preferring to reveal his true past only to a chosen few, but he left enough clues in his fiction for astute readers to join the dots. If journalists or casual friends delved too deeply into his emotional scar tissue they got their marching papers. This was the tightrope every public figure perforce had to tread: fighting for their privacy in life but going into the dark places of the soul on the printed page. To the end of his life, Hemingway never felt at ease with the dichotomy.

So tenuous was the distinction between his life and art that it was all too easy to see him not only in the heroes he created, but also their celluloid representations. The world recognised him in Gregory Peck stricken with gangrene on a Kilimanjaro summit, in Gary Cooper blowing a bridge behind Fascist lines in the Spanish Civil War, in Rock Hudson making his separate peace with Jennifer Jones. He threw his personality at the world and it responded by taking him into its heart.

There was even a Hemingway impostor going the rounds for a time - the ultimate accolade. It wasn't too funny, though, when he left a string of bills in his name scattered across the country.

He was a photo-journalist's dream, the ideal man to have pictured beside his buffalo even if he had never written a word. Quite apart from his literary prowess, his face sold magazines. It was like the tail wagging the dog. The cherub-faced Papa, as handsome as anyone from Central Casting, seemed a long way from the tight-lipped introverts of *In Our Time*. One also suspects such characters wouldn't have had much time for the elder Hemingway either. Neither would he himself at that time of his life. The grey beard made him look much older than he was, but then everything in his life thus far seemed to have been in fast motion, right back to the war wound when he was hardly out of school, or the literary fame others had to wait decades for, or that never came at all.

Some critics have wondered aloud why Hemingway, who could have held onto his fame easily on the basis of his work, insisted on upping the ante by advertising himself as a public figure. Was it for the money or simply a greed for notoriety? Perhaps both of these, but also, I think, a result of all the years of having his work rejected in the carpenter's loft in Paris. Editors had said no to him so often, he wanted to make up for lost time.

Either as a result of this kind of notoriety or a byproduct of it, his writing became flabby. There was a tendency to fall into lazy habits.

Fake European standards had ruined him.

His work deteriorated when he started 'putting in' the Hemingway style like icing you would put on a cake, or extraneous tissue inserted to shock.

After a time, this selfsame style became an affection that served more to distract from what he was trying to say than to amplify it. It attracted attention to itself to such an extent that it became decorative even in its lack of decoration. The ultimate unliterary voice had become literary almost by default.

On the surface his image appeared to be something that just happened, but in retrospect we can see it was carefully manufactured by Hemingway. He gave so much and then drew back, dangling friend and foe alike on invisible strings, dropping them and picking them up for equally enigmatic reasons.

A favourite Hemingway canard was the one alleging he had spent the Paris years in a freezing garret. It was also widely mooted that he had an aluminium kneecap inserted after the Fossalta wounding - and of course that he had been present at the Caporetto retreat. He added a few peaches of his own too - most notably a boast that he had bedded no less a luminary than Mata Hari.

Making love to this lady, would have required rare talent. Alongside his ability to fish, hunt, box, shoot, pontificate and write, it would have also required him to possess the gift of bi-location... because she died the year before he came to Europe.

Hemingway was content to propagate such stories until they outlived their usefulness, which meant that by 1932, when *A Farewell to Arms* was being filmed, he took pains to disclaim his own publicity puff, but by now he was even larger than his own protestations. As Dorothy Parker noted, 'People so much wanted him to be a figure out of a saga, they went to the length of providing the saga themselves.'

Consciously or unconsciously, he parlayed his literary fame into his life, and vice versa. The advantages, however, were short term, and by the mid-forties obscurity suddenly seemed highly desirable.

Suddenly he was tired of being the property of the cocktail party circuit, of the middlebrow chattering classes. He was even tired - momentarily, at any rate - of being a *bon vivant*. This is a phenomenon that assails most icons, and one has to believe Mary when she said that, as the years went on, her husband was forced to use the back exit of hotels to avoid a horde of fans mobbing him. To be sure, he never envisaged this in the Rue de Champs as he sat in cold rooms with Hadley pruning paragraphs he feared would never even see the light of day.

It's reminiscent of the rock star who spends twenty years trying to become famous and then goes around wearing dark glasses so nobody will recognise him.

Hemingway courted fame but, like others who have received perhaps more of it than they wished, he paid the price. He hated people who came up to him in pubs saying, 'So you're Hemingway, are you?' and then proceeded to paw him, and/or his wife or whoever he was with. 'If you admonish them, warn them or have to clip them, it gets in the papers,' he said, adding wryly, 'Henry James was not faced with these problems.' Indeed.

Such pugilistic endeavours hit the headlines, but not the way a writer got up at first light to work. Neither was it in the papers 'that you were wounded on twenty-two different occasions and have been shot through both feet, both thighs, both hands and had six bad head wounds due to enemy action.' Well actually it was, but one sees his point. In the age of image-makers, media machines and news-hungry paparazzi, the nuances of a Hemingway short story very definitely played second banana to a punch-up in Sloppy Joe's or Huck von Hemingstein decking an over-zealous acolyte.

The common view of Hemingway is that he was a man who was imprisoned by his fame. It's an opinion he wouldn't have totally disagreed with, despite the fact that he milked his celebrity status for whatever it was worth during his halcyon years. The irony of fame, of course, is that it's a one-way street. One can never decide to be 'unfamous' after becoming a household name. The best one can hope for is to retire to a bolthole somewhere and lie low. Ernest Hemingway had many such boltholes but he could hardly be said to have lain low in any of them.

When you're a living legend, you see, there really is no place to hide.

Problems with the Squaw

Hemingway left Key West for Cuba in 1939, needing a degree more anonymity than he was being vouchsafed there. His old home was fine, but he was too much of a public figure there rather than a writer who could give his books the time and discipline they deserved. The main problem was that he was sociable by nature, he said, 'and a writer doesn't have an office organisation to protect him from friends the way a businessman does.'

He moved to Havana, to a house just a mile from the Gulf Stream, where *The Pilar* lay docked. He hunted for marlin in it by day, and at night watched cockfights or drank rum and gambled. If Paris was the quintessential city of the bohemian in the twenties, Havana fulfilled that purpose for him two decades later. The mystique of Paris didn't have the Gulf Stream beating away at the shore all year, nor the isolation he needed for his writing.

Such writing wasn't going at all well for him by now, however, and neither was Martha giving him the support he needed to gee himself up for another burst of creativity to emulate *For Whom the Bell Tolls*. She was far too busy with her own writing for that, and not as much in awe of her husband as he expected. This led to many quarrels between the pair, and an even greater indulgence in liquor by a man who was already a huge tippler.

The union of the Great American Chauvinist and the Great American Feminist was always going to be doomed to disaster. She wasn't like Lillian Ross, who had a bemused attitude to his politically incorrect disquisitions, and she certainly wasn't a Hadley Richardson, whose love for him over-rode his boorishness. Nor was she even a Pauline Pfeiffer, who had been willing to sacrifice her career to his.

Hemingway could probably have had a whirlwind affair with Martha in the same way as he had with, say, Jane Mason, and left it at that. If, on the other hand, he had taken somebody like Mason - or

Duff Twysden - to the altar, the result would no doubt have been as disastrous as the Gellhorn marriage. Of course if his marriage to Pauline wasn't in such dire straits when he met Martha, that could well have been what transpired. They could have adopted a mate/relate/separate formula and shook hands as fellow chums of the idealistic left. Thrust into one another's arms at a time of heady socio-political ferment, and both feeling themselves to be lovers of lost causes, they really felt they could make a go of things, a pair of articulate, fun-loving crusaders who would champion underdogs wherever they saw them - in China, Finland, Cuba, Spain or even the U.S.A. That was the theory, at any rate.

The actuality was somewhat different. Apart from the obvious age difference, Hemingway was the man who had done it all when they met - at least in a literary sense - whereas she still had something to prove; to herself if not the world. The fact that she was using The Most Famous Writer In The English-Speaking World as her Svengali only compounded the problem. Let us not forget that Zelda Fitzgerald underwent a similarly disingenuous odyssey a decade or so before, when trying (vainly, as it turned out) to emulate Scott's success. Martha's resentment about living in Hemingway's shadow made her all the more obsessive about cutting loose on her own in her journalism, and even outdoing him as a hands-on war correspondent. Her advantage over him was that she wasn't likely to be mobbed everywhere she went, or importuned for autographs. Neither would she be sidetracked into taverns by over-enthusiastic aficionadoes anxious to hear Papa's latest war yarn.

Hemingway was more amused than impressed by her ambition. On one occasion in Hong Kong 1941, as he happily enaged in banter with a cadre of his buddies, Martha noticeably absented herself from such felicities only to hear her husband emote, 'M. is going take the pulse of the nation.' As for himself, he was taking a different kind of pulse by engaging in such chit-chat. It may have not have the *gravitas* Martha craved, but it could have been the guts of her next novel. 'M.

loves humanity' he declared on another occassion, in true Swiftean mode, 'but she can't stand people.'

A colleague from her youth gave this denunciation of her - which actually had many echoes of Hemingway in it: 'She claimed she loved the poor - actually she loved the rich. Whenever she came back to St. Louis to see her ageing mother, she always stayed with people who had swimming pools in their back gardens. She claimed she was a great lover of peace, but wherever there was war she rushed into the fray. She loved her mink coat, and claimed it was her *entrée* into any office.'

They had happy times together, to be sure, and she slotted very commodiously into the role of stepmother to the children Hemingway had by Pauline whenever they visited. She was also content to go riding and playing tennis with Hemingway in the early days; it was only when journalistic rivalry raised its ugly head that other bones of contention between them became aggravated.

Their life in Cuba was a mixture of fun, conflict and chronic incompatibility.

Martha renovated the Finca Vigia from its original decayed state, but even when it was habitable she grew enraged by Hemingway's slackness with his servants, and the foul-smelling tomcats he allowed to roam anywhere and everywhere - including up on the eating tables. She finally had them neutered, which he looked on as a kind of vicarious castration of himself. This was more of a joke than anything else, but it was also an ironic commentary on their bed-life together. She lost her physical attraction to him soon into the marriage, so all she could do was lie back and think of literary fame. Hemingway for his part lost everything *but* physical attraction for Martha. Making love - or what passed for it under these circumstances - was guaranteed only to drive them further apart.

Hemingway looked on her refusal to try to have a child with him as an indirect way of letting him know her career was more important to her than her marriage. 'When I got to know Marty,' he remarked once, 'I knew she collected things. She collected bric-a-brac, oriental rugs and paintings. It took me some time to realise I was part of the selection process too.'

If one reads the love dialogue between Robert Jordan and Maria as deriving from conversations between Hemingway and Martha - an obvious temptation considering the fact that Maria is physically based on Martha, and Jordan a clear-cut Hemingway clone - this is to overlook the fact that their relationship was more an expedient arrangement than a gesture of mutual passion. To be sure, there was early excitement, but much of it was of the forbidden fruit variety considering Hemingway was still married to Pauline. (The early excitement with Pauline had also revolved around secrecy, Hemingway still being married to Hadley at the time).

If truth be told, Hemingway was much more likely to say 'When shall I see thee?' to Martha than 'I love thee truly'. She was like a part-time wife to him, forever disappearing on assignments from *Collier's* to Europe and the Caribbean. 'What old Indian likes to lose his squaw with a hard winter coming on?' he asked rhetorically.

Martha would never be his squaw, however, unlike his former wives, who were less confident than she was, possibly as a result of feeling themselves too old for their husband. Martha had all the brazenness of youth, and let Hemingway know in no uncertain terms that she was never going to compromise her identity to his. It was like an action reply of his own parents. With one exception - Hemingway wasn't going to take such treatment lying down.

In 1940 she told *The Kansas City Times* in an interview 'Right now I'm the war correspondent in the family.' Suddenly, it was getting a little crowded in there.

Arguments also flared up frequently between the pair - usually about writing. Hemingway regarded her as his pupil with regard to things literary but she didn't see things this way, setting herself up on a par with him. Gregory said that his father once shouted at her in a rage, 'I'll show you, you conceited bitch. They'll be reading my stuff long after the worms are finished with you.'

'When you were with my father,' Patrick added, as if to endorse the point, 'it was the Crusades. He was Richard the Lionheart and my mother the woman left behind in the castle with the chastity belt.' Clearly, this was not a man who could take kindly to a wife at the business end of war correspondence as the years gained on him and he started to fall in love with sitting out the years in the Finca Vigia.

Martha was a firebrand and an independent spirit, and while this was fine in small doses, after a while the allure wore off for the chauvinistic Hemingway. 'I need a wife,' he moaned after she went off to Finland for yet another journalistic junket, 'and not in the most widely circulated magazines.' He might have been echoing Marilyn Monroe, who said that a career was a fine thing, but you couldn't snuggle up to it on a cold winter night. Hemingway had snuggled up to Hadley and Pauline whenever the need took him, but dammit, these women like Gellhorn, they didn't understand that a man needed them to be around all the time, not jetting off to far-flung places for bogus contracts when a world-famous author needed them to unwind with.

The fact that his mother kept her maiden name perhaps irked Hemingway more than he would be willing to admit. He liked independent women, but in moderation. He would hardly have been happy with somebody like Brett Ashley for long. Martha was more in this mould than either Hadley or Pauline, and neither was she as awed by his celebrity status, being an author herself. Likewise for Mary, who was distinctly underwhelmed by him when they first met.

He often said that his marriage to Martha was his greatest mistake. After she had been away from him at the end of 1943 on yet another assignment, he described her as 'the Unknown Soldier.' It wasn't really the done thing for a Hemingway wife to have a career so vibrant that it threatened to obscure his own. He also needed his squaws to be on hand to curb an almost pathological tendency towards loneliness.

From Martha's point of view, she entered the marriage loving him for his charisma and high sense of fun (if not his sense of hygiene), and they did have some spirited years together, but she never could and never would tailor her personality to suit his, as he demanded - whether overtly or covertly. A small example may suffice: he wanted her to publish her stories under the name Martha Hemingway and she declined. This caused him no small degree of chagrin. Even though she was publishing stories before he she met him, he wanted to be seen as a Svengali of sorts to her, by the world if not by herself. (He actually got his wish, because anything Martha Gellhorn published after she married him invariably invoked the name Ernest Hemingway somewhere in the resultant reviews).

When he was young, he told A.E. Hotchner, he never really wanted to get married, but after he had done so, he could never be without a wife again. There was only one marriage he regretted, he said. After the ceremony was completed, he went from the licence bureau to a bar nearby. When the barman said 'What will you have?' he replied, 'A glass of hemlock'. Significantly enough, he didn't specify which marriage that was.

According to Archibald MacLeish, Hemingway didn't so much hate Martha for herself as for the fact that she took him away from Pauline. Maybe he felt the same way about Pauline at the end of *that* marriage.

The marriage between Hemingway and Martha was like two ships passing in the night - a steamer and a dinghy that wanted to be another steamer. When she tried to climb aboard his boat he threw her overboard. What he wanted was to have her travelling alongside him, available if he should need to get closer, but otherwise firmly in the background. It was this sexism that frequently caused her to lose her reason.

Her fiery temper can be illustrated by an incident that happened in 1942 when he was driving her to their Key West home. She accused him of being drunk and took the wheel instead. He slapped her with the back of his hand for her accusation and she retaliated by crashing the car into a tree, thereby making Hemingway walk home. He wasn't used to being taken on like this and he didn't like it. But he still had to live with it. Hadley and Pauline would have been much more lenient with him, though it's unlikely he would ever have been tempted to slap either of these women in the first place.

His lack of hygiene was another major bone of contention between them. When she accused him - and his cats - of being malodorous he counteracted by telling her she was trying to run the Finca Vigia like a hospital her father might have worked in.

She adamantly insisted on more tidiness about the house than he was used to. He compromised on this because he was reasonably happy with her for a time and glad to be getting a third shot at marriage. Being married to such a young woman, however - in theory she could have been Hadley's daughter - was a culture shock for him.

Martha was the only one of his four wives who didn't humour, indulge or flatter him. Some men are attracted to women who play hard to get in this way: not Hemingway. He might have married three journalists, but he didn't want to be betrothed to a literary critic. There were quite enough of those about without having them under ones's own roof.

Though Martha admired *For Whom The Bell Tolls*, she also found much of it trite and self-serving. When she said as much to Hemingway he wasn't so much shocked as astounded, having been accustomed to a degree more respect from his previous wives for anything he ever committed to paper.

He was fascinated by Martha because she posed the kind of intellectual challenge to him that neither Hadley nor Pauline could approximate to, but in the end the challenge proved too formidable for him. To preserve his macho dignity he took to pillorying her in everything from *The Fifth Column* to *Across the River and Into the Trees*.

He once told Lillian Ross, in a revelatory moment, 'Would never marry an actress on account they have their careers and they work bad hours'. Gellhorn certainly fell into that barrow - on both counts.

Aubrey Dillon-Malone

He would have have adored a daughter by her but this wasn't to be either. Not only did she not want children: she looked on books as a replacement for them. *For Whom the Bell Tolls*, she said, was 'probably better than looking at a brand new child'. Neither did a hard-working journalist-cum-novelist have to get up in the middle of the night to feed a book.

Martha, like Brett Ashley, didn't want to be one of those bitches that ruin children. She preferred readymade families like Ernest already had. These required less effort considering the children were already raised.

After the war Martha adopted a child, so it's probable it was the actual pyrotechnics of childbirth that bothered her rather than the end product. This was Job's consolation to him. (Mary Welsh would also fail to deliver a daughter to him. She had a tubular pregnancy in 1946 but the tube ruptured and she miscarried.)

On the other hand, as Christopher Ricks pointed out, he was so volatile in his relationships with the opposite sex, having daughters might not necessarily have been a good idea. 'It was a disaster for Hemingway that he had no daughters,' Ricks said, adding, 'It might have been a disaster for *them* if he had.' The point is well taken, but one imagines a little girl would have brought out the best in Papa - and subdued the worst.

Along with Grace, Martha was the only woman who ever took Hemingway on. She admired his discipline and he her pluckiness, but that was as far as it went. She probably did him a favour by letting him know that he couldn't take it as axiomatic that a Hemingway wife would drool over him so much as to ignore all his shortcomings. She matured him by humbling him in this regard. But he still sought out the obsequious sycophants whom he knew would feed his legend. It was like a drug fix he craved - all the moreso whenever he felt his creative powers were failing. He needed his fans to tell him he was still 'The Champ' even when he couldn't tell it to himself.

Or *especially* at these times. With Martha he was only as good (or bad?) as his last novel, his last short story, his last journalistic assignment. He had to prove himself anew each day for her, had to push the boat out like Santiago. And sometimes he just wasn't able - or willing - to do that. He was older than her by as many years as Hadley had been older than *him*. And he was getting tired, too. He was unable to match her enthusiasm for those Finland trips, that Normandy landing. He was at an age where he wanted to be cossetted by his woman. She would have been ideal for him in Paris in the twenties or even Key West in the early thirties. As it was, however, this eager beaver who had it all to do was unawed by an author to whom she had once been compared in her literary style.

'Hemingway cannot teach her much,' a reviewer of one of her books wrote. And he didn't, much as he would have liked to. She broke out of the tyro/tutor mould early. And before long they were hollering at each other, practising oneupmanship both on and off the page.

She described him as a cobra, never knowing when his temper was going to erupt. His hangers-on enjoyed his boorishness, or at least put up with it because of the thrill of being with him, but he got under Martha's skin when he became pompous, or launched into one of his he-man yarns. The situation was something like what would happen a few decades later with that other American icon of a different field, Elvis Aaron Presley, when his wife Priscilla found herself having to vie for his affections with his bodyguards. Hemingway had no bodyguards but he did have disciples and as his talent dimmed he seemed to need them more than ever to massage a rapidly-deflating ego. Martha certainly wasn't going to do it. Far from feeling sympathetic towards the sometime hero on the ropes, he made her flesh crawl.

She refused to feed his heart on fantasies, as this man-child demanded, preferring to jerk him out of them with a sharp tug. His drinking and fishing friends, on the contrary, felt that his legendary past earned him the right to be obnoxious betimes. It was all a question of attitude, but Martha's fuse was almost as short as his own, which meant that their relationship was like two pieces of rusty metal scraping against each other... and often igniting.

Hemingway once actually drew up a mock contract for 'Marty' which more or less suggested she devote herself to him body and soul like some kind of feudal chattel. 'I, the undersigned,' it went, 'hereby guarantee and promise never to brutalise my present and future husband in any way whatsoever...I recognise that a very fine and sensitive writer cannot be left alone two months and sixteen days during which time many trying and unlikely things are put upon him.' And so on. It was addressed to 'Mrs Martha or Mrs Fathouse Pig' and witnessed by a Judge R.R. Rabbit and P.O. Pig. The tone was straight out of the kind of thing he did for *The Tabula* in High School, but Gellhorn wasn't deluded by that tone into realising that a very serious desire to possess her (if not deny her total identity) underlay the humour.

Hemingway had many affairs while married to Martha; maybe the surprise is that the pair of them actually stayed together for seven years. It wasn't so much that his marriage with her failed, but - as someone once said about Christianity - it wasn't even *tried*. For the first time in his life Hemingway had been slotted into a subsidiary role. No longer was he the object of an adoring woman who would give up everything to tend him; instead he was like the lesser half of a writing cartel, a househusband like his father, subject to the disparate whims of a globetrotting wife.

He created a character close to her in *Across The River and Into the Trees,* writing, '(She had) more ambition than Napoleon and about the talent of the average High School valedictorian'. He accused her of having had affairs with generals, and of marrying him to advance her social and literary standing. He also believed she exploited war from the relative security of the sidelines. Martha, for her part, retaliated by asserting that Hemingway was one of the cruellest men she had ever met, and speculated that he was losing his sanity as early as the early forties. By the end of their marriage she had lost total respect for him as a man if not as a writer. But then she had really married the writer rather than the man so this shouldn't have caused her too much distress.

In many ways Martha had more of a social conscience than Hemingway. She went on assignments to see injustice at first hand round the world and report on it, whereas he went on them to write books and thus assure himself a place in history. This is to state the situation baldly, but the young Hemingway, the assiduous reporter who flushed out boors and buffoons like Mussolini, was a much more conscientious soul than the man Martha married. After he threw in journalism for literature (which Ezra Pound described once as 'news that *stays* news'), he had his eyes firmly fixed on posterity. Martha was more firmly focused on the job in hand and gave more authenticated accounts of what she saw and felt. 'Ernest's commitment to the Spanish Civil War was the last time he cared about anything beyond himself,' she said after they parted, 'If it wasn't for that, I wouldn't have been hooked.'

After they had split up he said, 'I hate to lose anyone who can look so lovely and who we taught to shoot and write as well.' The placing of the priorities is interesting (did it matter what she was like *inside*?) as is the use of the royal plural. There's no mention of bonding, no reference to the good times they had together as he had done after his previous marriages broke up. Hadley's love was pure and Pauline's hot and cold, but the liaison with Martha was largely null. From *both* of their perspectives.

'I made a very great mistake with her,' he wrote to Patrick in 1944, 'or else she changed very much. I think probably both - but mostly the latter.'

Gregory had a different take on the marital split. His father tortured Martha, he believed, and when he had finally destroyed her love for him, told people she had deserted him.

Up until Martha Gellhorn, it was unthinkable that a woman would walk out on the great Ernest Hemingway. Unthinkable to the world and unthinkable to Hemingway. But The Squaw did it. Just like that. And a severe blow was struck to that gargantuan ego. Maybe he never quite recovered from it.

As well as feeling betrayed that she had walked out on him he also felt, as he said, 'damned lonely'. Neither was it a loneliness that could be assuaged by another woman. No, it was *Martha* he wanted back. He had never been deserted by a wife before and never imagined it could happen. But as he said to Pauline when he deserted *her*: 'He who lives by the sword shall die by the sword'. It was easy to say that when you were delivering the blow; something else entirely when you were on the receiving end.

On November 22 1945, just one day after their fifth wedding anniversary, she filed for divorce from him. In retaliation he charged her with abandoning him. In effect this meant that under Cuban law he was entitled to everything they owned. He interpreted such a law to the letter, laying claim to everything from Martha's typewriter to a pair of cashmere underpants he had once bought her as a present. (One of the few presents he had ever bought her, incidentally).

After the divorce they became like a pair of bickering children badmouthing one another both in print and verbally, each one claiming the other got the thin end of the marital wedge. There was neither the pathos of the Hadley split or the deeper acrimony of the Pauline one. This was more like high farce played out by two juveniles...with Hemingway generally coming across as the more juvenile. But then of course he had more of a reputation to protect. As for Martha, she felt she could close the book on that chapter of her life and move on, but - as was the case with other Hemingway women like Agnes and Adriana - she came to realise that life with Hemingway was a moveable feast. Or rather a moveable headache.

This was particularly galling to her since she set such store by her own achievements, both literary and sociological. As somebody who asserted her independence right from the day she dropped out of Bryn Mawr - and who would publish not only five novels in her life, but also seven prize-winning collections of journalism - she always saw herself as a more *engagé* war correspondent than her husband, and that applied to her work before, during and after her marriage to him. (After he died she became an outspoken commentator on every global issue from Vietnam to Nicaragua, but she continues to be remembered chiefly as his third wife).

When they divorced she said she lost total interest in Hemingway's reputation or welfare. She occasionally skimmed through newspaper articles about him with a vague curiosity, but most of them only confirmed what she already knew: that his talent was decaying almost as soon as she had met him in Sloppy Joe's, and continued to do so as the years went on - almost in inverse proportion to his fame. The more his writing degenerated, she felt, the more opinionated and extravagant his defences of it became. She saw him as a desolate wreck of a man, and thanked her lucky stars she got out of the marriage when she was still young enough to explore life - and the world - with some degree of vivacity and youth.

In years to come she adopted a whimsical attitude to the marital state in general, at one stage declaring that some couples would improve things between themselves if they shot each other.

She would subsequently tell Hemingway's biographer, Jeffrey Meyers, that she couldn't think of her former husband without getting stomach pains.

Adriana and the Colonel

Hemingway met Mary Welsh, the woman who would become the fourth (and longest-lasting) Mrs Hemingway, in 1944 during the London blitz.

Immediately after meeting her he told her he wanted to marry her, even though both of them were already married. Another woman would have been scared off by this overture; she was merely amused by it. (He had made a similar pronouncement to Hadley after meeting *her*).

He slept with her while still married to Martha in the same way as he had slept with Pauline while still married to Hadley, keeping the two relationships going in a psychological and moral quandary. Martha was much quicker to shout 'Divorce' than Hadley, who wanted to keep her husband at any cost. After she was gone, however, he was philosophical and looked at the bright side of their parting. 'Going to get somebody who wants to stick around with me,' he told Patrick, 'and let me be the writer of the family.' Mary Welsh filled that particular credential with alacrity.

Mary was the only one of his wives who didn't appear in his fiction. He seems to have lacked a certain passion for her, as indeed he did for Martha. Both of these women arrived in his life when he needed a permanent woman, and were pragmatic exercises to that extent, whereas his first two started from love.

Scott Fitzgerald said Hemingway needed a new woman for each new book, but maybe it would be truer to say he needed a new one for each new *war*. Agnes fulfilled that function during World War One, Martha for the Spanish Civil War, and now Mary was doing the honours for World War Two. Bearing in mind, however, that both love and war seemed to inspire him creatively in roughly similar doses, maybe it's all part of the one strain.

They argued fiercely but usually made up swiftly afterwards. It was as a result of this dynamic to-ing and fro-ing that they got to know one another so well. Hemingway said of her: 'She is an excellent fisherwoman, a fair wing shot, a strong swimmer, a really good cook, a good judge of wine, an excellent gardener, an amateur astronomer, a student of art, political economy, Swahili, French and Italian, and can run a boat or a household in Spanish.' He called her his 'pocket Rubens'. She was one-half Irish and one-half Kraut, he said, 'and that makes a merciless cross and a lovely woman.'

Marlene Dietrich insisted he never really loved Mary, nor she him. It was a marriage built on shifting sand, she suggested, and mutual convenience. He spent more time with her than any of his previous wives but there were glitches. He flirted openly with Adriana Ivancich before her, for one thing. On another occasion he called her 'a goddam smirking useless female correspondent.' And she, after he slapped her one time, dubbed him 'a poor fat feather-headed coward'.

In May 1950 Mary wrote Hemingway a letter which said 'My view of this marriage is that we have both been failures. Therefore let us end it.' He didn't really take her ultimatum seriously and a simple 'Stick with me, kitten' from him seemed to placate her.

Mary gave up her journalistic career to be with him, something Martha was never willing to do. Part of the package of being Mrs Hemingway entailed being someone who could muck in with the lads, or at least one lad. This Mary Welsh, a Jolly Hockey type if ever there was one, was more than willing to do.

She was obviously worried about whether the marriage would work, however. Did he really love her or was he seeing her, as she once put it, in the guise of a practical nurse for him in his old age?

Mary was like the best of Hadley and Martha rolled into one. She was both sweet and outdoorsy, and content to accommodate his whims in the same way as Hadley did. Cynics said the union wouldn't last (not an ingenious prediction considering his track record with wives) but Mary had other ideas. She was bent on going the distance, warts 'n all.

He boasted to Buck Lanham about his past sexual conquests in front of Mary, and both of them were equally embarrassed at his arrogance and bad grace, but Mary took it all in her stride, suffering his indulgences in a way that would have driven Martha - indeed, *did* drive her - away from him as fast as her legs could carry her.

The common view of Mary is that she took an inordinate amount of emotional punishment from Hemingway, and put up with things none of his other wives would have stood for. This is only partly true. All four of his spouses had to endure him flirting (and indeed sleeping) with other women, but none of them left him for this. Hemingway was 'poached' from Hadley by Pauline, and 'poached' from Pauline by Martha. If Adriana Ivancich, Jigee Viertel or Valerie Danby-Smith (to name but three) had tried to poach him from Mary, one senses he would have departed from her too. All his marriages were serial ones, it must be added. None of them broke up as the result of an affair, only because another wife-to-be waited in the wings. The relationship with Mary was stormy, but ultimately more stable on that account.

If the marriage was steady, however, the writing was anything but. By 1950 he was on the ropes artistically, having published nothing of note for a decade. He was also suffering from sporadic bouts of depression. He wrote a letter to Lillian Ross that year in which he confided that, after taking a dive off *The Pilar* some time before, he was tempted to let all the air out of his lungs when he was under the water until he decided that in doing so he would have been letting his sons down.

A book also kept him vibrant: an autumnal love story set in Venice. He wrote to Buck Lanham in September 1950 telling him he left his heart there 'and haven't been able to find the son of a bitch ever since'. His heart was in Venice because of a woman called Adriana Ivancich, the youngest daughter of an aristocratic family. He found it difficult to conceal the fact that he was besotted with her almost as soon as he met her. Mary, meanwhile, looked the other way.

Ivancich - who, like Hemingway, would commit suicide in time

- had a kind of beauty you had to look twice to see. She was like a Renaissance painting, a languorous porcelain model come to life. Hers was a static charm; she had an exotic inaccessibility which enthralled the ageing icon. And of course her youth was a draw. She was a whopping thirty-eight years younger than Hadley and, at that, a fantasy figure for anyone undergoing the male menopause as Hemingway was. Each of his wives were progressively younger than the last, but this time the thirty-one year age gap between them made it into more of a 'father-daughter' thing.

As previously mentioned, Hemingway always dearly longed to have a daughter. The fact that he didn't led him to gather round him a crew of adoptive ones in the same way as Stein and Pound became his adoptive parents in the early years in Paris. Ava Gardner was one, as was Ingrid Bergman, but none moreso than Adriana Ivancich.

He met her at the end of 1948 near Fossalta, where he had been wounded thirty years before. She was nearing her nineteenth birthday, as he would have been then. As was the case with Marlene Dietrich on the *Ile de France* in 1934, their first meeting had a romantic overtone. She was drying her hair by a fire and asked Hemingway for a comb. Instead of giving it to her outright he broke it in half, a significant gesture of bonding on his part. Sadly, it wasn't reciprocated.

It's interesting that his first encounter with Adriana concerned hair, as this is a topic Hemingway was fascinated by ever since his mother made Marcelline and himself adopt similar cuts in their youth. Extravagant discussions of hairstyles occur not only in *A Farewell to Arms* and *For Whom the Bell Tolls* but also, to an even greater extent, in the posthumously-published *Islands in the Stream* and *The Garden of Eden.*

He wrote over sixty letters to Adriana over the next few years, and even asked her to design the dust jackets for *Across the River and Into the Trees* (which features her as Renata) and *The Old Man and the Sea* (which he claimed she partly inspired). Mary watched on helpless-ly as his infatuation played itself out.

In her innocence, she looked on his fascination with Adriana as an attempt to try and become Colonel Cantwell, the hero of *Across the River and Into the Trees,* in real life. Little did she know that the inverse was closer to the truth: Cantwell and Renata had come about precisely *because* of his dalliance with her.

Though Hemingway was besotted with Adriana, and would have left Mary for her in the same way as he had left Hadley for Pauline and Pauline for Martha, he knew it was hopeless to imagine he had a chance with her. 'I would ask you to marry me if I didn't know that you would say no,' he told her on one of their last meetings, and she didn't argue with his interpretation of their relationship. In fact she was mightily relieved by his attitude. His heart hadn't been broken quite this forcefully since one Agnes von Kurowsky so many decades before, and then at a remove. Both women saw him as attractively immature, so maybe not too much had changed between Milan and Venice, between cavalier obscurity and extravagant fame.

Hemingway would appear to have tried to buy Adriana's love by getting her the contract to design his book covers. She was no Picasso, to be sure, but he strong-armed Maxwell Perkins into accepting her artwork, which was so poor it had to be re-designed almost out of recognition by the in-house graphic artists in Scribners. Hemingway also showered Adriana's brother Gianfranco with favours, and gave him a free run of his house in Key West.

He courted Adriana without the traditional pay-off of a bed scene. She accepted his fawning on her but made it clear that things would go no further. Amazingly, he seemed content with this state of affairs. Either he had the relationship on such an idealistic footing he felt a carnal relationship would spoil it (very unHemingway) or else he feared the wrath of Mary if such an eventuality transpired (this was infinitely more likely). Either way it was never going to happen as Hemingway didn't interest Adriana in the least in this regard. She toyed amicably with his affections but that was as far as it went. To press the issue further would merely have been inviting ridicule on himself.

Dora, Adriana's mother, sometimes acted as if she were outraged by this old (and married) man courting her beautiful daughter, but like Adriana it's safe to assume she wallowed in the attention his interest provided. Nonetheless, after *Across The River* was published, Hemingway forbade its release in Italy to protect Adriana's honour. Exactly why he chose to portray her exactly as she was, and not with a fabricated appearance and nationality, isn't clear. He could well have been involved in a wish fulfilment syndrome. How often had he told Scott Fitzgerald that if you wrote something well enough, it would come true later? That was never likely to happen with this lady, however. Her purity of purpose can be gleaned from the fact that she even sold his love letters to a New York opportunist after their tryst was over.

Across the River is like a love letter too. It is also, it must be said, the most embarrassingly trite book its author would ever compose. For a writer who once said prose should be like architecture, this was more like a condemned building. One can only understand his lapse on the grounds that he was writing it as a kind of valentine to Adriana, which blunted his critical apparatus. Even to the great Ernest Hemingway, love could be blind.

What we have here is a clapped-out character mainlining on reminiscences about ducks, sausages, wine and war with almost the same degree of misplaced *gravitas*. Hemingway has written worse books than this, to be sure - *Green Hills of Africa* and *To Have and Have Not* being the two obvious examples that spring to mind - but they weren't bad in such a patent manner as this one is. It's a book that says baldly to the reader: 'Hit me: I'm a target'. Not only does it wallow in its own ineptitude; it seems fascinated by just how fatuous it can be when it puts its mind to it.

It's the pulp fiction version of *Death in Venice*, a meretricious example of Hemingway 'lulled and dulled by the fable of himself', as one critic expressed it. The sleeping bag of *For Whom the Bell Tolls* has been replaced by a U.S. army blanket for the (anti) climatic love scene on the gondola, but the dialogue is as maudlin as in the other book, and equally contrived.

This is emotion recollected in pedantry. Cantwell is like a scratchy record as he fulminates against his superiors. It might well have been subtitled *The Torrents of Autumn*. There's one sentence too many in all of the paragraphs. Hemingway has taken his eye off the ball and let too much of himself show. If it were written by a satirist one would have been tempted to say it wasn't even a good lampoon.

Everything in the book is treated like a military operation: shooting duck, eating, making love and so on. Even reaching for the champagne has to be done 'accurately and well' by the bumptious Cantwell. Digesting a good lobster, for Cantwell, eventually seems to become as important as storming the beach head. Is it possible to take a man like this seriously? (He even keeps his flanks covered in the bar: his latest battle zone.)

Love always clouded Hemingway's artistic judgement. He was brutally clinical in his creation of male characters, and even female ones he disapproved of, but when he was modelling a heroine on somebody he loved - e.g. Catherine Barkley, Maria, Renata etc., the writing suffered. He never really recognised or acknowledged this fact. He got away with it to an extent in *A Farewell to Arms* and *For Whom the Bell Tolls* because these were such superbly crafted novels *anyway*. Because this book was structually suspect, the weakness of the female became thrown into high relief and was all the more meretricious (if not actually laughable) on that account.

In fact the best character is neither Adriana or Colonel Cantwell (some have justifiably dubbed him Colonel Cant) as the city of Venice itself, which is described with the love Hemingway had once shown for Paris. It also seemed able to return that love to him immeasurably more resonantly than Adriana Ivancich ever could.

If *A Farewell to Arms* was his Hamlet, *Across the River and Into the Trees* was a stab at playing Lear - but sadly a rather buffoonish one.

There's also an element of *Othello* in the book, but one mentions these Shakespearean echoes merely to throw them out again. Unless one is John O'Hara, a critic who did his best to rehabilitate Hemingway's ailing reputation by comparing him to the Bard of Avon on the strength of this effort - not realising that by doing so he was only making a laughing stock of both of them, considering the circumstances.

Details which might have been pregnant with possibility in another book, or another context, seem merely laughable trifles here, as indeed does the Colonel's entire relationship with a woman who acts like she's humouring him for fear of hurting his feelings rather than being head over heels in love. Hemingway's defence of the book, flying in the face of a landslide of abuse from all quarters, smacked more of panic than anything else, as did his summary denunciation of his most flagrant critics. Unfortunately, this was one struggle that couldn't be settled by a rifle or a pair of boxing gloves.

It's hard to believe that he felt a limp yarn about an old colonel who shoots duck, courts a contessa aboard a gondola and then dies of heart failure in a car could have entranced the readers who grew up on his cerebral stories and pulsating novels.

There's no way Maxwell Perkins - who had died in 1947 - would have allowed the sloppy prose on view here to pass his eagle eye unedited, but Perkins' demise gave Hemingway a free rein to rant on as he might, to everyone's loss. Up until now he had always kept his fictive hands close to his chest, but now there was *only* the chest. And he was playing with a stacked deck.

He would have been far better advised to publish *Across the River* as a long short story along the lines of the brilliant *Snows of Kilimanjaro*, where passages of straight narrative could have been interspersed with Cantwell's heady ruminations. The resulting format would have given him a degree of much-needed distance from his material.

Cantwell is really talking to himself in the book. Renata's 'Go on please' and 'Tell it to me' etc, are little more than jaded attempts by

Hemingway to inject an illusion of dialogue into the proceedings. Such promptings give his lapidary reminiscences a cosmetic justification, but there it ends.

Here as in *For Whom the Bell Tolls* the woman acts as the pupil to Cantwell's teacher as he expounds. In the earlier novel, however, Maria performed the function a lot less consciously because there was so much plot, and the relationship between herself and Robert Jordan was that much more credible as a result.

What surprises one most about *Across the River and Into the Trees* isn't that it's a bad book - but that he didn't *admit* that it was bad. Did he even realise the fact himself? He had never been one to take criticism on the chin, but he was now entering a phase of his life where even the vaguest negative vibration sent him into a tailspin.

For some inexplicable reason, he even talked of it as being his greatest acheivement to date. How off can one's radar be? Was it that his famous 'built-in, shock-proof, shit-detector' was seriously malfunctioning or had infatuation clouded his literary judgment so much that it became virtually non-existent?

The book goes nowhere and nobody cares about Colonel Cantwell except Colonel Cantwell. The fact that the only plot resides inside his cloyingly self-obsessed head only adds insult to injury.

On paper, the romance between a fifty-year-old colonel and a beautiful young woman of nineteen could have had a kind of *Lolita* style appeal, but Hemingway's personal involvement with Adriana was so foremost in his mind that it fails to take off on its own steam. It's also sad to see the sometime master of laconicism and stoic forbearance throwing his heart across the pages in a manner that seems more pathetic than full of pathos. The book is like a geriatric version of *A Farewell to Arms* as Cantwell, our valedictorian Frederic Henry, agonises about a woman he loves but can't be with forever.

Hemingway often castigated the likes of Dos Passos, Scott Fitzgerald and Peter Viertel for what he called 'whoring', i.e. selling their talents short for the fast Hollywood buck, but he was well aware that he himself had gone for a kind of literary shorthand too when his talent failed him. In his case, however, the reason wasn't money. The book was indicative of the decline of his powers, and a lapse into prose that reminded one of derivative rather than vintage Hemingwayese.

There's no fool like an old fool, to be sure, and in Colonel Cantwell's sententious attempt to recapture past glories he appears like Santiago without the grace. Hemingway loved this book like a mother would love a handicapped child: i.e. not so much despite its faults as *because* of them, but few readers could empathise with the idea of a self-obsessed old soldier swanning around Venice like a fop when all his wars were over except the one inside his own head.

If we're in any doubt as to how much he identified with the plot of the book, it might help to note that in letters to Adriana, he addressed her as 'Adriana Hemingway', and signed himself 'Ernest Ivancich' at the end. (He had originally intended to call Renata 'Nicole', as if casting her in the role of a female Nick Adams.)

The presumptuousness of signing correspondence to her thus would surely have scared off all but the most ardent of lovers, even if he wasn't old enough to be her grandfather, and twice as eccentric. When he called her Renata in the book, the allusion to a rebirth could be taken two ways - either as his own renaissance or a reappearance of the Hemingway of some forty years before, who had also fallen headlong for a woman (Agnes) and who would have his advances rejected in similarly bemused fashion.

Such a renaissance is as unsuccessful on the page as it was in life, unfortunately. Whatever about the Hemingway of *Death in the Afternoon* wearing false hairs on his chest, as Max Eastman opined, Cantwell really does. He epitomises all the very worst qualities his author embodied - the empty *bragadocchio,* the wild yarns, the preciousness, the incorrigible self-indulgence. Not forgetting the signature tune of all pedants everywhere: the feeling that, because you yourself went through something, it will, *ergo,* be of interest to others on that account.

If the book fails on artistic grounds it's still an interesting porthole into the psychological condition of its author, who was the same age as Cantwell when he was writing it. Fifty-one isn't geriatric by any means, but it seemed to be for Cantwell, as it was for his creator. Hemingway would stumble on for a decade longer than his bruised and battered colonel, but in the avuncular tone of this book we see death putting in its first brushstrokes. Through Cantwell, Hemingway is really bidding adieu to his loyal faithful as he is to a life that he felt betrayed him as much as it had Cantwell - and not only on the battlefield either.

Evelyn Waugh had a different approach to the Colonel. 'He is one with the baffled, bibulous crew of *Fiesta*,' Waugh commented, 'men who thought they were plunging deep into the heart of Europe by getting on friendly terms with barmen; who thought their cafe pick-ups the flower of decadent European aristocracy.' Waugh said of Cantwell: 'He believes he is the sort of guy for whom the Old Masters painted - and to hell with the art experts.' In other words, not very much has changed at all since Hemingway launched his one-man crusade against the eunuchs in the harem.

The book is also reflective of Hemingway's lack of involvement in the Second World War. He didn't have the intensity he had in World War One, which gave us *A Farewell to Arms*, or the dynamism he showed in the Spanish Civil War, which produced *For Whom the Bell Tolls*. In a sense, we didn't have the *right* to expect a great World War Two book from him since his participation in it was so marginal.

After Japan invaded Pearl Harbour in 1941, Hemingway, who loved war even if he hated what it did to people, decided he wanted to be part of it all. It was like 1918 all over again. He may have been forty-two years of age now, but the lust for action was still alive and well. Unorthodox as ever, he didn't apply to the Red Cross this time, but rather to the U.S. Embassy, receiving permission to turn *The Pilar* into a submarine chaser. The idea was that, having sighted enemy submarines, he would either explode them by flinging grenades down the spouts or else ram them with his fishing boat. The Embassy, amazingly, bought the idea, probably because he was who he was. He continued such Intelligence activities through 1942 and 1943 with commendable enthusiasm, even if he didn't succeed in destroying any enemy vessels.

One doesn't doubt that the forever gung-ho Hemingway would have been in his element dropping grenades into enemy subs under the auspices of being a fish salesman, but even Jack had to admit that the whole enterprise seemed 'somewhat surreal'.

Martha, like many another, remained unconvinced that the sub-hunting lark was anything but a juvenile excuse for him to go gallivanting with his disciples while preserving the illusion that they were doing something for the war effort. Never before had he put fishing on such a grand scale.

It's very tempting to take Martha's view on this one, to see him as a kind of military transient putting out his begging bowl to the likes of Buck Lanham for any sniff of World War Two that he could muster once his own U boat/Q boat escapades ceased in the spring of 1944. Just as he was a frustrated writer in search of a theme (he now found himself eating humble pie by contributing to *Collier's,* which was really Martha's baby), so also was he a frustrated pugilist in search of a war. *Any* war. The Right Honourable Lanham allowed him do his thing in Huertgen Forest for a time when his own troops were deplet-ed, but one suspects his motivation for this wasn't so much reverence for a fellow soldier as affection for an old buddy with an itchy trigger finger.

He went to Normandy for D-Day but wasn't allowed to go ashore. Martha was, which irked him hugely. The way she managed to achieve this was by posing as one of the stretcher-bearers. Hemingway, meanwhile, watched the action from the landing craft, furious that she had upstaged him in what could have been his finest hour - or at least a delayed stab at some latterday mythmaking. By way of consolation, he became an honorific captain of a unit of Resistance fighters in

France.

He also mixed his drinks in this guise, getting himself hauled up for a military interrogation in 1944 by George Patton's Inspector General after several unarmed men squealed that he had abused his status as war correspondent. He had taken command of the French Resistance forces at Rambouillet, the Inspector General alleged, and thus abused his journalistic status. Hemingway answered the charge gamely, being highly flattered to be questioned in this manner. Just as he had warmed his hands at the military fire in 1918 by getting into the action under the wire, as it were, so also did he repeat the trick here, nearly thirty years on. At Fossalta he was an ambulance driver posing as a soldier; now he was a war correspondent doubling as one. Was it any wonder those who toiled in the trenches for their daily bread would accuse him of being a fraud?

Carrying weapons as a war correspondent, of course, was a serious breach of the Geneva Convention. Hemingway knew this, but thought that he could work his way around it, maverick that he was. He might have argued that he had lived most of his life thus far with a gun in one hand and a pen in the other, so why stop now?

He became proprietorial about the war after it ended, and bragged incessantly not only about his own contribution to it (which was minimal) but also the manner in which he claimed to have captured it in his book. He continued to defend this stoutly, at the expense of infinitely superior war novels like James Jones' *From Here to Eternity* and Irwin Shaw's *The Young Lions*.

Of course it's not difficult to see why he was aggravated by *The Young Lions* considering Shaw had drawn a caricature of Mary in it, portraying her as an opportunist both romantically and in her military career. (He also hated Shaw because he had slept with Mary in the past).

It's hard to know why he was quite so vicious about *From Here to Eternity*. He wrote to Maxwell Perkins saying (among other things) 'If you give (Jones) a literary tea you might ask him to drain a bucket of snot and suck the puss out of a dead nigger's ear.' (Interestingly enough, this is the kind of tone critics tended to adopt for the young Hemingway in parochial magazines and newspapers when he first became famous.)

He was similarly dismissive of Norman Mailer's novel, *The Naked and The Dead*, despite the extravagant praise heaped on it by the critics. Mailer would go on to model much of his life on Hemingway but the pair never met, despite repeated efforts on the part of Mailer to interest him in his work.

Mailer actually sent an inscribed copy of a subsequent novel, *The Deer Park*, to Hemingway in Havana hoping he would give it a puff. The book, amazingly, was accompanied by a defensive note from Mailer saying that if Hemingway thought the book was 'crap', then 'Fuck you' - a classic case of biting the hand you hope will feed you before you know what it's going to do.

Hemingway never got this parcel, but he did eventually buy a copy of the book, which did even less for him than *The Naked and the Dead*. All the more surprising, then, that Gregory tells us his father once said to him, 'Mailer's probably the best post-war writer... Chances are he won't be able to throw another fit like *The Naked and the Dead*. But if he does, I better watch out. There'll be another Dostoevsky to contend with.' This contrasts dramatically with his earlier description of Mailer's novel (which he never even got around to finishing) as 'poor cheese pretentiously wrapped'.

Whatever their mutual feelings about one another, however, Hemingway had always been a role model for the impressionable Mailer. In Harvard his hero-worship of the older writer amounted to something of an obsession. He fought like him, drank like him, tried to write like him, became combative in the same way and even had multiple wives. In both their cases, early and fairly extravagant success (with war novels) made them create personae which eventually became like albatrosses round their respective necks, probably making them rue the very thing they lusted after when it began to devour their artistic integrity.

In the Introduction to *Advertisements For Myself*, a book Hemingway was courteous enough to describe as 'a ragtag assembly of ramblings, shot through with occasional brilliance' (high praise by his standards), Mailer wrote: 'Every American writer who takes himself to be both major and macho must sooner or later give a faena which borrows from the self-love of a Hemingway style.'

Such an ambigious testimonial is particularly applicable to *Across the River and Into the Trees*. While the *cognoscenti* laughed aloud at Colonel Cantwell's endless tirades, Hemingway continued to defend his novel as a kind of Americanised *Death in Venice*. The fact that it didn't quite measure up to that grand ambition was due to the specious attitudinising of much of the text, which made even the decent bits look ridiculous, sandwiched as they were between nonsensical diatribes about hair, food and hoary old war yarns. It wasn't too surprising, then, that the critics, who were always adept at smelling blood, kicked the great man while he was down. He himself added fuel to the flame by refusing to admit the novel had any flaws. It was left to Raymond Chandler to steer an honourable middle course. 'It's not the best thing he's done,' he wrote kindly, 'but it's still a hell of a sight better than any of his detractors could do.' Perhaps, but was that the point? Since when were critics supposed to be novelists? Chandler hit the target better when he said that very little actually *happened* in the novel, and therefore Hemingway's mannerisms 'sort of stick out'.

He dedicated the book to Mary 'With Love' but she was hardly impressed. How could she be? First of all, it was his worst composition in her (and the world's) eyes, and secondly the dedication flew in the face of the attentions he was showering upon Adriana during the writing of it. She must have been reminded that he dedicated *The Sun Also Rises* to Hadley in similar fashion, just after deserting her to marry Pauline. The blurb, in other words, went to one woman; the heart to another.

The reading public denounced the book just as the critics had.

Nobody bought the idea of an eccentric old warhorse having a May-December tryst with a glamorous young damsel who hung on his every word as they travelled through Venice on a gondola. They'd waited ten years for a big Hemingway book, but this self-indulgent miasma was hardly what the doctor ordered. Maxwell Geismar crystallised the feeling of most readers when he wrote, 'It is not only Hemingway's worst novel: it is a synthesis of everything that is bad in his previous work, and throws a doubtful light on the future.' Hemingway felt he was getting the same kind of raw deal from the press as Cantwell had received at the hands of his superiors during the war.

Just as Cantwell had been demoted by idiotic generals, so also had Hemingway fallen from the vanguard of American letters. By 1950 he was a humble foot-soldier bringing up the rear, but hopeful of averting the slide down the slippery slope to oblivion with one last gasp novel.

Contrary to what we're generally informed, it's not Hemingway's love for Adriana Ivancich that mars the book so much as his unstinting devotion to Cantwell - which is really an extended form of *self*-love. If Cantwell had been drinking in the left Bank cafes of Montmartre in the twenties, one can fairly easily imagine how he would have been lambasted by Jake Barnes and his bohemian cohorts. Robert Cohn would almost have been a hero by comparison. But then the issues the book dealt with were far too close to Hemingway's heart for him to see them clearly. He too could have been a three-star general of a different type if he hadn't sold out, or so he thought. The irony was that the selling-out was taking place precisely in a book about a man who refused to do that.

The reviews hurt him deeply but he tried his best to overlook them. Critiques of books, he told Leicester, were 'about as interesting and constructive as other people's laundry lists.'

Upset by those critics (they were many) who complained that nothing happened in the book, he countered by exclaiming, 'All that happens is the defence of the lower Piave, the breakthrough in

Normandy, the taking of Paris and the destruction of the 22nd Infant Regiment in Hurtgen forest - plus a man who loves a girl and dies.' Most of these events, however, are related in flashback, and the love of a man for a girl is hardly 'plot'.

Despite the rumours about Hemingway and Adriana that dogged public perception of the book, he afterwards invited both Adriana and her mother to be his house guests in Cuba. Mary went livid when she heard about this, and accused him of drooling over her like a pimply adolescent. Hemingway responded by throwing Mary's typewriter on the floor and flinging wine in her face. He finally told her he wanted her to go away to Havana so as he could have some privacy with Dora and Adriana. Another woman would have divorced him for this kind of carry-on, but she suffered it all in the hope that it would blow over with time. Her course of action proved wise, not only because Hemingway was the kind of man who would do what he wanted *anyway,* but also because it meant she saved herself from one of those fearful temper tantrums he was subject to when rebuffed.

From another point of view, the fact of Mary holding her counsel and manifesting the patience of Job during such marital lapses must have decimated his respect for her. Hadley grasped the nettle quickly when Pauline showed her true colours. She lost him physically as a result, but always possessed his soul. Perhaps the obverse was true for Mary Welsh, who spent many years with him, but inhabited an emotional territory that could hardly be described as ecstatic.

In the final analysis, the damage done to his public reputation by Adriana and the book was more lethal (and long lasting) than the not inconsiderable damage to his marriage. Suddenly he wasn't the darling of the public any more. The long knives were coming out and he wasn't liking it.

The fact that his career blossomed under intense public scrutiny meant that it was always destined to falter in the same way. Hence his almost paranoid hatred of newshounds, gossipmongers and journalists. (In another generation it would have been the paparazzi who got to him: he once confessed that the click of a camera lens reminded him of a rifle shot). So thin-skinned was he, he never learned to take the bad with the good. Pampered by the superlatives of hangers-on from a young age, not to mention the literary establishment for whom his pronounced anti-intellectualism acted as a pleasant antidote to his forbears, he expected such superlatives to continue unabated even when his work wasn't up to snuff.

Amazingly, he didn't seem to have been aware of the fact that academics tended to specialise in tearing down icons with the same speed and enthusiasm with which they originally built them up. Hemingway was a veteran of war at twenty and a world famous author a few years later with a best-selling novel and a couple of short story collections under his belt. There was a hiatus after *A Farewell to Arms*, and another one after *For Whom the Bell Tolls*, but people expected *Across the River* - which had all the hallmarks of being his last major novel - to restore his credibility. Maybe that's why critical opinion of it was so merciless; it had come with the weight of huge expectations.

Another event happened around this time to which he had mixed reactions. On June 13 1950, Lillian Ross did a profile of him for *The New Yorker*. The article which was subsequently published in book form, confirmed many people's prejudices about Hemingway the poseur, the charlatan, and the irascible old (or at least aging) coot. What they missed was the affection with which Ross imbued the character portrait. It was never meant to be comprehensive, merely a hands-on, from-the-hip vignette.

It had Hemingway declaiming on life, love and the whole damn thing - as was his wont. He drank, philosophised, said 'How do you like it now, gentlemen?' to no one in particular, spoke about defending his writing title against the young pretenders and generally disported himself as the cheerful animal that he was. As he told Ross, however, if you don't act pompous, you didn't stand much chance of being taken seriously as a writer. He hated literary pomposity, but he also hated being trivialised. The American public denied him the right to have it both ways.

Ross caught the strange old man of half a hundred years offguard, but her comments on him were all the more precious for that. She also caught him at a time when he wasn't working, and to that extent it was an unbalanced portrait. He was a severe disciplinarian at his typewriter, but off-duty he was anarchic, self-parodic and quite often a pain in the neck. This was fine for those who knew (and suffered) him, but to the American populace at large there were some things which were non-kosher for Uncle Sam's most high profile literary tiger. Neither did it help when he said of *Across the River*: 'I think I've got *Farewell* beat in this one.'

Ross admired Hemingway hugely, which may be the reason she didn't realise that she was actually portraying him as a scoundrel. He makes something of an exhibition of himself at New York Airport when she meets him (obviously chuffed with the completion of his book) and thereafter in the cocktail lounge where he drinks like he talks. Unstoppingly.

This is a domesticated Hemingway, far from faenas and indian camps and safaris, but he still has to be *numero uno*. We see him buying a coat, turning down the offer of attending a boxing match, being proud of his slim waist, going a few metaphorical rounds with Chekhov and his pards. It's all very chummy and diverting, at least until you begin to wonder if he isn't only a legend in his own lunchtime, if the man behind the image isn't as phoney as those he has spent his life castigating.

From another perspective, both Hemingway and Ross show a lot of bottle in giving it to us straight from the shoulder, without frills or pretensions. There may be snobbery but there's no subterfuge. Even the role-playing is amiable. Better a devilish Hemingway, one concludes, than a Hemingway who conceals his warts. And one can be sure Dr Hemingstein said and did many more reprehensible things in his life than he says and does here.

Hemingway seemed to like the profile when he saw it in proof form, but after it appeared on the shelves, and people started telling him he was 'ruined' because of it, he suffered a sea-change in his attitude and started describing Ross as shrewd and devious.

She was neither of these things. She took the ball on the hop and wrote accordingly, not knowing enough about her subject to be able to sift through his outpourings for a larger perspective. The upshot was a portrait that read to some like a character assassination and to others as an innocuous thumbnail sketch of a writer at play.

The timing of the sketch was important. Hemingway was resting from his labours on *Across the River* and was hungry for laughter, but Ross - and her readers - could have been forgiven for seeing this as the whole person. If that indeed was the case, it could explain why some critics were so vicious over that book, synonomising Colonel Cantwell with the Hemingway who spoke to Ross like 'a half-breed Choctaw' (his own words) as he shopped at Abercrombie & Fitch, or chewed the fat with Marlene Dietrich and other members of his elite inner circle.

Ross herself called the profile 'a sort of Rorshach test' in which readers found what they wanted. Dwight MacDonald felt it 'gloried in the grotesque but virile philistine' that Hemingway had become. Arnold Gingrich said Ross saw 'the Emperor's bare behind, while everyone else was oohing and aahing over the cut of his new clothes'. Some even saw it as representing the beginning of his deterioration.

According to Bumby, the portrait was accurate *per se*, but it looked different written down than it had sounded when it was happening. Ross failed to create the *mise-en-scene* for her article, with the result that all of the kidding around that was going on as Hemingway spoke was left out. As a result she missed the spirit of the man. Ross also broke with journalistic integrity by quoting Marlene Dietrich confessing that she used towels from the Plaza Hotel to clean her daughter's apartment, so Hemingway wasn't the only one who was caught with his pants down. But he accepted the fact that it was written in good faith so he gave Ross a fool's pardon.

Anyone who found Ross's portrait tedious would have found

Hemingway himself tedious. And vice versa. The profile was the man, albeit writ small. Ross was a diligent fly on the wall, but she *was* only a fly - and flies don't capture tigers. She did glimpse him observantly though, and it's a glimpse that has lasted, acquiring added resonance with time. It's interesting to set this profile off against more controversial reports from those who knew him less well but crowed more about him. The acid test was that their friendship outlasted the article. In time it became a storm in a tea-cup. There was nothing as stale as yesterday's newspaper. Or even last month's *New Yorker*. The beat went on.

Whether the portrait affected people's reaction to *Across The River* is anyone's guess, but the article served to make Hemingway even more paranoid about journalists than he already was, which was saying something. A man as tetchy as he was could gave gone under as a result, but he chose fight rather than flight, hitting back not with words or fists, but, yet another novel.

It was the book which had been in gestation inside him for some twenty years: the simple story of a man, a boy, a fish and a boat.

Colonel Cantwell was already history. His creator was returning to basics, retreating back to the frugal diction that was his signature tune. The groggy champ may have been on the artistic ropes, but he was still punching - albeit with a problematic right hook.

Hemingway had actually written a synopsised version of the story of *The Old Man and the Sea* in a 1936 piece called *On the Blue Water*. Now, twenty years on, it was coming home to roost. Maybe the stories you carried round in your head rather than the ones you simply wrote, he mused, were what made the difference.

His ambition in *Across the River,* he once said, had been to go from arithmetic into calculus, but to many readers he hardly got beyond the abacus. The point is that Hemingway shouldn't have *wanted* to go beyond arithmetic. It was simple arithmetic, after all, that would create the primitive potency of *The Old Man and the Sea*, the book which would introduce him to a whole new generation of readers and enable him to reclaim his place at the top of the literary totem pole. Renata wouldn't give him re-birth so much as Santiago.

Before Santiago hit the shelves, however, there were some niggling problems to be got out of the way. One of these was a young Yale lecturer called Charles Fenton, who was digging up Hemingway's past for a proposed tell-all biography.

When Fenton expressed an interest in writing a biography of him in the early fifties which would focus on his early days, Hemingway warned him off the project, saying nobody had a right to investigate his life in Oak Park because he had never written about it himself. He had a wonderful novel to write about Oak Park, he said, but he refused to do it because he didn't want to hurt living people and 'I did not think that a man should make money out of his father shooting himself nor out of his mother who drove him to it.' He gave Oak Park a miss, he continued, and never used it as a target.

Anybody who has read Hemingway's work closely, of course, would realise that he never *stopped* writing about Oak Park. He may have never mentioned it (or its denizens) by name, but it was implicit in almost all the early stories, implicit in the pastoral ambience, his own personal experiences and the many familial references.

He said he would never write a novel about Oak Park because he didn't wish to hurt people's feelings, but if that were the case why did he openly inveigh against the likes of Sherwood Anderson in print? A more likely reason he refrained from direct autobiographical writing was the fact that it might leave his own skeletons on display for researchers who were becoming more like detectives than scholars in their analyses of his work. He always steered biographers away from investigating his youth, so much so that when there was a suggestion his mother was about to give an interview to a journalist from *McCalls* magazine, he threatened to withdraw her allowance if she broke silence. The irony wouldn't have been lost on her. She had spent most of her life asking Ernest not to delve into sensitive areas: now he was effectively muzzling *her.*

Around the same time as the *McCalls* journalist expressed an interest in interviewing Grace, Hemingway asked her to forward him some photograph albums with pictures of him in the effeminate pink dresses he loathed so much. The timing of his request is significant, hinting at a fear that his mother would blow his macho image for keeps with one fell swoop. Thankfully for him, such an eventuality didn't materialise. He could deal easier with the written words of potential biographers.

He told Malcolm Cowley: 'I truly think that we suffer in our times from an exaggerated emphasis on personality. I would much rather have my work discussed than my life.' This was pretty rich coming from a man who had gone out of his way to make his life equally as exciting - if not moreso - than anything he ever wrote on a sheet of paper. As with many icons who courted publicity in their early days, however, Hemingway realised celebrity was a poisoned goldfish bowl that destroyed as many reputations as it created. The problem, as I've stated already, was that it was equally difficult to slough off as it was to originally win.

He was willing to suffer Fenton at first but started to become panicky when the Yale professor started to quiz Marcelline and Carol about his past. This was strictly off-limits and marked the turning point in his relationship with him. From here on in, it was 'cease and desist' time.

He wrote irately to him: 'I would no more do a thing like that to you than I would cheat a man at cards or rifle his desk or wastebasket or read his personal letters.' He then told Leicester he was fed up with authors 'trying to dig under my fingernails.' He said it was enough 'to disgust a guy to the point of tickling his own throat and making himself vomit.' Fenton apologised for badgering him with queries, saying he felt like 'a lush baiting an amiable stranger at the bar.'

Fenton's finished book, sad to say, is high on facts but low on insight. He's a surgical chronicler of the minutiae of a certain phase of his subject's life, but the book is so deadpan and bereft of anything approaching freshness or style, one wonders how it meant so much to him to garner Hemingway's support. What he vouchsafes us is a Hemingway gleaned from quotes and actions rather than anything more cerebral. His excuse for this was that, having gotten no help from his subject in its composition, all he could do was sketch an outline.

Six years after it was published, in any case, a depressed Fenton, for reasons yet unknown, committed suicide.

He actually threw himself out of a hotel window, a fact that didn't cause Hemingway too much chagrin. He probably wished more of his potential biographers would do the same, thus saving him many headaches about dirty linen that might be unearthed in haunts of his youth.

The irony of Fenton jumping to his death is like something from a Hemingway story itself. Here we have a man obsessed with an author's secret demons, but having perhaps twice as many himself. There had to be a moral there for critics the world over. No wonder Papa was chuffed.

He hated scholars with a vengeance right through his life. He saw then as people who would most likely have rejected his works if they had been literary editors when he was submitting them but who were now placing them under their precious laser beams. He baulked at the notion that there was symbolism in his work, but if the 'explainers' (as he called them) wished to look for such symbols, they were welcome to do so. They should remember, however, that a book was only as good or bad as whatever readers it found, the content being a function of what each reader brought to it. Other than that, he refused to run 'guided tours' through the more recalcitrant territory of his work.

When he learned that a course in Princeton had him as its chief subject, he confided to Jack, 'If I could disguise myself as a student and attend that course incognito, I'd bet anything I couldn't pass.' One is reminded of Oscar Wilde's dictum: 'Are *Hamlet's* commentators mad are they only pretending to be?' Or the mischievous boast of his

Aubrey Dillon-Malone

sometime friend James Joyce that he wrote *Finnegans Wake* merely to keep college graduates busy until the end of the millennium.

If there had to be criticism, he held, it should only be of the famous dead. That way they couldn't interfere with the process of creativity no matter what they said. Hemingway, however (like most writers) was willing to amend his views whenever he received a flattering review of his work. Critics were okay so long as they praised him. It was only when the long knives came out that they became eunuchs, whores, pimps, fakes, phoneys and jerks.

He said to Maxwell Perkins once, 'There are a lot of critics out there who really seem to hate me very much and would like to put me out of business. And don't think I mean it conceitedly when I say that a lot of it is jealousy. I do what they would like to do, and I do what they are afraid to do: and they hate me for it.' He also noted wryly, 'Sometimes I find out what I'm supposed to mean when I read the books on my work.'

As well as Fenton, he was also plagued with another biographer called Philip Young, whose main thesis was that he had never recovered from the trauma of the Fossalta experience and that such a trauma was evident in almost everything he did and wrote afterwards. He fumed at this kind of reductive reasoning, as might have been expected.

Apart from being fatuous - any old Hemingway theory would sell books by now - these people were like parasites to him, feeding off his droppings like so many demented sparrows chasing after a cart-horse. He despised them for their opportunism and also felt they inhibited his future writing by leaving him open to libel suits if potential readers 'saw' themselves in his works.

'Why don't they write books about dead authors?' he wondered aloud. But dead writers could never be as controversial as Ernest Hemingway, as he knew all too well, having been instrumental himself in embellishing his legend ever since his early twenties.

Young promulgated the theory that Hemingway was suffering

from 'repetition compulsion', and could only exorcise the evil demons of his wounds by acting them out in similar 'staged' circumstances. This in unlikely, though it's possible he felt some residual guilt in the manner in which he was excessively championed for his deeds in Fossalta, and spent the rest of his life trying his damnedest to retrospectively earn all his accolades and medals.

Young's thesis gains some credence from the fact that he spent most of his life entering situations of great danger, as if to expiate the trauma by exposing himself to scenarios which would help him to re-experience it and thus (the theory went) transcend it. But it's equally plausible he put himself into these situations in order to steel himself against an ever-present fear of death, a related phobia.

A psychiatrist called Yalom came up with yet another theory: i.e. that Hemingway's desire for virile pursuits resulted from an over-reaction against his parent's stuffiness. He tried to create a heroic alter ego, Yalom said, but could never quite live up to it. Theses like this were ten a penny, each increasingly more banal and tenuous than the one that went before.

'Everybody,' as Mary Welsh said, 'and his brother and cousin and his uncle and aunt all think they are the definitive authorities on Ernest.' He did have nightmares after being wounded, but this was to be expected. Author Max Schur described these as being 'attempts to master the stimulus retroactively, by developing the anxiety whose omission was the cause of the traumatic neurosis.' This is the kind of thing that entranced Young, and made Hemingway either chortle or explode with rage.

Young, according to Hemingway, had a fixation about his life that was like the Procrustean bed, 'and he had to cut me to fit into it.' This may have been true, but Young differed from the common run of analysts in the sense that he admired Hemingway's work from a literary point of view. He made it clear from the outset that he had a huge regard for his output, and also that his comments on his life and character would be deeply thought-out and never gratuitous.

Young was hardly expecting Hemingway to be overjoyed at the manner in which he was psycho-analysing his past, but he could well argue that the author had done enough psycho-analysing of himself in the past, and thus had to see himself as fair game for the other would-be hurlers on the Freudian ditch. (Hemingway had applied some of this kind of logic himself to justify his denunciation of Scott Fitzgerald in *The Snows of Kilimanjaro*). Young was surprised when Hemingway said he would block publication of the proposed book any way he could, but insisted he was pressing ahead anyway - with or without the author's help. The refusal of such help meant he would have to quote him only in paraphrase, he explained, which would be a disappointment to readers. Maybe this comment hit Hemingway's vanity. Whatever, he decided if he couldn't beat Young he might as well join him. Not only did he eventually give the project his blessing, he also offered Young $200 of a loan to ease his financial difficulties. (Young also mentioned that his University post was dependent on the book being published, which hardly caused his heart to bleed.)

Hemingway had nothing but contempt for what he saw as Young's trite over-simplification of his life, but he still allowed him permission to pursue his research. He hated academics trying to strangle his books into shapes to fit their theses. These weren't real people for Hemingway, just ciphers.

Princeton professor Carlos Baker was also in communication with Hemingway at this time regarding a proposed biography. He initially opposed the idea, even offering to refund Baker's advance from his publishers, but as time went on his attitude changed. He felt Baker would be more factual than speculative, as was the case with Young. Baker also warmed his way into Hemingway's heart by enthusing about *Across The River*. He was almost in a minority of one among critics in this respect. Either Baker really did admire the book (he compared it very flatteringly to Thomas Mann's *Death in Venice)* or had a vested interest in pretending he did so. Whatever, Hemingway was chuffed and sent him a draft version of *The Old Man and the Sea* by way of appreciation.

But then came another blast of news that shook him: the death of his mother.

His feelings were mixed when he heard of her passing. He allowed himself a moment to remember how beautiful she had been when he was young 'before everything went to hell in our family'. A few hours later, however, he said he wouldn't go to her funeral for fear the coffin was booby-trapped. Maybe that reaction said more about his neurosis than anything Grace had ever done or not done to him in the many years of their *mesalliance*.

'With bad painters,' he would later write in *A Moveable Feast*, 'all you need to do is not look at them. But even when you have learned not to look at families nor listen to them and have learned not to answer letters, families have many ways of being dangerous.' Perhaps, but from the grave?

No matter how many miles he travelled round the globe, her presence had always haunted him. She plagued him with letters that adopted the high moral ground, she criticised him for his 'filthy' writing and, when she was allowed, visited him in whatever abode he called home. Even after she died he told people he didn't feel safe from her.

His father had committed suicide as a relatively young man, while his mother lived to be a ripe old age. No doubt he would have preferred it the other way round. He had carried a suspicion about women with him right through his life as a result of her matriarchal influence. Such reservations were partly assuaged by Hadley, who was everything to him that Grace wasn't (including a mother?), but copperfastened by his subsequent wives, and also umpteen female colleagues, 'friends' and mentors like Gertrude Stein.

One feels Hemingway could have lessened, if not quite removed, his mother's influence over him if he grasped the nettle and told her bluntly what he thought of her. The fact that such a straight-talking man never did so is astounding. He called her 'the All-American bitch' to everyone he knew behind her back, but his letters to her right up to the day she died are formal and polite. Did the domination of the early years still exert some kind of a pull even on a middle-aged man?

Pauline also died in 1951 and you can almost hear the choke in his voice as he writes to Charles Scribner, forgiving and forgetting all the bad times: 'The wave of remembering has finally risen so that it has broken over the jetty that I built to protect the open roadstead of my heart and I have the full sorrow of Pauline's death with all the harbour scum of what caused it. I loved her very much for many years and the hell with her faults.'

Pauline died from a stomach aneurysm at a hospital where she was visiting her sister Jinny. She had been ill for many years with high blood pressure and headaches caused by an undiagnosed adrenal tumour.

Her death was almost certainly accelerated by an incident that occurred on September 30 involving Gregory. After he was arrested for a misdemeanour in Los Angeles, Pauline rang Ernest to tell him what happened and he fumed, blaming her for the way Gregory was turning out. Later in the night she woke up with abdominal pain and was rushed to hospital with high blood pressure. One of her blood vessels ruptured then and she died of shock. Both father and son tried to lay the blame on one another instead of grieving together; the result was an irrevocable split between the two of them. Pauline's death in effect meant the death of Gregory as well as far as Hemingway was concerned.

He always had to scapegoat people for events. Gregory was to blame for Pauline's death, not he. His mother was the cause of his father's suicide, not health or financial worries. And Pauline 'stole' him from Hadley. Much of this was the result of an over-active imagination. The novelist, as he well knew, was never very far from the downright liar. Fiction was a euphemism for mendacity as often as not.

In her will, Pauline left nothing to Hemingway and everything to her sons. He did, however, succeed in cajoling from them the original manuscript of *A Farewell to Arms* after some gentle persuasion.

Some years later, Hemingway met the playwright Tennessee Williams at a party and Williams asked him how Pauline died. Hemingway paused a moment and then said 'She died and now she is dead', which is like a sentence from one of the characters in his stories. It stands in marked contrast to the manner in which he wrote to Scribner.

One imagines he spoke to Williams this way for either one of two reasons: his increasing fatalism or his guilt over the manner of her dying.

Or both.

The Old Man and the Prize

He was an old man now and he had written many books, but they had not received the attention they deserved, he felt, especially the last one about a Colonel and a young woman. It was a true book, and one that was deeply felt, but they made fun of it, these critics, and they made fun of him too, the author, as critics who knew nothing about writing would always make fun of him. He was hurt by this, and he was even tempted to give it all up, but he said that he would make one last try and maybe it would come right for him.

He put his energy into the story of a fisherman, a fisherman like one he had known once in another country many years ago, but the memory had stayed with him and he knew that if he wrote it truly and well it would find its readers and he might be lucky again with the people who knew he had it in him to write a good book about the things that meant something to him, even though he had many health problems now, and his luck with marriage hadn't been great, and the labouring at his craft wasn't showing much fruit. He had gone eighty-four months now without success, so what chance was there for him with this old man who wanted to fight the moon and the stars, and a big fish that would pull him out farther than where he wanted, out to where the sharks were, who would pick his bones clean, leaving him with nothing at the end of it all except his dreams?

B ecause of the vicious critical reception unleashed upon *Across the River and Into the Trees*, Hemingway galvanised himself for one last lyrical surge to pacify the beast within himself and write a book that, as he put it, 'would not go bad afterwards'. The simplicity of the title gave it all away: *The Old Man and the Sea*.

We were back with primary colours again, with elemental delineations. Like Colonel Cantwell, Santiago was a bruised and battered soul, but his almost hieratic ability to soak up suffering contrasted deeply with the Colonel's world-weary denunciations. The stylistic clutter of the other book had also been dispensed with, so what we were left with was a man, a boat, a boy, a fish, the sky, the sea, the sun, the moon and the sharks. The test of a good story, he had always said, wasn't what you put in, but how much you could afford to leave out.

It was all of twenty seven years ago since Nick Adams had fished the big two-hearted river, and he was hardly recognisable in the Bible-spouting Santiago, but the same dynamic was at work, the same therapeutic odyssey, the same Emersonian struggle of man against the elements.

Hemingway pared things to the bone in this little book, but it still sold five and a half million copies within forty-eight hours after it was serialised in *Life* magazine, which perhaps proved some kind of a point. The friends of the old master, the aficionadoes, felt he had one last great book in him, or at least they hoped he had, but who would have believed it was going to be such a tiny one? Yet if what you said was right, you could do it quickly. Every novel he had ever written had started out as a story, but this one ended as a story as well. A long short story. Or, as the purists would say, a nouvelle. Whatever they called it, it netted Hemingway over a hundred letters a day in fan mail. The dethroned heavyweight was fighting one last bout. He would have another shot at 'the title'.

Across the River had been an unmitigated disaster, but now Papa had another kind of Renata. After an *interregnum* that had lasted the best part of a decade, the king was back.

Fitzgerald's theory about Hemingway needing a new woman for every book applied to this one as well. He would confide to Robert Emmett Ginna in 1962: 'I wrote it for a dame. She didn't think I had it left in me. I guess I showed her.' The woman, again, was Adriana Ivancich.

He told Ivancich that as well as being the model for Renata she had given him the motivation to write another book. 'It will be my most beautiful book,' he promised her, 'It will be about an old man and the sea.' Well, he was as good as his word, even if she wasn't around to help him with it. One assumes her reaction would have been more positive than the one she gave to the ill-fated Venice book.

This was a development of a story he wrote some fifteen years before, just as *A Farewell to Arms* was a development of *A Very Short Story*. The latter was somewhat less recognisable. He had perhaps been writing *The Old Man and the Sea* in his head for those fifteen years without realising it, but now it flooded out of him with the simple passion out of which all great art springs. It would be the last book he would publish in his lifetime, even though he lived for seven more years, and worked vigorously (if erratically) on a number of manuscripts during that time.

It wasn't as if it contained anything startlingly new either in style or content, but it crystallised all of his classic themes succinctly. The critics, of course, would have no truck with this kind of simplicity and went overboard looking for symbols. Santiago was Hemingway, they said, the marlin was his savaged books and the sharks were the critics themselves. Or something like that.

Hemingway himself begged to disagree. As he wrote to Bernard Berenson: 'The sea is the sea. The old man is the old man. The boy is a boy and the fish is a fish. The sharks are all sharks. No better and no worse.' No good book, he insisted, had symbols arrived at beforehand and stuck in. If they emerged in the process of the composition they were allowable, but only then.

The book had a fair number of classical as well as Biblical echoes, but it's chiefly memorable for the manner in which it enabled its author to return to his miniaturist roots at the age of fifty-three. The most obvious question it posed was: why did it take him this long to leave out so much? It must have been a source of amusement to him, as it was to all his readers, that he had spent so many years looking for success through major projects, only to find it in a fragment which had been lying in his mind in ferment for so long.

The book could have been over a thousand pages long, he claimed, with every character in the village in it, and all the processes of how they were born, educated, bore children, etc. That kind of thing was done excellently by other writers (Tolstoy is probably the foremost one that springs to mind) but Hemingway preferred to work by a process of exclusion.

It was originally meant to be a part of a bigger opus, a trilogy of sorts that Hemingway had been preparing, comprising *The Sea When Young*, *The Sea When Absent* and *The Sea in Being*. Thankfully such titles went no further than the work-in-progress stage, becoming replaced with *Islands in the Stream* and *The Garden of Eden*.

Dos Passos said its style was so clever 'I could hardly judge the story. It was like a magician's stunt - when he makes a girl float through the hoop, you don't notice whether she's pretty.'

Cynics would call it pseudo-primitive, but it encapsulated everything he had been trying for since he perfected the 'less is more' prose-poetry of his most fruitful years. Many felt he was past it now, but a Spanish-Cuban fisherman and his young helper silenced the naysayers.

The world had broken Santiago like it broke all people, but he was strong at the broken places and would live to fish another day, even if it didn't net him a marlin. Once more, the winner took nothing. But he was still undefeated.

Santiago microscopes Hemingway's own philosophy of life as a struggle nobody can win; nevertheless there's pride to be gained in losing gallantly. It may be cold comfort, but it's all that's available to us, and to that extent we should make a virtue out of necessity. Oak Park's lousiest Catholic was really outlining the 'vale of tears' *zeitgeist* here. One became purified by suffering, having done one's purgatory in this life.

Santiago's botched fishing mission comes to us laden with ritual-istic overtones, as he himself does with messanic ones. He's a thinly-

241

disguised Christ figure all but crucified by the sharks. The only surprise is that he doesn't die at the end. Mary was largely responsible for this. Hemingway had intended to kill Santiago but she said this would be too easy and predictable a finale. The closing pages where he lies dreaming about the lions are stronger as a result of her astute suggestion.

The genesis of the book, as already mentioned, was featured in an innocuous 1936 *Esquire* piece. What he added on was the Biblical imagery, the overwhelming air of dignified failure, the cool but reverberative tone. The *Esquire* sketch, in comparison, was as bare as the skeleton of the marlin Santiago carried into the port at the end of the story.

The irony about the book is that Hemingway, unlike Santiago, liked to fish for bragging purposes rather that to eat. He also liked to write big books for the same reason. As fiercely competitive on the ocean as he was in the boxing ring, on the racetrack, at the corrida, in the boudoir or behind his typewriter, it's arguable that his best talent was for shorter fiction, a genre he all but abandoned after he became a major force in the literary firmament.

The Old Man and the Sea is like a book he would have written in his twenties rather than his fifties. *A Moveable Feast*, on the contrary, while purporting to be the work of a man in his twenties, is really that of a man in his fifties. If we view these books through such prisms it gives us a better perspective on where he was coming from when he wrote them.

He wouldn't live to see the publication of *A Moveable Feast*, but *The Old Man and the Sea* gave him his best notices for over a decade. Gone, thankfully was the self-conscious striking of poses. What we're left with was a book as elemental as the sea or the sky. Bernard Berenson said it was 'as unByronic and unMelvillian as Homer himself', a paean that would have pleased Papa after a decade of abuse from his detractors.

The book netted him the Pulitzer Prize in May 1952. He hadn't received it for his larger works, but they paved the way. This one was smaller but despite its size it packed an even bigger punch. The primitive posturing may have seemed stilted to some, but it was all so delicate in contrast to the declamatory excesses of recent years, readers were willing to overlook the stylistic daintiness.

It was appreciated as much for its weaknesses as its strengths. An upmarket tearjerker with one eye on a frugal yarn and the other on the headier reaches of posterity, it hit a nerve in the collective unconscious. Papa was back, bloodied but unbowed, the big two-hearted river having been replaced by the wide blue yonder. Nick Adams was never this melodramatic, but neither was he ever as serene or self-effacing. Santiago stooped to conquer.

The essential conundrum of the book was phrased eloquently by Hemingway's biographer Kenneth Lynn. How was it, he asked, that a book which 'lapses repeatedly into lachrymose sentimentality, and is relentlessly pseudo-Biblical, that mixes cute talk about baseball with crucifixion symbolism of the most appalling crudity, have evoked such a storm of applause from highbrows and middlebrows alike?' One theory he propounds is that people really wanted Hemingway to write a decent book after the debâcle of *Across the River and into the Trees*. Their generosity of spirit, he contended, was born as much from relief as adulation.

Buck Lanham was expectedly extragavant in his praise. 'It is truly, he said, 'one of the most breathless things I have ever laid eyes on or an ear to. It is knee-deep in beauty and in all the values that mean so goddammed much to jerks like you and me. It is written with an angelic pen and a heart as big as this lousy world.'

The world proved even lousier again, however, later that year when Hemingway was involved in two back-to-back plane crashes, the second one damaging him in a manner from which he probably never fully recovered.

He was on safari with Mary at the time. The first crash happened after a flight of birds crossed the path of his plane near the Belgian

Congo, forcing the pilot to dive, whereupon he struck an abandoned telegraph wire. Miraculously, his only injury was a sprained shoulder.

In order to miss the birds, he later claimed, the pilot had to either land on a sandspit where six crocodiles lay basking hungrily in the sun, or on an elephant track through thick scrub. He opted for the latter - with good reason.

Lightning struck again two days later, though, when another plane he commandeered caught fire on take-off, trapping all the passengers inside.

Mary was small enough to fit out the front window but Hemingway wasn't. In a classic example of gung-ho foolhardiness he head-butted the door open and suffered bad concussion as a result. Nobody seems to have known why he chose that particular part of his anatomy for the action, least of all himself.

His injuries were more substantial this time. As well as suffering from impaired vision and hearing, his sphincter was paralysed and he had multiple burns as well as crushed vertebrae and damage to his kidneys and spleen. He was also bleeding from practically every orifice. When he reached a doctor in Nairobi he was informed that it was a miracle he hadn't died. (He had been given primitive first aid in a local bar by a physician who poured gin into a hole in his head, after which cerebral fluid leaked out.)

A few days after the crashes he appeared at a press conference clutching a bottle of gin and a bunch of bananas as he told reporters, 'My luck, she is running good'. The quasi-Choctaw comment became the subsequent subject of Ogden Nash's poem 'A Bunch of Grapes', which was then made into a song. (The Hemingway industry, she was also running good).

Between the two crashes, he later quipped, all he worried about was the fact that Mary's snoring was drawing an unusual amount of attention from a group of elephants that were hovering nearby. He claimed that they were as large as 'moving mountains' but that neither himself or Mary were worried overmuch about them. There were wild dogs too, but Hemingway, making wild dog-howls himself, was able to gauge their whereabouts by sending out coded noises. Whatever damage he might have done to his cranium with the headbutting, his brain still seemed in good working order...

He had a second gag about his wife as well. 'Miss Mary had never seen a plane burn up,' he said, 'That's an impressive sight - especially when you're in the plane!'

Many stories circulated about the crashes, the most intriguing being the one from the German newspaper which stated that he had crashed into Mount Kilimanjaro while searching for the frozen carcass of the leopard he had immortalised in his famous short story.

Far from being morose, he spent the next few weeks in a state of elation reading obituaries of himself in newspapers from around the globe, news of his 'death' having spread like wildfire ever since the first plane was spotted without any sign of survivors. Reading the obituaries, he confessed, was 'a new and attractive vice.'

'In almost all of them,' he reflected sardonically, 'it was emphasised that I sought death all my life. Can one imagine that if a man sought death all his life, he could not have found her before the age of fifty-four?' It was a moot point, notwithstanding what was to come.

The personalisation is interesting, as is the gender. He had always seen himself as being involved in a duel to the death with death, but whether he saw it as his whore or his mistress remains a mystery - the most exciting mystery, to my mind, of his whole life. Anyone who can unlock it may well be able to unlock his true character. Personally, I think he saw it as his mistress. In this sense a search for death would be the supreme sexual experience, the ultimate orgasm.

Other articles regurgitated the old chestnut about him wearing false hair on his chest and/or whistling in the dark to try to prove to himself that he wasn't nervous. Or else they speculated (again) that he was a lifetime coward who sought out all those death-defying situations to try to allay his fears.

Such theories were, by and large, overly simplistic. If he felt fear in situations of danger, as any intelligent man must, surely this meant he was even *more* brave. One can't be truly courageous, as he often said to himself, unless there was fear present.

Robert Ruark made a very sensible point when he said that Hemingway went on safaris 'not because of any subliminal obscure psychological torment, but rather because he bloody well liked to hunt and shoot.' (One is reminded of Brendan Behan replying to an earnest interviewer asking him why he drank so much by telling him, 'Because I like the stuff.')

Cowardice, he once said, shouldn't be confused with panic. He defined cowardice as 'the lack of ability to suspend functioning of the imagination.' People ought to work on that ability, he felt, to live completely in the now, with no thought of future or past. He possessed that gift himself at times with often horrific consequences.

The need to continually prove himself perhaps hints at some inner insecurity, but to call it a deathwish is to be too clever by three-quarters. Nonetheless, papers wouldn't refuse ink. (For someone who was suspected of seeking death, though, he never acted like it in civilian life. His bathroom couldn't be painted in Cuba, for instance, because he had written on the bare walls all the details of his blood pressure, weight changes and prescription numbers, etc. Not exactly suicidal behaviour.)

When he survived both plane crashes, he must have felt that not only was his luck running good, but that he was well-nigh indestructible. From another point of view, though, they copperfastened his (already ubiquitous) intimations of mortality.

A welcome piece of news in the aftermath of the crashes caused such thoughts to retreat into the background because in October of that same year he was awarded the Nobel Prize. The world and his wife were relieved that Papa was back, even a saccharine Papa, and though Hemingway himself had trivialised what he called his 'Ignoble Prize', he was delighted to have landed the big one. Nobody who ever won it before, he noted wryly, wrote a damn thing worthwhile afterwards, but he hoped to be the notable exception to that rule. (The tragedy of his life, though he wasn't to know it then, was that he too would be a victim of the curse.)

He told journalist Robert Harling in December, 'They called me from New York to tell me I was to get it. I didn't think that was right. I don't think anyone should know about that kind of thing in advance. Then the journalists came. I don't know how many. A crowd. I'm not used to that kind of thing. I'm old, but shy. I'm more used to attacking than accepting. Prizes aren't good for writers.' Nonetheless this was one he had always coveted whether he admitted it or not. It was somewhere up there with hooking the biggest marlin the world had ever seen, or going fifteen rounds with Tunney. The old, shy man was secretly over the moon. No longer did he need to defer to writers like Faulkner, who always had more appeal for the connoisseurs than Hemingway. The quintessentially unliterary man had scooped the ultimate literary accolade.

With uncharacteristic humility, he confided to Harvey Breit that he thought the award should really have gone to Isak Dinesen, Bernard Berenson or Carl Sandberg. Suddenly he didn't at all sound like the man who told Lillian Ross he had won the heavyweight literary championship in the twenties and went on to defend it successfully in the thirties and forties.

A couple of years before, Hemingway's old friend Gary Cooper had also returned from the brink of oblivion with a movie called *High Noon,* which netted him an Oscar. Like *The Old Man and the Sea*, it was a simple story which worked the miracle. Cooper, like Hemingway, had done nothing different to what he had been doing all his life in his chosen trade. But somehow the formula worked, and *High Noon* was a critical and commercial bombshell. Will Kane, like Santiago, went out too far, out beyond where anyone could help him, but he still prevailed in the end.

After the momentary exultation of being awarded literature's finest honour had sunk in, he phoned Buck Lanham and said to him, 'I should have had the damn thing long ago. I'm thinking of telling them to shove it.' What stopped him wasn't so much prestige as the knowlege that with it came $35,000 - a sum of money a man could have a hell of a lot of fun with. Even at fifty-five.

Hemingway used the excuse of the plane crashes to avoid having to go to Stockholm to collect his prize, whereas the real reason was that he was suffering from depression at this point of his life. And of course he also hated the formality of the occasion. The thought of having himself measured up for a monkey suit didn't enchant him. 'Wearing underwear is about as formal as I get,' he quipped.

Even if he had been fit, he said he wouldn't have gone to the prize-giving as it would have stuck in his craw to appear in front of a congregation of stuffed shirts and mouth bromides. Still, he didn't stray far away from that in the acceptance speech he taped, which was a fairly typical example of the Literary Scout Leader on his soapbox again. But few would deny him his pontificating on this occasion.

Writing, he said, was a lonely life, and though organisations for writers palliated the writer's loneliness, they hardly improved his writing. As a writer grew in public stature, he said - the reference to his own cult status being resoundlingly relevant - he sheds his loneliness, but the writing often suffers as a result. A good writer, he finished, again foreshadowing his own final days, 'must face eternity, or the lack of it, each day'. Well Papa had certainly done that, but in latter times it was the lack which was foremost in his mind - and on the page.

The fact that he was hot property again brought the inevitable movie offer from Hollywood. Nobody expected him to be enthusiastic about such a project considering the mauling his books had received in the past when they were put on celluloid, but he seemed unusually interested this time. His interest rose even more when he heard that Spencer Tracy, an actor he respected, was slated to play Santiago.

Hemingway had a fondness for Tracy, perhaps identifying with his alcoholic streak if not his naturalistic acting style, but he was as unimpressed with Tracy's Santiago as he had been with any of the films made from his books before. For one thing, Tracy was much too fat to look like a hungry Cuban fisherman. He looked more likely to have just walked out of a five-star hotel than an adobe hut.

Tracy had loved the book, shedding tears when he finished it, but he was still nervous about the prospect of working with Hemingway. He feared he would be difficult to deal with, having heard many stories of his bullying and whatnot. (Maybe one would need to have been on holidays in Jupiter not to.) Screenwriter Peter Viertel tried to allay his fears by telling him Hemingway had mellowed with time, but Tracy was still nervous. With good reason: Viertel told Hemingway that Tracy had fallen off the wagon on his last film and Hemingway feared - understandably - that history would repeat itself.

The idea of Hemingway disapproving of somebody because he liked to drink was somewhat ironic, but work was work. No matter how much he liked the sauce, he forced himself to wind down when he was writing and expected the same kind of dedication from others - in any walk of life.

Even if Tracy had been ultra-sober, however, or sallow and gaunt, audiences were always going to see him as Spencer Tracy rather than Santiago. This was an occupational hazard bedevilling any novel brought to the screen and featuring - as it had to for box office reasons - a star. Gary Cooper was probably the best actor Hemingway had working for him because of his tight-lipped aura. Rock Hudson was always going to be a beefcake, and wilfully so. Errol Flynn - despite Hemingway's voluble protestations about him - worked in *The Sun Also Rises* because he was almost on his last legs. This wasn't the way Hemingway created him (all of the characters in the book are significantly younger than their celluloid counterparts) but it still had a positive side-effect.

Tracy may have looked 'fat and rich', as Hemingway complained, but even if he had looked thin and poor he would still have been Tracy, with all that called up in audiences' collective memories. As critic Philip Kauffmann observed, 'He has put on pyjama-like Cuban clothes, and he walks about barefoot, but he carries with him always fifty films in which he tipped his fedora back and was urbanely sage.' In a sense, the film was tagged with stellar echoes even before the first day's shoot.

Another opined, 'Tracy usually plays himself with a difference. This time he plays himself with *in*difference.' Amazingly he went on to be Oscar-nominated for the part.

Hemingway tried to catch a real marlin for use in the movie, but (in a way like Santiago), he failed. Many of the boat scenes were also shot in the studio to save money. Director John Sturges, who replaced Fred Zinneman shortly into the shoot, admitted that the film was 'technically the sloppiest picture I ever made.'

Once again, as was the case with every other Hemingway book which had the muted life-blood sucked out of it in favour of a blockbuster approach, in Hollywood's hands it turned from being a simple elemental story into, as the billboards disingenuously put it, 'Rugged, ripping and real drama as man meets tiger sharks head-on in the most exciting adventure ever filmed!'

'All hell and heaven and Hemingway break loose!' went another poster. It was always going to be more *Jaws* than Jesus in Sturges' hands.

Other slogans went: 'Man Against Killer Monsters of the Raging Seas!' and 'The Most Dramatic Man-Against-Monster Battle Ever Shown!' Once again, the spareness of Hemingway's diction had been compromised for the masses.

Hemingway didn't want to lower himself to become a 'mere' screenwriter for the film version, but he was happy to nominate Peter Viertel (a writer he both admired and knew) for the task. In order to entice Viertel to write a more inspired screenplay than he might otherwise have done, he put him into all of the situations in which Santiago would have found himself.

In a nod to the 'Method' style of acting which Marlon Brando was finetuning in other studios at the time, he seemed to want Viertel - if not Tracy - to do everything but hook the big fish as the cameras were running.

This was curious considering Viertel's brief was to work only with Hemingway's original words. Nevertheless, Hemingway put him into a dilapidated hut that resembled Santiago's and also brought him fishing for marlin. He was disappointed that he wasn't too successful at this, and also that he became seasick one day when Hemingway cut him loose from *The Pilar* so he could sample nautical loneliness. How could a man who suffered so much with seasickness, the fastidious Hemingway argued (with no trace of tongue in either cheek) get into the heart and soul of his beloved Santiago? Viertel put up with all this nonsense, because he liked Hemingway and felt that the less he argued with him, the more he would climb down on his demands. It proved to be a wise course of action and Hemingway's confidence in Viertel's talents grew as the film neared completion.

Viertel himself said the job of adapting the book for the screen was a cushy number - and one which 'an intelligent, movie-wise secretary' could have done as well as he.

He was all too well aware of the sparse material, however, and wanted to beef it up by adding on a scene where Santiago goes to Havana to find work, thereafter returning again in a depressed frame of mind. He also wanted a scene with Manolin's parents forbidding him to go into the boat with the old man. Hemingway strenuously objected to both of these changes, but there's every likelihood they would have enhanced the final cut, notwithstanding the fact that they could have compromised the film's purity.

The movie version was a financial disaster, as Hemingway predicted, despite its fidelity to the literary source. Hemingway was no screenwriter, and his presence on the set probably detracted from the film's chances rather than enhanced them. He had been unhappy with previous film versions of his work because of their unashamed commercialism, but somebody should have told him showbusiness *was* a business. The name of the game was to put bottoms on seats.

The book may have enthralled readers the world over, but the inescapable fact about movies - as Hemingway should have known - is that they need variety and perhaps a love interest. The plight of Santiago was unremitting, and it would have been difficult for any director to maintain audience interest in him over ninety minutes, evocative and all as was the semi-mystical brooding that came through the voiceover.

He was also singularly unimpressed with the actor chosen to play the part of Manolin. He was, he said, 'like a cross between a tadpole and Anita Loos.' The final fish chosen was also a rubber one, which didn't do much for the authenticity of the film. 'No movie with a rubber fish ever made a goddam dime,' he fumed. This one was no exception. It didn't have the commercial edge The Great Unwashed might have craved, nor the delicate purity that would have entranced the buffs. Between these two stools it malingered: a dull, pretentious lemon that totally betrayed its origins.

On the credit side, the whole Santiago experience put Hemingway's name in lights - and on magazine covers - for the first time in years.

What a pity that it would also accelerate a slide into depression, paranoia and near-insanity in the years to come.

A Horse Called Morbid

*Death keeps crooking its finger at me. But I go on banging
my typewriter anyway. When I go, I want to go fast.*
Ernest Hemingway

Hemingway's frailty in his later years was a shock to any of his former friends who hadn't seen him for some time. Somehow, it didn't jibe that the former bear with the physique to dream about was suddenly beginning to show the wear and tear of age - even if he had treated his body with contempt in a life that seemed like something out of one of his books. He aged almost visibly before people's eyes in the mid-fifties, becoming old and frail so suddenly it was almost as if he had lost the picture in the attic. He also started to think about death a lot at this time. Not the dramatic death of plane crashes or being gored by a bull, but death that was banal, domesticated and absurd.

The war injury in Fossalta didn't only make him an instant hero: it also gave him - understandably - a fatalistic attitude to death. When Tennessee Williams asked him how Pauline died, he answered as already mentioned, 'She died and now she is dead,' After Katy Dos Passos (John's wife) was decapitated in a car accident in 1948 he wrote to Marion Smith: 'She is dead and so will we all be and there is nothing to do about it.'

He began to be aware of his own mortality as early as 1941, what with the death of Joyce, Sherwood Anderson and Virginia Woolf all in that year. Ford Madox Ford had already died in 1939, as had Thomas Wolfe, and of course Scott Fitzgerald the year after. To avoid dwelling on these matters, he drank and worked, but such activities were, at best, only temporary alleviations of his black moods.

As young as nineteen he wrote, like James Joyce in *The Dead:* 'How much better to die in all the happy period of undisillusioned youth, to go out in a blaze of light, than to have your body worn out and old and illusions shattered.' Was this just one of those casual comments he tended to unleash on auditors willy-nilly or the ominous chronicle of a death foretold? Author Ivan Kashkeen, who translated two of his short stories into Russian in 1934, summed up the contradiction between his renaissance zest for eclectic experience as well as his underlying sense of tragedy in a succinct phrase: *Mens morbida in corpore sano.*

'I'm not a depressed rat naturally.' he said to Pauline Pfeiffer in 1926, but depression was always there burrowing down inside him. He wasn't so much a congenital depressive as a reactive one, not so much manic as situational. But when the situation became chronic, as it did in the late fifties, he was on a collision course with disaster in some shape or form. William Walton insisted he was a manic depressive all his life, but managed to conceal it under alcohol - at least to the outside world if not his wives and others who knew him intimately.

If he hadn't been so much a man of activity he might well have accommodated himself better to retirement. He once called it 'the ugliest word in the language'. Hyperactivity and workaholicism didn't make him good fodder for it, but a boozing lifestyle can't go on forever. Neither could he accept the fact that his body was wearing out. There was a time for every purpose under heaven in the kingdom of God, or so the saying went, but Hemingway didn't belong to the kingdom of God. He was his own man and he would choose his own exit. When the time came.

The decline was apparent in his writing too. The emotion was becoming emotionalistic, the sentiment sentimental. He was getting to be like his character in *The Snows of Kilimanjaro*: 'dull and repetitious.' In that story he had written about a leopard that managed to intrigue everyone by being found on a mountain's uppermost peak. He was like a human leopard himself now, but from his own peak he saw only devastation.

Hemingway's pride was such that he couldn't admit to himself that he was sick. After all those war wounds he couldn't accept the fact that he was falling prey to nerves like his father. Nerves were for wimps in the Hemingway canon. To acknowledge he had them was tantamount to resigning his status as role model for a generation of thrill-seekers. All he could do was practise the old 'grace under pressure' ploy. Or, failing that, at least *silence* under pressure.

But silence was really his death knell. Silence meant the wound festered rather than relieved itself. He couldn't even share it with Mary, his soulmate. She too had become an enemy of sorts. He was left to sort it out inside his schizoid self. Or not sort it out ...

'He has not lived who has not conceived life as a tragedy,' said Yeats. Hemingway would have agreed. Nobody could overcome this tragedy, but it was possible to learn to live with it, or in it, by adopting certain behavioural stratagems. Some of these involved denial and/or escapism; others were confrontational attacks on the eye of the storm - a different type of escapism. In boxing, battle and bull-fighting Hemingway saw a way to challenge his demons, and the demons of an adventitious fate, and sometimes he seemed to conquer these demons, either directly or through his characters. But other times the demons won.

Sometimes they *seemed* to be conquered but were actually just lurking in the subconscious, waiting to pounce. He acted cavalier about them in an attempt to render them impotent but such an attitude seemed to have a counterproductive effect. By trying to assert himself above his sensitivities he set standards he couldn't live up to. Which meant that when his powers started to diminish and his health failed him he had no fundament of resilience left. The bigger they are the harder the fall, and this man took the full force of the tumble.

In youth his discipline acted as a buffer against this kind of punishment, but by middle age it was suddenly no joke being battered and bruised. Something terrible was happening to his insides, and even he wasn't quite sure what. Bewilderment mixed with rage inside that big, childish heart. He started to give vent to feelings he had suppressed during the years he was so busy showing everyone how macho he was. It's as if he was going through a protracted adolescence, but with no tutor to guide him through it. He could find his way through deepest Africa without a compass, but left to negotiate his own inner traumas he was desolate and lost. The old philosophy of *Il faut d'abord durer* was a thing of the past. He was approaching a personal Gethsemane, but unlike the Jesus of 'Today is Friday' he wasn't at all sure if he was going to be 'good in there'.

He was a man, as his friend and translator Ivan Kashkeen would phrase it, who had been 'reduced to stupor by having gazed too long at the repelling and yet fascinating mask of Nada.' That mask was now staring back at him unforgivingly, perhaps even with malicious glee. He had descended into his Nietzschean abyss once too often and, for once, lacked the climbing equipment to ascend back out of it again, having rejected the efforts of any potential allies to effect his return, or rehabilitation. Charging bulls or lions had always been much easier to negotiate than this disease of the intellect, which left you with no matador's cape or long-range rifle lens. Depression, he learned, was a beast that sneaked up on you when you least expected it, demanding ultimate submission even without a struggle. You were beaten even before you started. And then, horror of horrors to one so proud, stripped off any vestiges of past dignity.

Despite the number of people who surrounded him, and/or cared about his welfare, he was at this point in life quite profoundly alone. As alone as Santiago stripped of his booty, as alone as Frederic Henry having lost a wife in childbirth, as alone as Robert Jordan lying on the pine needle floor of a forest awaiting certain death. He wasn't going to the wars anymore, but they were still to be found inside his head. But could you say 'Quo vadis' to your own cranium?

His eyes were also shot to pieces - the result not only of a congenital weakness but also many years spent reading in poor light and without glasses. This was one of the reasons he asked Aaron Hotchner to help him edit one of his last journalistic assignments, *The Dangerous Summer*. (At this time, the only book he could comfortably enjoy was a large-print edition of *Tom Sawyer*.)

He was overweight even though he looked frail, and his liver was showing the effects of a lifetime of abuse. His kidneys were damaged too. His hair was also thinning and he found himself combing it to the front to hide the bald patch in a rare example of vanity.

His eyes had developed a hunted, haunted look. Things fell apart for him; the centre couldn't hold. He was tired of riding out the storms, or bellowing at the fates like a domesticated Lear. And he had a fear of impotence. 'A man alone,' he might have said with Harry Morgan, 'ain't got no fucking chance.'

Neither were matters helped by the fact that his doctors ordered him to cut down on his drinking habits - or else. He had always struggled against drinking when he was working on a book, with varying degrees of success. In 1945 he told Mary, 'This non-drinking thing is a bastard to have to do by yourself, but it pays off terrifically in the writing thing.'

Alcohol had almost been as much a part of his life as writing was. Buck Lanham said of him, 'Before he wrote a book he'd go into training. That is, he wouldn't take a drink before noon.' Henry Villard, the fellow patient in the Italian hospital mentioned earlier, claims he was lowering fairly vast quantities of cognac, vermouth and cointreau as early as 1917.

His drinking habits finally began to catch up with him after the two plane crashes. His sheer bulk had helped him get away with a lifetime of abuse, but the damage done to his kidneys and liver made this unfeasible anymore.

'I wish I lived in the old days,' he said, 'before all the books had been written and all the stories told for the first time. In those days it was no disgrace to drink and fight and be a writer too.'

Apart from the ravages of drink, Hemingway's body was brutalised by a barrage of mishaps that had taken place over the years. Not only was there was the war wound, which must have left a lot of residual pain, and the aftermath of the two plane crashes, but also a car accident in 1944 which necessitated forty-seven stitches to his head, a 1952 bust-up aboard *The Pilar* which required stitches to the head as well, a freakish 1954 fall into a brushfire which resulted in him burning himself all over, and the 1935 business where he accidentally shot himself in the leg while trying to kill a shark. Add to that the time when he cut a finger to the bone due to over-exertion with a punchbag, and a riding accident in Wyoming after his horse bolted. And so on. He downplayed these because his code demanded that, and his incredible strength no doubt helped him bear the pain better than other mortals, but as he went into his sixtieth year he was starting to run out of reserves to combat the mental fatigue.

'My luck, she is good' were his famous words after he survived the second plane crash, but was it? In retrospect, he might have done better to have died on a high that day. If he had, neither he nor the world would have been privy to the Stygian darkness of his last years.

'The real reason for not committing suicide,' he said in 1926, 'is because you always know how swell life gets again after the hell is over.' But the hell came back once too often in 1961 - and neither were there enough 'swell' times between the black periods. 'No horse named Morbid ever won a race,' Colonel Cantwell had noted, but Hemingway wasn't in the race-winning business anymore. He was a non-runner.

Maybe his main tragedy was that he couldn't accept the process of ageing, seeking out his youth even as an old man, like a kind of reconstructed Scott Fitzgerald. A more insightful portrait of him suggests that he never grew up *at all*. From this point of view he wasn't so much seeking to *return* to his youth as to continue it.

As Clive James put it, 'His premature old age was brought on by his relentless pursuit of a young man's sensations.' These weren't particularly easy commodities to aquire after a lifetime of abuse, accidents, war wounds and the other thousand natural shocks his flesh was heir to.

The miracle was that he didn't die even before Fitzgerald. If the jungle didn't get him, or the plane crashes, you felt cirrhosis of the liver at Sloppy Joe's *would*.

His life could never reprise the grandeur of the early years, despite his frenzied efforts to roll back the clock. He returned to Spain in 1953 to see if he could recapture the excitement of Pamplona that he portrayed in *The Sun Also Rises*, but the *frisson* just wasn't there. The same year he went back to Africa, the scene of *The Green Hills of Africa* also twenty years before, and again he was frustrated. In the forties he visited Fossalta with Mary, intent on defecating on the spot where he had been wounded in 1918; instead he buried a 1,000 lire note there. Which gesture would have been more significant, one wonders. Had the wound made his life excrement or lucrative - or both?

'Where the hell does a man go now?' he asked desperately in 1951. For the next ten years, some glorious moments apart, he was merely going through the motions. Cynics would put it more crudely: they would say he was simply waiting to die. And when it didn't happen to him in the many life-threatening situations he entered with such zeal, he had to do it himself. The party was over, but as Jake Barnes might have said, 'What the hell.'

The irony was that, while unable to accept the inalienable fact of ageing, he accentuated it by growing a beard that became a trademark. It suited his paternalistic demeanour, though he preferred to tell people he wore it because he suffered from skin cancer from the sun's rays and wanted to hide his pockmarked skin. In a sense he seemed locked in a timewarp between two - if not three - separate generations. He was before his time as a young writer in Paris and now he felt he had outlived his welcome on the planet.

It was never in him to bask in the afterglow of fame. Aaron Hotchner asked them why he didn't simply retire when the writing wasn't coming any more, but that was never his style. Like Santiago he had to go on proving himself every day. You were only as good as your last book, he felt. It was acceptable for a boxer or a bullfighter to retire, but not a writer. No one would accept that a writer's legs were shot, or the whiplash gone from his reflexes. They just kept asking the same question over and over again: 'What are you working on?' And he had to have an answer for them. Even if he knew his creative powers - and his eyesight - were in rapid decline.

Archibald MacLeish once said that he never saw a man 'go through the floor of despair' as much as Hemingway did. Norman Mailer added, 'He carried a weight of anxiety with him which would have suffocated any man smaller than himself.'

A man who epitomised the Byronic ideal of the artist-adventurer against sometimes apparently insuperable odds throughout his life, he was now at the end of his rope both medically and creatively. He may have landed the big marlin like Santiago, but the sharks of his own psyche were about to wrest it from him with merciless force.

Adios Pamplona ... and Ketchum

In 1959 the rivalry between Hemingway's friend Antonio Ordonez - the son of Cayetano, who was the model for Romero in *The Sun Also Rises* - and Miguel Dominguin, his brother-in-law, was reaching fever pitch. It was like the world heavyweight boxing championship of toreros and he dearly wanted to see his man win, and thus prove himself to be the greater bullfighter alive. It was almost like an obsession with him. He tried to write about the subject with the same elegance as he had done in *Death in the Afternoon* all those years ago, but his concentration wasn't what it used to be now and he found himself unable to edit his own ruminations, much to his bewilderment. The creative flow was going, but he couldn't admit this to himself. If anybody else suggested it, he flew into a rage.

He bought a house in Ketchum in 1959, and it was here he returned to after the trip to Spain to verify details of the bullfighting piece that was to appear in *Life* magazine. It was during this trip he evidenced the first signs of the paranoid tendencies that would dog him until his death. Whatever about Paris in the twenties, the Spain of 1959 most definitely was *not* a moveable feast.

When he went back to Pamplona, a quite different spectacle greeted him than the one he expected. The place was over-run with tourists, for one thing. Non-aficionadoes were jumping on bullfighting bandwagons and the purists were becoming an endangered species. He couldn't re-heat the *soufflé*. All he could do was try to live with the slivers of grandeur his memory called up. If indeed, there were any.

The Pamplona Hemingway visited in his youth had maybe two dozen tourists. By the late fifties (thanks to him making the place famous through his writing?) that figure had leaped into the league of a hundred thousand. Suddenly, it was time for the purists to make an exit. They were like cowboys on a mesa dotted with Pan-Am jets. Except it wasn't technology that made them anachronistic - it was mediocrity.

The country overall was transmogrified. The magic was gone, and the new breed of bullfighters weren't what they used to be either. They were superstars now, celebrities rather than romantics going into the valley of death. The corrida was in danger of turning from ballet into pop art.

He was returning to the scene of former glory, but as a shadow of his former self. He was a legend now - maybe he always had been - but unable to capitalise on it. The profusion of tourists annoyed him, as did the hangers-on, the autograph-hunters and the pedantic expats. There was still the beauty of the corrida, of course, but he drank too much to apprieciate it properly now. He was also insulting to Miss Mary, and she wasn't going to stay too long suffering the abuse. Eventually she went back home and left him alone with his bulls.

He again recruited the services of Hotchner to help him edit down the sprawling *Dangerous Summer* article for *Life* magazine but was crabby and confrontational about Hotchner's proposed cuts. His own judgement, he knew, was off, but he still couldn't countenance the input of this literary midwife, probably for that reason. He wanted to be told he still had 'the juice'. That he could still get the gen on those toreros without being shepherded along by an intrusive mentor. Hotchner was always going to be a cosmetic item, someone he liked having around as a buddy rather than a fastidious editor who would guillotine his little masterpiece. Like a fractious child, he wanted to be told it was fine and inspired, that you couldn't change a word without changing all the other words, that the Ford Madox Ford tesselations were still intact. Woe betide Hotch for daring to be critical of the Grand Master. And woe betide the editor of *Life* too if he tried to alter the precious copy. The more turgid it became, the more his defensiveness increased. Nobody had edited him down in the glory years of *Death in the Afternoon*. He would not be silenced.

The *Life* essay was originally supposed to have been one of 5,000 words, but Hemingway's final tally reached a whopping 120,000. Even after he cut it down to half that length, with Hotchner's assistance, it had to be run over three separate editions of the magazine. He resolutely refused to condense, even though such condensation had been his *forte* in years gone by.

The Dangerous Summer was subsequently published in book form, but it wasn't really much more than *Death in the Afternoon: Mark Two*. The beauty or the finca is there, and the sweep and swirl of the language and the avoidance of tricks - all those Hemingwayesque ideals - but hadn't we been here before? And had that much really changed?

If *Death in the Afternoon* was a paternalistic lecture, this is more a diary. It also lacks human interest for those not fascinated by male codes of honour as practised in a circular arena under the hot glare of the midday sun. The irony is that it could actually have benefited from editorial cuts, but the increasingly irascible Hemingway didn't know how to go about making them.

His eyes were worse now too, and he was suffering under the ravages of God knows how many aches and pains - of body and soul alike. ' It's like living a Kafkaesque nightmare,' he said , 'I'm bone tired and beat up emotionally.' He must have known it would be his last Pamplona. The lion needed to retire to his lair to lick his wounds. He had been watching this dance of death for too many years. It was time to go home.

Before he did that, however, he would have one last fling. In 1959 he employed Dublin-born journalist Valerie Danby-Smith as his secretary. His interest in her, however, went well beyond that.

He was fascinated by Valerie both for her fiery temperament and her undisguised adoration of him. In time she became the Adriana Ivancich who didn't rebuff his overtures - though she wasn't as physically alluring. Mary feared the relationship would go beyond platonic affection, but, as ever, kept her fears under wraps. Instead, she joked about her husband 'kidnapping' the impressionable young Dublin lass. Hemingway went along with this, enjoying casting Valerie in the role of illicit plaything.

His fascination with her youth was part of a pattern with him. In his teens and twenties he had fallen in love with four woman who were older than him: Hadley Richardson, Duff Twysden, Agnes von Kurowsky and Pauline Pfeiffer. When he was in his thirties and forties he fell for younger ones - Jane Mason, Martha Gellhorn and Mary Welsh. And in his fifties he fell for two women young enough to be his daughters: Adriana Ivancich and Valerie.

Valerie may have been a poor interviewer of Hemingway - that was how she originally met him in Spain - but she was a good secretary and formed a strong friendship with Mary that outlasted her husband's death. (She also, intriguingly, went on to marry Gregory after meeting him at his father's funeral and then starting off an unlikely friendship that eventually blossomed into love).

Hemingway often humiliated Mary with his attentions to other women, even in her presence. Either she was abnormally thick-skinned or was desperate to hold on to her famous husband at any cost, but she let it all wash over her: she endured Adriana and Valerie, and even a Havana prostitute with whom he arrived home drunk one night.The more he got away with this kind of thing, of course, the more he was going to try it on. Maybe she felt it was a kind of male menopause phase that would burn itself out. Time seems to have proved her right because they stayed with each other until he died - though Marlene Dietrich felt Mary contributed to his suicide.

Hemingway's sixtieth birthday party was a gala occasion liberally attended by anybody who even had a tenuous relationship with the genial old bear. The only person missing seemed to be Scott Fitzgerald. Much hell was raised, and the fire brigade had to be called after a firecracker got stuck in the top of a palm tree near the house and set it ablaze.

Miss Mary put great care into its preparation, even going so far as to set up a shooting booth she had hired from a travelling carnival. Maybe she was trying to get her husband to forget he had just hit the three score mark. In actual fact he hit a different kind of score as the party went on, passing the time shooting cigarettes out of Antonio Ordonez' mouth. Hemingway would probably have played the game all night, but Ordonez must have been getting slightly nervous because he said at one stage, 'Ernesto, we've gone as far as we can go. The last shot just brushed my lips.' (His luck she was still good). He diverted himself in a different manner afterwards and, by his own admission, refused to shoot at George Saviers 'because he was the only doctor in the house'. By noon the next day the last of the guests were still straggling out. A good time was had by all - including the host.

Maybe it was the last truly happy night of his life. Not long afterwards his spirits went downhill for a multiplicity of reasons, most of them to do with nervous tension...

When he left Cuba for New York later that month he already had a paranoia about being stalked by the FBI. After having employed Valerie as his secretary in February of the same year, he was terrified he would be hauled over the coals by the immigration authorities simply because she mislaid her passport.

He had many other paranoias during his final months. Perhaps the most risible one was the fear that his friend Bill Davis was planning to murder him by boobytrapping his car.

He bickered with Mary about trivia, becoming as petty as some of the fidgety women in his early stories. Over-riding most of his 'black ass' moods was the omnipresent worry about money. One night he noticed the lights of the local bank on after hours and concluded that the skeleton staff were combing his accounts for irregularities. Most likely it was the cleaning lady doing overtime, but there was no point in telling him that; his fears wouldn't be quelled.

He was also worried about the fact that he might be put in jail as a result of a minor accident on the road one day, his car having barely tipped against another one. A more concrete concern was the fear that Mary would one day have him permanently committed to some psychiatric institution if his demons got worse. And he felt sure they would. He also feared the arrival of burglars after a storm had blown down a cottonwood tree below his house. And he told Mary he felt the vice-president of his bank was trying to fiddle his account. His preoccupations, she wrote in her book *How It Was*, seemed to enclose him 'as the tentacles of an octopus envelop a mollusc.' (After he died, she found a letter he wrote to the FBI denying her complicity in the mismanagement of his financial affairs - which shows us just how deeply his worries went.)

By now he was starting to lose weight, his clothes almost hanging off him. Either Mary didn't notice or didn't pretend to, but those around him did. His posture became sunken too, and his voice lower. He was like a pathetic creature from one of his early stories - or one of those timid recluses Sherwood Anderson captured so vividly in *Winesburg, Ohio*, the book he took as his Bible after *Huckleberry Finn* could teach him no more.

He was terrified his weight loss was due to cancer, and expressed a fear of lawsuits over the book that was to become *A Moveable Feast*. More absurdly still, he feared the wrath of the law after a day in which he drank wine in his car.

So Hemingway was worried about the fact that he might be hauled into a police station for having a hip flask of wine in his glove compartment. Was this really the man who fought with the Loyalists against France? Who was given a medal for valour in Fossalta? Who spent his whole life giving the two fingers to powers-that-be?

It was as if all the emotions he hadn't allowed his characters - or himself - to feel right through his life came tumbling back to him to exact revenge for such subjugation. He reverted back to the small child in the summer dress, the Dutch Dollie rather than the Pawnee Bill. He was his mother's compliant son again, the one she wanted to be a daughter. It was as if he was back in 1902 in Oak Park, as if the fifty-eight-year interim was a sham. The old warhorse had reached his nemesis. The oak tree had become a weeping willow, the craggy hulk a piece of broken porcelain.

The Ketchum house he lived in at this time seemed to reflect his own mental state. Perched on a hill overlooking a barren landscape, it was as forbidding as a fortress, in an area as desolate and derelict as his own tired heart. In a strange way, this may have suited him because it imposed few demands on him. He didn't have to compete with it, or live up to its expectations of him. It allowed him to cower into a corner, far from Pamplona's madding throng, or the prettier seascapes of Bimini or Key West.

It was a place to retire to - for the man who defined retirement as the ugliest word in the language. Jack said his real tragedy was that he couldn't cope with the simple fact of ageing. This was a moot point: when you're Ernest Hemingway, youth was always going to be a tough act to follow. The pain of a battlefield had a certain legitimacy attached to it, but old age was an ignominious form of suffering for him. It had no rationale, to his way of thinking. It was something imposed upon him from without, a dull chronological evil that only pedants could countenance with equanimity. Ernest Hemingway was never a candidate for dying in his bed at eighty-five. He would leave that dubious benison to the Paul Mowrers of the world, or the Grace Halls.

He also betrayed one of the classic symptoms of depression by telling people his whole literary career was a fiasco, that he had never written anything that was 'worth a damn.' This, mind you, not so very long after he had been accorded literature's especial honour. Other things being equal, he was on the verge of a new decade with many unfinished novels waiting to be worked on. Other things weren't equal, though, and he contemplated the sixties not so much with hope as dread.

Every decade seemed to begin slowly for him. The early twenties produced some of his best work, but it wasn't until *The Sun Also Rises* that his reputation was secure. He ended that decade with a novel, and would also end the thirties at work on a big book. The forties both began *and* ended badly for him. The fifties inverted the usual pattern, starting promisingly and fizzling out with panic-stricken re-writes and half-baked projects that were postponed indefinitely or junked. Maybe if he had given the sixties a chance something would have come of that decade too, but he couldn't. He had lost faith in his ability to put words on paper.

Most of the paranoias of his last months came from this source: the decline of his creative verve. Frustration with this kind of impotence left a haemorrhage in him that became filled up with the neuroses we've mentioned: the IRS, the FBI, his financial status, illegal immigration of minors, the bugging of his room, etc. Now no matter child the name, sorrows springs are all the same. And this spring was dry. The man who could once crank out 5,000 words a day, and then maybe reduce that to 500 if his radar wasn't on the blink, was sterile. It wouldn't come any more.

He tried to make the sentences work for him, but they wouldn't bend to his wishes. He chopped paragraphs up in an attempt to breathe life into them but they only mocked him with their emptiness. There was no life in them, nor in him, their creator. They lay inert and lifeless before him, refusing to yield the old riches. The white spaces between the lines were just white spaces now, not implications. The iceberg was visible in its totality now, and it was dull. It was as if the ringmaster at the circus had lost control of his animals and they were rebelling against him - or refusing even to turn up. In the absence of inspiration he tried to re-create old tableaus, filling up his mind with dead visions of a half-forgotten past.

In January the winter of his discontent worsened. He rang Hadley with an enquiry about the Paris years which he hoped to include in his memoirs. (These would eventually be published as *A Moveable Feast*.) She couldn't help him, so the call went nowhere. As she left down the phone, however, she found herself in tears. A woman who knew him better than any other, she sensed his depression through his words, even though it was unvoiced. She had obviously been trained well by her master to read between the lines of his speech. But this time it wasn't in the pages of a book. It was for real.

The early months of 1961 exacerbated his decline. In January

John F. Kennedy invited him to his inauguration but he refused. Not only did he feel unable to attend this, but the sometime exemplary wordsmith was at pains even to articulate his reasons. This was the pass his life had come to: the author of *For Whom the Bell Tolls* found it such a challenge to compose a missive of some ten lines he almost gave up on it. Small wonder then, that the Bay of Pigs episode which would follow in the not-so-distant future would wash over his head. The great lover of Cuba was in his own hell by this time, as was JFK. And within a couple of years, both of them would have departed the planet as a result of a shot to the head.

In February he was asked to write a tribute to President Kennedy which took him the best part of a week. Only Mary knew the real score. But she also knew his pride was too great for him to admit the full extent of the psychological scars he had. She was a better nurse to him than anyone since Agnes, but then she had to be. She knew she was dealing with a timebomb.

He refused to sign himself into a psychiatric clinic for fear the public would say he was losing his marbles - which he was. But vanity had always been one of his greatest vices. His bravado wouldn't allow him to admit he suffered from his nerves. That was the disease of wimps and he wouldn't have any truck with it. 'Many must have it,' as the line went in 'A Clean, Well-Lighted Place' - but not Ernest Hemingway. To be classified as a psychiatric case would have been the ultimate ignominy for him. Neither did it help that he had always harboured a healthy cynicism about 'shrinks'.

He finally went into the Mayo Clinic in Minnesota, registering under the name of George Saviers, his doctor. (He was even concerned that this might be deemed a felony by the FBI). He entered on the pretext of having tests for a blood pressure problem. This hospital was chosen because it treated both physical and psychological maladies. It was here that he underwent multiple electro-convulsive therapy sessions. In retrospect, this was probably the worst thing that could have happened to him.

Having befriended the doctors and nurses at the clinic he arranged for Scribners to send them copies of his books. He was in his element in this guise, playing the role of The Writer to his (now uniformed) fans. From a medical point of view things also appeared to be going fine. Dr. Howard Rome dealt with his psycho-neurotic problems and felt he was getting somewhere. What he didn't realise was that he was dealing with a master psychologist in his new patient.

According to Hotchner, Hemingway was now washing down pills with vodka to kill the pain of a lifetime of hellraising - or maybe to anaesthetise himself to the psychic shock of his depression. An added worry was the fact that the psychiatrists caring for him didn't individualise his problem. They doled out the bromides and the electro-convulsive therapy but really only succeeded in destroying his memory and panicking him. Hemingway felt his best shot would be a shrink who had done a creative writing course. Who knows; maybe the old warhorse was right.

The cure in any case, seemed worse than the disease. His alienation grew, as did his tendency towards delusional behaviour. He even felt one of the hospital interns was a 'fed' in disguise. Exactly why the Feds should be after him was never properly explained. His tax affairs were hardly that awry.

The fact that he allowed himself to succumb to ECT resound-ingly demonstrates just how desperate he was. His main therapists heretofore had been booze and writing, but the booze was taking revenge after a lifetime of abuse and the writing had gone AWOL. At the same time, submitting himself to the care of a breed of people he had never respected was radically out of character. It would have been equivalent to asking a literary critic how he should approach his next book.

It was also incredible that the clinic persisted in the shock treatment after it became palpably clear that it was ineffective. He showed no sign of improvement after each set of treatments and yet he had eleven in all. If anything, the treatment seemed more insane than the patient. But Hemingway was hardly in a position to object. He was straw-clutching now.

His dignity was stripped from him too. Items with which he might decide to kill himself were removed from him, and other inmates had the freedom to enter his room whenever they liked, even when Mary and himself were making love.

Nobody knows for sure why Hemingway had a total of eleven shock treatments when it was obvious to one and all that they simply weren't working. ECT has developed dramatically since the sixties, but even now it's not seen as a panacea. It's always been a hit-and-miss type of therapy, but surely after ten treatments somebody should have got the message that it was more likely to kill him than cure him.

Howard Rome swore by it, however. According to Hemingway's biographer Jeffrey Meyers, 'If somebody came in to Rome with cancer or a hanging nail, he'd probably get shock treatment.'

Instead of solving his problems, the clinic intensified them. Hemingway had been depressed before he was admitted but he never actually tried to kill himself until hospitalised here.

The shock treatment played havoc with his memory, and what was a writer without that? If observation was college for a writer, as he once commented, memory could be described as High School. But now he was losing both. Frustration with his memory loss also increased his depression. If he had been more patient there's a strong likelihood it would have come back with time but patience was never one of his virtues.

He was also paranoid about his room being bugged, and about federal agents coming after him for impairing the morals of a minor. (In actual fact, the FBI *were* aware of his admittal to the clinic and did indeed 'tail' him there, so he wasn't altogether delusional in this respect. What was surprising wasn't the content of his comments, but their drama.)

His predicament became even more bizarre when he succeeded in making the doctors release him prematurely. The Old Artificer convinced them all he was cured. Only Mary knew what was really happening but she was powerless to do anything about it. It's difficult in retrospect to know if a longer incarceration in some institution could have reversed his downward psychological spiral, but no way should a man with a history of morbid depression behind him - not to mention a few suicide attempts - have been allowed home this nonchalantly.

Another matter was also dragging him down: Gary Cooper had cancer and the prognosis didn't look good.

Cooper, like Hemingway, was another daredevil who converted to Catholicism for his wife's sake. Being a card-carrying Catholic was a private joke they shared between them. Not only were there no atheists in the trenches; they were absent from hospitals too. After Cooper converted to Catholicism, Hemingway wound him up by saying, 'Now, Coop, you can have all that money *and* God'.

When Cooper died in May it was like the last straw for him. The two, allegedly, had a long-standing bet whereby each promised the other he would win 'the race to the barn.' Coop won, but only by a short head. Hemingway's own High Noon was approaching fast.

The pictures taken of him round this time show a man who looks dazed by life, someone who's looking through the camera rather than at it, like a rabbit caught in the headlights of a car. A gaunt old man smiling genially, but lost and confused inside himself as he searches his memory-banks for the treasures that won't come. He could never scowl, but the smile is painted on to pretend to us that everything is quite fine, really. Nick Adams would know the feeling. The post-ECT Hemingway, patched up once too often for comfort, looked geriatric before his time.

It was as if all the tragic sensibilities that had only been hinted at previously came back with a vengeance. As if he had somehow willed his life to this horrific pass, as if it was somehow implicit in every self-destructive character he ever created, or hid himself behind. No longer could he numb himself with sex or booze or a new blockbuster; no longer did his rhetoric of emotional numbness apply. He was on his own now, whether losing his marbles or not, and no doctor or wife or confidante could alleviate the gnawing of his insides. If he was a character in one of his books he would probably have killed him off, so there was a kind of poetic justice thinking of doing it to himself. He was now Harry Walden and Colonel Cantwell and Robert Jordan and Frederic Henry and Santiago all rolled into one heated mass of panic. But one bullet could end it.

Had he been suicidal all his life? Perhaps. In small doses, at any rate. In between the faenas and the big game hunts and the deep sea fishing. Or even during such pursuits. How else could someone capture the dark night of the soul so adeptly? Was 'A Clean Well-Lighted Place' the promissory suicide note of a self-professed 'lousy' Catholic all those years before? Would Papa too have said 'Our nada, who art in nada, nada be thy name' when his luck was bad, or the writing not coming, or things not well with Miss Mary - or Miss von Kurowsky or Miss Mason or Miss Ivancich? Was the dark emotion there like the hyena in *The Snows of Kilimanjaro,* waiting for the esteemed Dr Hemingstein to slip up so it could get out? Was this what his whole life had been leading towards, this empty morass?

In *For Whom the Bell Tolls* he had written: 'Dying is only bad when it takes a long time and hurts so much that it humiliates you.' Earlier still, in an unpublished fragment he wrote in the thirties, he said: '(My old) man was a coward. He never had any fun and was married to a bitch and he shot himself. (I) am not a coward, have had a damned good time, plenty of fun, been married to two good women...and I think I will shoot myself.' The dark humour of the final comment is tellingly prescient and illustrates just how graphically (and early) he saw suicide as an eventual escape-hatch if the pain of life got too bad.

He wrote in a letter to Chink Dorman-Smith, 'I believe I would have stayed in the kite that burned in Butiaba, once Mary was out, if I could have seen the rest of 1954.' He had rarely been as explicit about the psychic disintegration that would finally see him off.

By 1961, as Dwight MacDonald put it - in the kind of asyndental prose Hemingway would have appreciated - 'the position is outflanked the lion can't be stopped the sword won't go into the bull's neck the great fish is breaking the line and it is the fifteenth round and the champion looks bad.'

He had spoken of suicide as a way out of life almost jocosely since his twenties. He even talked of it as a possible solution to the loneliness of being without Pauline pending his divorce from Hadley.

Some worthies would argue that he had been committing slow suicide for years, not only in his drinking binges, but also because of his danger-laden safaris and deep sea fishing exploits, and the manner in which he popped pills with such abandon. Norman Mailer said that he probably struggled with 'a secret lust to suicide' all his life. Probably, but he hadn't been totally secretive about such tendencies whenever they assailed him.

In *To Have and Have Not* he speculates extensively on suicide when he says: 'Some made the long drop from the apartment or the office window; some took it quietly in two-car garages with the motor running; some used the native tradition of the Colt or Smith and Wesson. The 'long drop' from the apartment window or office was messy indeed, but so was death by gunshot wound. Hemingway would know all about that.

'And then it occurred to him that he was going to die.' Hemingway though, wouldn't go out on a whimper. He wouldn't shuffle off the mortal coil because a thorn had nicked his finger and the planes didn't come in time, as was the case for Harry Walden. No, he would go out like his father, like Hadley's father. *Nada y pues nada y nada y pues nada.* Many must have it. But none as intensely as he.

'When a man is in rebellion against death,' he had written in *Death in the Afternoon*, 'he has pleasure in taking to himself one of the godlike attributes: that of giving it.' Now the failed torero was about to test that theory to its limits.

He wanted to get out of life at any price. He had seen his body and soul alike wracked with pain. He had a date with destiny and when the bell tolled for him he answered it.

He was like an animal with his foot caught in a trap, a tethered lion without the facility to scream. The thrills of yesteryear held no allure for him because he hadn't the emotional equipment to give himself to them anymore. The intensity with which he had lived his life up to this was catching up on him with a vengeance. He was entering an almost surreal vacuum, but he couldn't admit it, not even to himself. It was a vacuum had its roots as far back as the Nick Adams of 'Indian Camp'. His final end seemed to be fated even from that early story, with its blunt existential edge. From his youth he had seen his father deal with brutal scenarios; now such precocious visions were coming back to haunt him... from the inside.

The unmitigated disaster that was *The Dangerous Summer* probably decided him not to go to Pamplona in 1961. He was ashamed of it, and ashamed of the man he had become as a result of it. It seemed to prove to him that he could no longer write eloquently about his favourite subject, and if he couldn't do that, what point was there in going at all?

Instead he returned to his lair in Ketchum to suffer a self-imposed *cornada*. There was no grace in this one, however, unlike a goring that might have been suffered by Ordonez, or Dominguin. This would be perfunctory, a desperate lust for oblivion. He had staked a place in posterity, that much he knew; it was the present that was the nightmare.

His end didn't come in in a plane crash, or facing a lion like Macomber, or fishing for marlin or hunting antelope or in a war or a boxing ring. No, just as he had used his gun to kill cleanly and purely in the heat of pursuit, so he would turn it on himself in keeping with the family tradition.

Not many men have had their deaths wrongly proclaimed by the world's press like this one. Not only did this transpire after the 1954 plane crashes, but also a decade earlier when he was involved in a car crash in London, and again in 1960 when he was alleged to have died in a bullring in Malaga. The real end, however, when it came, was muted. Not so much *grand guignol* as Theatre of the Absurd.

On April 21, Mary came down the stairs of their Ketchum home to find him in the sitting-room with a shotgun in his hand and two shells standing upright on the window-sill in front of him. Instead of getting hysterical, which most women would have done in the circumstances, she casually suggested she would like to go on a fishing trip to Mexico. She was using a stalling tactic on him because the doctor was due to call and she felt he might pacify him.

'Honey,' she said simply, 'you wouldn't do anything harmful to me as well as yourself, would you ?' That seemed to work. He put down the gun and then the doctor arrived and took him to a hospital and had him sedated. It was, however, merely a temporary remission from his depression. (Years after he died Mary wondered 'if we had not been more cruel than kind in preventing his suicide then and there.' In the light - or darkness - of subsequent events, she was probably right.)

Before the doctor left, he made another half-baked attempt to run to the gunrack but was dispossessed without too much ado. He then travelled by plane to a hospital in Rochester and after they stopped en route for re-fuelling he went for a walk during which he allegedly searched the glove compartments of parked cars at the airport looking for firearms. He also tried to walk into the propellers of a plane coming down the runway towards him. He was then re-admitted to the clinic and received more electro-convulsive therapy.

Such therapy was as ineffective as previous doses, but Hemingway didn't admit this. He proved himself to be an adept actor once again, fooling the doctors into signing him out while he was still unhinged.

We can blame the medical establishment if we wish, but it's also a tenable theory that he fooled everyone he ever knew with his high good humour. Jack once said that most of the biographies about him neglect what great fun he was to be with. And he was. His dark moods he generally kept to himself. His temper tantrums were public, by definition, as was his waspishness, but how many black nights of the soul did he have before July 1961? I would hazard more than a few. Nobody commits suicide without without having thought long and hard about it, or without having suffered at a deeper level than most of us will ever know about.

He left the clinic for the last time on June 26. Mary protested at his untimely release, but nobody listened. As Gregory put it 'What was one woman's intuition compared to all that medical expertise?' On the other hand, as Gregory also said, cerebral tissue splattered all over the walls a week after a patient is discharged can hardly be classified as a therapeutic triumph.

The fact that he was terrified by a cable TV version of *Macbeth* which he watched with Mary a few days before he killed himself says all we need to know about his mental state at this time. Somehow, one feels the man who built his reputation on his almost nonchalant depiction of horror wouldn't be expected to be fazed by the stylised violence of a Shakespearean moral fable.

On the last night of his life he dined with her at a restaurant in Ketchum. A pair of travelling salesmen sat at a table opposite. He panicked again, believing them to be FBI agents. He insisted they leave the restaurant.

All that matters in life, he had always held, was to die well. His father didn't, and he might have thought that he would improve on that, but when it came to it, whacked out in Ketchum at sixty-one going on eighty, the old-fashioned cure of a gun to the head would have to suffice, messy and all as it was. It wasn't ideal, and it wasn't pretty, but it seemed somehow inevitable. As inevitable as his rising blood pressure, or his cholestrol, or disenchantment with fame and its accoutrements when your body wasn't able to enjoy them anymore, or when all your friends were dead.

At 6.30 a.m. on the morning of July 2 1961, Hemingway came

down to his Ketchum kitchen while Mary slept upstairs. It was Sunday, a day he had always hated. Maybe it reminded him of his mother's piety and cello practice and everything lifeless and sanitised about his early days in Oak Park.

He had woken early as was the case most days of his life, his thin eyelids making him susceptible to the early light, and made his way down to the basement where Mary had locked all the guns. (He said he never missed a sunrise in his life, no matter how many glasses of absinthe or tequila he consumed the night before).

He then filled his favourite rifle with two shells he'd been hiding. 'I was certain,' his friend and biographer Jose Luis Castillo-Puche would later write, 'he had picked up the rifle as he might have picked up his pen - quite willing to sign his autograph for the very last time, with a bold flourish.'

He couldn't have killed himself in Spain, Puche believed, because he had too many fond memories of there. The only place he could do that was Ketchum, 'a cold, neutral zone where he had no guardian angel'.

He was both destroyed and defeated, and he would kill himself exactly as the man who had taught him to shoot did, by a bullet to the head. *Tels pere, tels fils.* He had done it all and now there was only one more thing to do. Better to burn out than to rust away; better to extinguish the flame quickly than rage against the dying of the light. Drink, women, sex, safaris, corridas and clean, well-lighted places could only stave off bleak thoughts for so long.

He knew he was an ace marksman; he had to be. No more than firing at a lion, you only had one shot so you had to make it count. To only partly do the job, to have to live with a gunshot wound, that would have been even more nightmarish than the original demons.

He put the rifle to his head and fired. The shotgun with which he had killed so much wild game he finally turned on himself. Both barrels. And that was it.

He had found his island in the stream, his sea in being, his 'gen'.

He had finally fucked 'the oldest whore in Havana.' But once again, the winner took nothing. Like the Pablo of *For Whom the Bell Tolls*, he had taken death as an aspirin. The silver cord had broken.

It was almost like a promise he was fulfilling, an appointment he had said he'd keep many years before and was now honouring. The man who had always attacked life with such great zest and ferocity was ending it now by attacking himself. He was about to achieve his separate peace. It was a fitting end to a larger-than-life life.

Clive James summed it up: 'He could never have enough of killing living things. Finally he did it to himself. He had bagged his last trophy.'

There was no better man at facing down a physical challenge, but there was no bravado involved in negotiating a dismal old age or its concomitant side-effects. What could you do with old age exept shoot it to hell? So he did. James was right.

It was just two and a half weeks before his sixty-second birthday. He departed the world he had given so much to and taken so much from. He died as he had lived, with a flourish, and there was a horrifying predictability to how he did so. For those who said he spent most of his life attempting suicide in some shape or form it was an endorsement of their trite thesis. As was the case with many other twentieth century icons who went before him and would come after - the Presleys and Clifts and Monroes and Deans - fame exacted the ultimate price.

He died like his father had, and his sister and brother and granddaughter too, like all of those the world broke, the very good and the very gentle and the very brave, the beautiful and the damned.

He couldn't go on living with anything less than a perfectly healthy body. Life had betrayed him by destroying that body and it deserved no better from him than that he put the finishing touches to that destruction himself.

To those who insisted his death was the culmination of a half century full of attempts at self-destruction, I would have to disagree.

He may have gone into life-threatening situations ever since his teens, but never with a death wish. The danger may have been the buzz, but he loved life too much to want to end it. At the age of sixty-one, however, the goalposts had shifted. He wanted do die with his boots on and thus cheat death. By taking the initiative, in a sense, he asserted himself over it. Even killed it, if you like. By doing himself in, he stripped the Old Whore of her authority. He wouldn't let her set the time or the place.

Mary would later compare the report of the shotgun to the sound of a bureau door slamming shut. (Leicester had heard a similar noise in 1928 as he sat in his bedroom listening to his father seeing himself off.) The scene that greeted her when she finally awoke on that fateful Sunday morning wasn't pretty. In fact there were pieces of her husband's face all over the floor. This would not be another botched suicide attempt or a cry for help. He had meant business.

He left no suicide note, but in one sense his whole life (and even work) had been one.

She blamed herself for leaving the key to the basement - where he got the rifle that killed him - in the kitchen. She knew he was aware it was kept there, which made nonsense of hiding the rifles downstairs.

She shouldn't have blamed herself, however. She did everything in her power to keep him in the clinic. Even though he talked of suicide, she probably felt this very fact was a buffer against him carrying it out. Also, any attempt he had made to kill himself thus far was a public (and, indeed, theatrical) one, so she may have felt there was some reassurance in this too. It was as if Papa, grabbing rifles when others were present or trying to throw himself off planes, was still being the childish exhibitionist.

But now he was gone and it was as if the world had lost a father. The instantly recognisable face that zoomed its way across the globe for so many decades on all those magazine covers would now be captured only in repose, in a freeze frame. Morley Callaghan described hearing the news as being like hearing the Empire State Building had fallen down.

The man who preached courage and endurance all his life had not been able to endure this final hurdle of his life. The people who looked to him for guidance, and who felt he had led them to the promised land of self-realisation, felt direly short-changed. Maybe it had all been a mirage, they thought, maybe the Hemingway detractors had been right all along. Was he really yellow? Had it all been an elaborate sham, the whole paternalistic soapbox?

In another sense, maybe the courage he displayed in ending a life he had once loved so much was greater than anything else he had done during that life. The condition he was in made it nothing short of a miracle that he had produced so much good work so often, presuming suicidal tendencies had dogged him since his twenties.

After he had narrowly escaped death in the plane crashes in 1954, Robert Ruark commented, 'The man is unkillable. He has been trying for years to polish himself off the hard way and never quite succeeds.' But this time he did. This time he wouldn't be around to read the obituaries.

When Peter Viertel heard that he was dead on a news flash in Biarritz, he didn't believe it either. The report said he had been killed as a result of an accident with his gun, which Viertel found difficult to credit. Besides, how many false reports of the man's death had he heard before? When it was finally confirmed by Art Buchwald, however, he felt it had a frightening logic to it. 'He's gone,' said the bullfighter Antonio Ordonez to Viertel, 'It's better for him even if it's bad for us.' That simple statement summed it up. 'He's done the job,' Juan Belmonte said, all too well aware it had been on the cards for many years. (A year later, Belmonte would also shoot himself dead.)

Living life to the full was like the safety-catch on his rifle, as Jose Luis Castillo-Puche contended. Once his capacity to do that abated, there was only one way out. Puche claimed he died as he had lived: 'like a pagan, like an agnostic, like a nihilist, like a brooding romantic, like an absolute fool.'

Jack put it more piquantly the night before the funeral as he sat with Mary wondering where it all went wrong for him. 'Poor papa,' he muttered quietly into the night, 'poor old papa.'

The newspapers said it was a shot that rang out around the world - a cliché, but a true one. The bullet cut straight into the heart of the century he was synonomous with. People felt they had lost a brother, a father, a confidante, a friend.

As had been the case with President Kennedy, people would remember what they were doing when they heard the news. He graced so many newspaper and magazine covers over the years, he had all but entered the national psyche. This was both the blessing and curse of being a cult hero for the masses. Even in hibernation (and semi-retirement) he was still the king. A seer, a sage, a bear and a lovable hulk. And now he was no more. He had failed to cheat sleep's elder brother after a lifetime of Houdini acts and Lazarus-like uprisings.

He was commemorated in Russia, France, Sweden and - of course - Spain. In Cuba and Key West people wept on the streets when they heard the news. No longer would they be able to shout out 'Papa' to him in Sloppy Joe's or La Floridita, or accompany him in search of that elusive fish, or bird of prey.

'He had written so frequently about the meaning of death,' said author John Raeburn. 'It seemed somehow appropriate he embrace it by an act of will.'

He was buried on hallowed ground, Mary having told the priest who performed the funeral service that he had died accidentally. She wouldn't admit it was suicide for five more years, and then only because Aaron Hotchner's biography of him - which she tried her damnedest to block - was about to be published, furnishing the reading public with a portrayal of her husband that went into the dark places she had left out of her own memoir. The next day, Bumby and Patrick destroyed the rifle with which he had killed himself so that it could never be used as a grisly souvenir. (Hemingway himself had dispensed with the weapon that killed his father by throwing it into a lake).

The *Louisville Courier Journal* wrote in its obituary. 'It is almost as though the twentieth century itself has come to a sudden and premature end.'

John Donne said in the poem that gave Hemingway the title of his most famous book, 'Each man's death diminishes me'. Yes, but Hemingway's death diminished *everyone:* his friends, enemies, family, ex-wives, ex-lovers, heads of state, gamblers, criminals, fishermen, soldiers, hunters, drinkers and ghost poets the world over.

The universality of his appeal may also be gleaned from the fact that after he died, there were letters of condolence from the White House, the Kremlin and the Vatican: three strange bedfellows but all oddly relevant to his esoteric *oeuvre.*

Though telegrams came from all over the world, however, only a handful of people turned up at the actual funeral. Apart from family members, such a handful comprised many hangers-on. They were people who, according to Gregory, 'had enjoyed the periphery of greatness because they knew that was the closest they would ever come to it.' So maybe the old cliché was true: no matter how famous you are, the size of your funeral generally depends on the weather.

The slim turn-out could also have been a result of Mary's wishes. She didn't even want Marlene Dietrich, the most loyal female friend Hemingway ever made, and one he never even came close to falling out with, to be there. Perhaps she was still feeling jealous of her dead husband's remarkable chemistry with his beloved Kraut.

Afterwards she placed a monument to him in Sun Valley. In Petoskey, Madelaine gave him the unlikely honour of a stained glass window depicting the Nativity in the local Episcopalian church. No doubt Oinbones (her pet name for him) would have been amused at the gesture.

In the aftermath of his death literary gurus the world over queued up to give their spin on the reason (or reasons) for his suicide. Every nickel-and-dime psychologist, it seemed, had The Answer. Most of these theories, it must be said, were either melodramatic or overintellectualised. Anthony Burgess surmised that there may have been 'a self-disgust in his inability to live up to his youthful, Joycean ideal of total artistic dedication; he had become a mass of public muscle and, corrupted by the wrong kind of fame, found it too late to retreat.'

This kind of psychobabble, while preferable to the hand-me-down Freudianism that usually passes for learned post mortems, seems to trade on a portrait of Hemingway already vouchsafed us in *The Snows of Kilimanjaro* by himself - and also to ignore the huge pride he felt in winning both the Pulitzer and Nobel Prize not so very long before. The kind of crisis Burgess refers to, if indeed it bothered him at all, would have been a feature of his forties rather than his fifties or sixties. It was already too late for Hemingway to retreat from the 'wrong kind' of fame almost since he gained it, but I doubt he would have wished to even if he could. Few writers enjoyed the public platform as much as this man did, and fewer were more sure of their talent. No, he killed himself because he was spun out, not because he felt he had *sold* out.

In 1959 he said: 'Without pride I would not continue to live nor to write.' The association is interesting. Writing was living to him, and writer's block a living death. He had always seen it as an adventure, an investigation into the safari of the heart. In 1954 he told Hotchner, 'Writing is the only thing that makes me feel I'm not wasting my time sticking around.' When the inspiration went, he wanted to go too. In a world of absurdly adventitious coordinates, it was his one tenuous lifeline to an inner nirvana.

The theory has even been floated that he killed himself as the ultimate humiliation of Mary, a woman he humiliated in every other way in the last decade or so. This is a sad example of how low Hemingway 'experts' will stoop for a sensationalistic tidbit. If he ever made Mary feel bad, it was against his wishes. Falling for younger women wasn't done with sadistic intent; it was something he couldn't help.

After his father had shot himself he expressed incredulity as to how anyone could be so selfish as to leave a mess like that for others to clean up, but when he fell into the belly of the same beast himself, he realised that it wasn't selfishness as much as desperation.

It's my guess that he wouldn't have shot himself if his father hadn't. This act hung above him all his life like the sword of Damocles. His father had set a dangerous precedent. He became for his son a kind of inverted role model, with suicide a very real option if life got too tough. Other peoples' parents found different solutions, but the drama of this one appealed to him. Shooting oneself, after all, was the only proper way for a hunter to commit suicide. In killing himself ritualistically as his father had done he was almost exonerating it as a way out of an unbearable life. It completed the cycle.

He felt he had to die because he was an idealist, and the world kills all its idealists sooner or later. He put on a facade of toughness, but it was from the sensitivity that the writing came, and when it stopped coming he was gutted. He had always prided himself in killing cleanly - you don't shoot a lion, he said once, until you can smell its halitosis - and this he did on July 2 1961.

A Dangerous Friend

Hemingway was jovial, big-hearted, generous, outgoing and charismatic. He was also vengeful, violent, insecure, jealous, unfaithful, self-obsessed, manipulative, bigoted and tortured.

He once told Hadley he would love to have been a king, which will come as little surprise to anyone who knew him well. Nonetheless, he must have been one of the few liberal/socialist psyches to have been born with such a fantasy. Failing to realise it, one assumes he settled for the raiment of literary and behavioural demagogue. Or, in his domestic life, the Papa persona.

One of the main questions that intrigued people about him was how such an ostensibly jolly man could write such bleak stories. And how a man who appeared to be so charming could go out of his way to alienate his friends time and time again?

Hadley said there were so many sides to him 'you could hardly make a sketch of him in a geometry book'. She admitted he had a cruel streak, but added that his kindness 'went just about as far in the other direction'.

He made friends easily, but his susceptibility to criticism made him lose them nearly as fast. His ever-expanding circle of acolytes changed almost with the seasons, and people soon learned exactly what it was they had to do to remain within that charmed circle. Those who broke the rules didn't usually get a second chance.

There were some people he never lost respect for: James Joyce, Ezra Pound, even Scott Fitzgerald. When he turned against a former acquaintance, however, the viciousness of his reaction almost paralleled the original adulation.

While he gave off a sense of having an easygoing personality, this was far from the truth. He craved his fans and even his hangers-on, and if you crossed him it was usually for life. He never forgave his parents for criticising his books, nor Marcelline for berating him after he left Hadley, nor Ursula for marrying a man he disapproved of. Nor did he forgive Zelda Fitzgerald for saying he was 'as phoney as a rubber cheque', nor Max Eastman for accusing him of wearing false hair on his chest, nor any of those litcrit merchants who lionised his books. (A good critic, in Hemingway's definition, was one who admired Hemingway.)

He professed to set much store by friendship, but he wasn't especially good at it over long stretches, any more than he was good at going the distance with his wives. One suspects that the termination of relationships was as much a function of his vexed temperament as it was of the changes he saw in his colleagues, but I'm not sure if that condones or condemns him. Suffice to say that even in his fiction male bonding tends to have a finite life-span, despite all the noise he makes about Men Without Women. Frederic Henry and Rinaldi from *A Farewell to Arms* are about the only pair who seem to last the pace, and even their relationship is largely composed of sardonic banter.

As Matthew Bruccoli noted, he had the ability to draw people to him and make them feel that they had been accorded memembership in an exclusive club. Such membership, however didn't always guarantee tenure.

Many have called him a 'dangerous friend', and it's obvious he was one, as is evidenced by the vitriol he poured on those who put a foot wrong with him. But if you didn't, his loyalty knew no bounds. Reading his letters, one is overcome by the affection that oozed out of him for the likes of Bernard Berenson, Arnold Gingrich, Buck Lanham, Harvey Breit, Archibald MacLeish, Ezra Pound, and so on. He loved as he hated, with undiluted passion. His tears were at least as rich - and as close to the surface - as his bile.

His saving grace was always his sense of humour. No matter how 'black-assed' he became, he could retrieve any potentially disastrous scenario with a quip. In *A Moveable Feast* he wrote: 'They say the seeds of what we will do are in all of us, but it always seemed to me that in those who make jokes in life the seeds are covered with better soil and with a higher grade of manure.' Indeed. But maybe the manure buried him finally.

The waspish Hemingway only became apparent in the last two decades of his life, and then only intermittently. The lion's share of his friends never saw him being anything but courteous and affable, despite the occasional poisoned barb directed against a *bête noir*. Such barbs were usually provoked and afterwards he tended to be contrite, reverting back to cheerful mode after the poison was exorcised.

His charm was so great he could sell ice to eskimos. Like Arthur Miller's Willy Loman he spent most of his life not only selling ideas and novels, but himself. Dorothy Parker compared the experience of meeting him with how a tourist might feel upon seeing the Grand Canyon at sunset for the first time. Flattery didn't come more rose-tinted than this, but she meant it.

Humanity, he claimed, could be divided into two classes: the bastards and the sons of bitches. It wasn't a very idealistic concept of the human race, and neither did he specify which half he himself belonged to, though most of those he knew had their theories about this anyway.

'I try to be kind and Christian and gentle,' he told Robert Cantwell in 1950, 'and a lot of the time I make it and when I don't it gets in the papers.'

His namesake Ernest Walsh described him in a poem once as 'papa soldier pugilist bullfighter/ Writer gourmet lionhead aesthete'. He left out one word: 'romantic'.

When he entered a room he sucked the oxygen out of it. Neither was all his energy thrown into talking or amassing an audience around him. Few great writers got where they were without being avid listeners as well.

The French novelist and critic Pierre Drieu La Rochelle only met him once, but still divined his essence. 'He is a man who is at once a camera and a phonograph,' La Rochelle noted, 'but who is none the less a man. He has the shoulders of a porter and the soul of a hunting-dog, desperately aware of every living scent, pursuing every quarry with a tender and implacable desire.'

'He was Clark Gable,' as one commentator said, 'with biceps.'

Archibald MacLeish said he was a man he couldn't get along with or without. Such an antinomy produced both his attractiveness and the edge of unpredictability he carried round with him.

He could dish out criticism but he couldn't take it. After he published *Death in the Afternoon*, Max Eastman rubbished it in the same satirical vein with which Hemingway himself had rubbished *Dark Laughter* in *The Torrents of Spring*. Sherwood Anderson forgave him, but Hemingway was made of more fiery stuff and Eastman was lucky to escape from him in one piece after *Bull in the Afternoon* was printed.

He satirised Dos Passos in *To Have and Have Not*, but when Dos Passos had the temerity to reply in kind, portraying Hemingway in decidedly uncomplimentary fashion as George Elbert Warner in his novel *Chosen Country*, he went ballistic, referring him as a 'one-eyed Portuguese bastard'. (Dos Passos had lost an eye in a car accident in which Katy died, having nearly been decapitated by a truck that tore the top off the car in which they were driving).

He was pathologically sensitive. When Thomas Shelvin passed some mild criticism of *To Have and Have Not* as he was writing it, he threw the manuscript out a window and into the snow outside, refusing to retrieve it for three days. It was the first and last time he ever showed Shelvin his work-in-progress, and the experience made him stop doing that to others as well. Talking put the hex on great writing, he believed. A writer's job was to write.

His character was beset with contradictions. He was both vulnerable and unforgiving, selfish and magnanimous, conniving and philanthropic, messianic and banal. A bashful exhibitionist, he revered macho ideals and then came to believe all ideals were bogus.

Cursory readings of his books reveal him as being engaged in what James Gray called 'a pantomime of muscle-rippling and shadow-boxing'. It's only when we explore more deeply that we see a man engaged in such activities primarily in order to convince himself rather than the world that he is indeed brave. Neither he nor his characters suffer from egotism so much as a deep-seated insecurity about themselves which necessitates proving each day that they can still rise to an occasion of danger (like Santiago) or fear (like Francis Macomber).

The issue of his bravery, or lack of it, is a continuous bone of contention among Hemingway scholars - or those who pass for Hemingway scholars at fashionable seminars. Was he pre-eminently courageous or a coward who took elaborate pains to camouflage that fact? Andy Rooney said he was a man who 'either didn't understand danger, or was so taken up with his own image of himself that he ignored it.' According to this classification, Hemingway wasn't a brave man in his eyes.

If we want to be really Freudian about it, we could argue that Hemingway over-reacted to his father being browbeaten by becoming a bully so history wouldn't repeat itself in his own marriage(s). But it wasn't really his nature to behave like this, which was probably why he was so bad at it.

When people talk about Hemingway's apocryphal boasts, what they don't realise is that he rarely bragged about admirable feats like his generosity, his big heart or his physical bravery. He admitted the wounding at Fossalta was accidental; he hadn't rushed into the line of fire - rather he merely found himself in it and did the best he could to help a fellow soldier and stay alive. When he showed off his medals and his bloody uniform, it was with a sense of adolescent glee rather than anything else.

He was proud of his bravery, but never ranted on about it. He placed more emphasis on his sensitivity - his soul seeming to leave his body after he was hit, having to sleep with the light on for months afterwards, the insomnia, nervousness and general disorientation. It was only in later years that he became obnoxious, making up stories that were juvenile in the extreme. One of his more colourful boasts was that he killed 112 people in the war. He also claimed that he shot a German through the head which resulted in his brains coming out through his nostrils. This was ideal locker-room banter, and people took it with a grain of salt. It's difficult to imagine him killing even one man, never mind 112. There's a school of thought that suggests the only shot he ever fired in World War Two was at a picture of Mary Welsh's previous husband, which he had first thrown down a toilet bowl. It seems more likely than the phenomenon of a gun-toting Hemingway taking on all comers in the trenches.

He was, in fact, much more content killing soulless creatures like lions and marlin and quail, and even then with some reluctance. He never killed an elephant, feeling such an act would be an abomination. When asked why he condoned witnessing cockfights in Cuba, he said, with exemplary logic, 'What else does a fighting cock like to do except fight?' His violence was never gratuitous or sadistic; it was either Hemingway pitting himself against nature in a test of his *savoir faire*, or against his fellow man in official or unofficial boxing matches. The official ones took place with people like Ezra Pound, Harold Loeb and Morley Callaghan; the unofficial ones with Robert McAlmon, Wallace Stevens, Max Eastman and any other number of people you care to mention who raised those famous hackles.

The manner in which he over-reacted to being bested in a boxing bout with Callaghan in 1929, however (he blamed Scott Fitzgerald, the time-keeper, for letting a round go on too long), shows just how thin his skin was.

After Callaghan drew blood from him at one point, he spat in his face in retaliation. It was probably due to frustration, but Hemingway - who had an excuse for most of his actions performed in a temper - afterwards explained that it was part of a hallowed ritualistic tradition among bullfighters. Perhaps, but one suspects he wouldn't have been too pleased had the tables been reversed. In any case, he never forgave Fitzgerald for being remiss in his time-keeping duties. (As the years went on and the story changed in the telling, the round eventually became a thirteen minute one).

He never hit people for the sake of it, or as a result of having consumed too much alcohol. Most of his bullying was of the intellectual variety. He pummelled people more with his words than his fists. His pubstool pronouncements, outrageous and all as they often were, demanded to be seen as informal encyclicals. He was always insecure in the sense that he needed people to agree with his views, if not hero-worship him as a result of them. Such a strain became all the more incredible as his fame and celebrity grew, when he had absolutely nothing to prove to anyone anymore. But then nobody's basic nature ever really changes. The Nobel Prize merely copperfastened his truculence and tenacity, couched as it was in that pristine *patois*.

He loved to make fun of himself both on the page and in the Real World, whatever that means. A soldier asked him during World War Two why he had never been promoted beyond the status of captain despite his many scars gained in battle, and he replied, tongue lodged firmly in cheek: 'The reason, young man, is a simple and painful one. I never learned to read and write.'

He went from being an anti-christ in the public eye to a writer enshrined at the centre of the literary pantheon, from one who posed a danger to public morality at the outset of his career to somebody featured on even relatively prudish college courses. There was a transmogrification from inside too. As a young man he grabbed at life with both hands, but in middle age all he wanted was a corner to cower in and be allowed die. Like a wounded animal, he wanted some humanistic doctor to put him out of his misery by euthanasia or any other means.

His contradiction was summarised in a comment he made to Charles Scribner in 1950: 'I try to win always until I die,' he said, 'but afterwards I am not proud of winning and I try to be a good modest boy - without success.'

As far as Gertrude Stein was concerned, his shield of brutality was merely a cover for his acute shyness. Like the characters in his fiction he was like a coiled spring waiting to erupt. He remained an adolescent all his life, as is evidenced by the manner in which he boasted about fabricated sexual conquests and derring-do in the war.

He was always able for those who would impugn against his military endeavours, with a burst of carefully-chosen self-deprecation. When a member of a shooting club he belonged to came up to him in 1945 and said, 'Ernesto - you were never actually under fire, were you?' he replied gamely, 'Shit no. Do you think I'm crazy?' This is reminiscent of the mood he was in when he asked for the publicity puff advertising *A Farewell to Arms* to be watered down. Only the very secure can trivialise their own machismo.

He also liked to trivialise that of others. The two obvious examples that spring to mind are Scott Fitzgerald and James Joyce, two men who were happier at their desks than in a jungle. Neither could either of these two men hold their drink like Hemingway, Great Bear that he was. One night Joyce asked him if he felt his work was suburban. Nora Joyce, who was also in the company, piped up, 'Jim could do with a spot of that lion-hunting'. Joyce agreed that would be fine, but with his bad eye, he probably wouldn't be able to see the lions. 'Hemingway would describe them to you,' Nora advised, 'and afterwards you could go up and touch them and smell them. That's all you'd need.' Is this a joke against Joyce or Hemingway? Maybe both of them...

He often said he would prefer to have one honest enemy than all his friends put together. He either fell out with his friends or they with him, or else a kind of mutual treachery seemed to take place. This happened with Stein, Fitzgerald, Ford Madox Ford and countless others, including members of his family.

Hemingway wasn't always unforgiving to those who crossed him, it must be said. He did a favour later on in life for Wyndham Lewis, for instance, interceding for him to get a portrait commission in the mid-forties many years after Lewis had portrayed Hemingway as a 'dumb ox'. Likewise, though he locked horns with Robert McAlmon after being accused of being a wife-beater and homosexual, he afterwards tried to persuade Maxwell Perkins to publish one of his books. (It's important to mention, however, that at the time of the allegation, Hemingway knocked McAlmon down, calling him a 'half-assed fairy asslicking fake husband.')

Donald Ogden Stewart gave an unusual reason for his disavow-al of his friends. 'I think it was a psychological fear,' he said, 'that you might ask something of him.'

There's an old showbusiness adage to the effect that you should be nice to everyone, because the people you meet on the way down are the same as those you meet on the way up. Hemingway wilfully accepted favours from the likes of Scott Fitzgerald and Sherwood Anderson when he was a struggling author but when he reached the top of the totem pole and their stars faded he had no conscience about abusing them. He got away with it too, at least with these two gentle-men (for they *were* gentlemen) but others - like Gertrude Stein, for instance - were less gracious. All in all, however, Hemingway was a person nobody could stay angry at for too long. He was forgiven for his transgressions in the same way as a drunk or a small child might be forgiven. Indeed, he often behaved like both, so maybe this was the reason. His satire, even when dipped in vitriol, seemed to come from a deeply troubled part of his psyche, and often its victim felt more pity for him than rage.

He eventually turned against most of the people to whom Sherwood Anderson had given him letters of introduction. The collec-tive wisdom is that he did so because he had got all he needed out of them, but this is to ignore his development both as a writer and person. When he came to Paris first he was something of a literary nobody, a literary nobody intent on becoming a somebody in record time. The fact that he courted the attentions of such as Gertrude Stein and Ford Madox Ford is neither surprising nor reprehensible - and the fact that he subsequently fought wars of words with them as much a function of their own boorishness as his. (Stein, for instance, all but accused him of being gay in *The Autobiography of Alice B. Toklas*).

I don't agree with Scott Fitzgerald's comment that Hemingway 'would always give a helping hand to a man on a ledge a little higher up'. Perhaps this is the outpouring of a man who was himself snubbed by Hemingway in the thirties. As a fledgling scribe anxious to make his mark, it's arguable that he was more tolerant of his friend's shortcomings than he would later be, but I doubt he was as ruthless and manipulative as Fitzgerald implies. He rarely crossed swords with somebody without a reason, and if he found if hard to forgive transgressions, that was just part of his character. The thesis, in any case, founders when we consider his lasting friendship with Ezra Pound, right up to the latter's psychological collapse. The point was that Pound had something Ford, Stein and (most of all) Fitzgerald could only dream about: *cojones.*

The friendship with Pound over-rode their personal problems, allowing both men to indulge their mischievous sides. Pound was also one of the few writers he admitted he learned from. He was the man, Hemingway said, who taught him to distrust adjectives - advice he took to heart in the lion's share of his early work. He also stood foursquare behind Pound when he developed psychological problems which necessitated his incarceration in St. Elizabeth's Hospital. And he was financially generous to him, sending him a cheque for $1,000 one time when Pound was low on funds. (Pound never cashed it, preferring to keep it as a memento.)

With other luminaries, it was widely implied that Hemingway tended to court their favours if they were more famous than he, then became involved in kerfuffles with them which often resulted in a punch-up, and finally went on to rubbish their work (and/or personal-ities) in print. It was almost as if his natural instinct was to get very intimate very soon, which meant he had to develop a shell of obnoxiousness to protect himself against involvements he might later regret. Needless to say, the process of alienation happened much more quickly - and more dramatically - if the person he was involved with didn't like him, or annoyed him by denouncing his work, but even if this didn't happen he seemed to be able to invent reasons to turn against former allies.

His repudiation of those who helped him was really a disguised form of disapproval of himself - for having needed them. This kind of need was an assault to that gigantic ego, and aggression was his best way of dealing with it. Having said that, the actual amount of people who helped him on his career path has been wildly exaggerated by posterity.

There's no doubting the fact that Hemingway had many contacts in Paris in his early days, but the number of people who have claimed they were instrumental in getting Horace Liveright to publish *In Our Time* is like a roll-call. Not only did Sherwood Anderson claim credit for this groundbreaking publishing deal, but also Don Stewart, Harold Loeb and Henry Strater. 'Apparently it took half New York to place my stories,' Hemingway told Loeb one day in a bemused mood.

Fitzgerald, as already mentioned, was probably his most influential friend in this regard, but Hemingway failed to acknowledge his debt to the older man. If anything, Fitzgerald tended to act as if he was the one being helped.

Hemingway's relationship with Fitzgerald was irreparably damaged after he mentioned his crack-up in *The Snows of Kilimanjaro*. He believed he was entitled to do so considering Fitzgerald had expounded on it at some length in his own writings. He also felt it might give him a 'jolt', and force him to take account of the way his life was going. Much the same effect could have been achieved in a personal letter, however. Once again, as with Anderson, he was taking the law into his own hands to try and reform his friends. Fitzgerald couldn't believe he would stoop so low. When he read it he tried to overdose with morphine, but vomited it up before it could do any damage.

It smacked of kicking a man when he was down and Fitzgerald found it difficult to forgive. The relationship between the pair of them continued in this 'foggy' fashion right through the thirties but never became open warfare. Hemingway hated what Fitzgerald was doing to his talent but liked him too much to say so in as many words. Fitzgerald admitted to being madly jealous of Hemingway's fame and fortune but added that it couldn't happen to a nicer guy. One wonders if the latter comment was tinged with irony in view of Hemingway's falling from grace in Fitzgerald's eyes after - as Archibald MacLeish put it - 'fame became of him'.

When Fitzgerald said he was going to visit Hemingway in Paris in 1929 he baulked at the prospect, ever-mindful of Fitzgerald's former behaviour with him under the influence of drink. He had got him into too much trouble with his landlords for Hemingway to ever totally relax with his old buddy. Fitzgerald had to contact him through a third party and they arranged to meet at a neutral venue. The age of miracles and art and excess, to be sure, was a thing of the past.

In April of 1935, Fitzgerald wrote to Max Perkins to say that the friendship with Hemingway, despite its intense brilliance, had run its course and the two men were now going their separate ways.

This pattern of growing away from those he had been close to was a continuing motif in his life. It was perhaps most apparent of all his relationships with members of his family.

In time he broke the connection with all of them except Ursula - who became like a second mother to him after his war wound. Marcelline he had never liked, though Grace's twinning methods may have had as much to do with this as anything in Marcelline herself.

Marcelline was like a mini-Grace to him, someone who appeared to know the score. And, what's more to browbeat him with it. Madelaine he saw as being selfish and self-centred like his mother. He became bitter with Carol after she insisted on marrying John Gardner against his wishes.

He seems to have had little against Carol except for her fondness for Gardner. Indeed, in a letter to her once he expressed a wish to shoot the man, giving absolutely no reason why. After she defied his wishes in choosing her marriage partner he virtually disowned her, like an irate father whose daughter had 'married down'. When people asked him about her he replied that she was divorced - or even dead.

Nobody has ever been able to explain why he took such a dislike to Gardner considering he had such an affable personality and proved such an ideal husband for Carol. They had a thoroughly happy marriage together, which vindicated her decision, but he never kept up contact with her afterwards. Some critics have speculated that he had unconscious sexual feelings for her, which meant he would have disapproved of her marrying *any* man.

Leicester wasn't really virile enough for him, but they had a working friendship within its limited parameters. Another problem with Leicester for him was that too he resembled his mother. Everytime he looked into his eyes he saw Grace, which distressed him greatly. The only way he could be warm to his kid brother was to keep his eyes shut as he talked to him.

He always reserved an especial spleen for the graceless Grace. He told Mary he hated her for her financial extravagance and her lack of sympathy for his father. She would buy a $55 hat, he said, even as his father was trying to scramble a few dollars together for house expenses when his patients weren't paying up.

In a letter written to Malcolm Cowley in 1948, he said, 'My mother is an alltime American bitch and she would make a pack mule shoot himself, let alone poor bloody father.' But Hemingway was always more like his mother than he would ever care to have admitted, and as author Bernice Kert observed, 'The qualities he thought admirable in a man - ambition, an independent point of view, defiance of his supremacy - became threatening in a woman.'

His ever-beloved Ursula was the notable exception to all this. She had an almost umbilical bond with him all her life, right from the days shortly after the war when, understanding his emotional distress, she would sit over him until he fell asleep, thereafter slipping under the covers with him and leaving the light on, as he always liked, fearing that if it were turned off 'his soul would leave his body'.

He had complex relationships to his children too, oscillating between extravagant displays of affection and glowering rages.

In March 1955 he made two promises to Jack. The first was that he would never kill himself as his father had done, the second that he would leave him a large inheritance in his will. He probably made both promises with good intentions, but kept neither. In fact he left nothing to his sons, surprisingly enough. Everthing went to Mary, who, whatever problems he may have had with her stuck by him to the bitter end. And it *was* bitter.

Gregory said you could only love him if you had known him in youth, but if you also knew him when he was old you could only be sad and bitter, because the contrast was too stark and disturbing.

'He never could develop a philosophy that would allow him to grow old gracefully,' said Gregory, 'but if I had had all his talent and experience, and could imagine as profoundly as he could what awaits us all, maybe I couldn't either.' When his father was young, Gregory admitted, he was neither a bully, a bore or a professional celebrity. In later life, however, he had even started telling tall tales to people who were there when the original incidents took place: the last refuge of an apochryphier. (This is a Gellhorn term).

Hemingway adopted a paternalistic attitude to Gregory in the same way as he did with all of his sons, both real and adoptive, but after a while the novelty of being lavishly entertained by somebody who was becoming a bore - and a boor - wore off. 'It's fine to be under the influence of a dominating personality as long as he's healthy,' he moaned, 'but when he gets dry rot of the soul, how do you bring yourself to tell him he stinks?'

One person who didn't have any problem telling him he stank was Gertrude Stein, a woman who went from angel to demon in Hemingway's eyes. His relationship to her is interesting as a kind of prism from which we can view the ever-changing filter of his reactions to other former friends as well. Stein appealed stupendously to him after he arrived in Paris, but things deteriorated so much by the thirties that he tore strips off her to Arnold Gingrich. She was, he said, 'a fine woman until she went professionally patriotically goofily complete lack of judgement and stoppage of all sense lesbian with the old menopause'. (Now there's a Steinian sentence if ever there was one.)

He put a huge responsibility on Stein in the early days. She shouldered the responsibility of proving to him that strong women didn't have to be bitches, like his mother. For a time she passed the test, becoming not only his literary midwife but a friend and confidante as well - if not a surrogate mother. But when Stein fell from grace (or developed *into* Grace) there was no way back for her into her protégé's heart.

She turned against him rather dramatically in the end - either as a result of the menopause, as he suspected, or Alice B. Toklas' 'evil' influence. A more likely reason was jealousy. She was willing to accommodate him while he was still the rough diamond, but once his reputation started to outstrip hers she became defensive and insecure and took to sniping at him to conceal her frustration.

Stein, he said in 1948, 'had a necessity to break off friendships and she only gave real loyalty to people who were inferior to her. She had to attack me because she learned to write dialogue from me, just as I learned the powerful rhythms in prose from her.' This seems to be a pretty fair evaluation of their respective literary debts - and an answer to those who claim he never acknowledged any influence on him, however slight.

Some critics have theorised that he turned against her simply as a result of his homophobia. Stein was a nice woman, he wrote to Harvey Breit in 1956, 'until she had a change of life and opted for fags and fags only.'

In 1933 he wrote to Janet Flanner: 'I never cared a damn about what she did in or out of bed and I liked her very damned much and she liked me. But when the menopause hit her she got awfully damned patriotic about sex. The first stage was that nobody was any good that wasn't that way. The second was that anybody that was that way was good. The third was that anybody that was any good *must* be that way.'

Stein demonised Hemingway in her book *The Autobiography of Alice B. Toklas*, portraying him as a clumsy, accident-prone coward who wrote as stupidly as he boxed. He's alleged to have replied to her allegations with the classic words: 'A bitch is a bitch is a bitch.' He took a similar potshot at her in *For Whom the Bell Tolls*, but kept his most vehement spleen for his letters and *A Moveable Feast*.

The immediate cause of their split was a lover's quarrel he accidentally overheard between herself and Toklas. The surprisingly prudish Hemingway was shocked by their language and attitude. Stein must have sensed his presence because she was uncomfortable with him afterwards. It's incredible that he would have reacted like this to any kind of conversation between Stein and Toklas, be it racy or not, considering he knew full well they were practising lesbians. Maybe he was using the incident as a convenient way of ending his friendship with them, which was on the ropes anyway.

He once said he would like to have had sex with her, a distinctly unlikely possibility in view of that lesbianism. She sometimes told him of her revulsion to male homosexuality, arguably to bait him considering there's some evidence she thought him to be gay himself and thus in need of being 'outed'. Robert McAlmon probably gave her this view. Whatever its source, Hemingway never forgave her for the accusation. He had, after all, cut people out of his life for much less.

His relationship to Stein is interesting because it acts as a kind of showcase for much of his sexism - the sexism we see writ large in so much of his shorter fiction. Most of his stories about male-female relationships deal with 'the end of something' - not only the one bearing that particular title. Much the same could be said of the relationships in his novels, though it's less obvious here because of the more convoluted circumstances.

Women in Hemingway's books are largely killjoys. They spoil

the fun, cutting in on all that male bonding. This is a strain apparent all the way back to the early Nick Adams stories like 'The End of Something' and 'The Three Day Blow'.

He generally expected his women to be housewives rather than working mothers. His own mother infuriated him with her narrow-mindedness and the manner in which she bullied his father, but he may also have been thrown by the fact that she was an independent spirit at a time before it was *kosher* for women to be like this. There's a line between being assertive and being bitchy, and his mother traversed that line according to her son, but the feminists would argue that the two terms were pretty much synonomous for this chauvinist. Remember we're talking about somebody who once said: 'There is only one thing to do if a man is married to a woman with whom he has nothing in common, and that is to get rid of her. He might try to whip her first, but it would probably be no good.'

If we're looking for another example of his misogyny we can find it in spades in a letter he wrote to Bernard Berenson in 1953. 'God deliver us all from women's brains,' he wrote. 'They have a lack of imagination and when anything hits them they think they are the first person it has ever happened to.' Whores, he decided, were the best types of women, and the most emotionally trustworthy.

As Bernice Kert commented in her book *The Hemingway Women*, 'The conflict between his yearning to be looked after and his craving for excitement and freedom was never resolved.' He seemed to need the security of marriage but despised its claustrophobia. The Oak Park side of him needed to legitimise his romances, whereas the bohemian in him, which was forever threatening to take over, needed frequent breaks from the crippling routines of domesticity.

Any man who allowed himself to suffer from women, he also said 'had a disease as incurable as cancer'. He had been too aware of what Zelda Fitzgerald had done to Scott, and indeed what his mother had done to his father, to ever allow a woman run his life for him, no matter how besotted he was by her. This is one of the reasons his marriage to Martha Gellhorn failed.

His life would have been less complicated - and of course more affluent - if he had had less marriages and more affairs. Mary showed a common-sensical awareness of his polygamous tendencies when she said he was basically a victim of his time in this regard. When he was young, she said, 'people were more or less committed to marry the woman they wanted to shack up with. That was the custom. It would seem to me that someone of Ernest's wide interests and exuberance, a normally healthy fellow, would be interested in more than one woman. He'd naturally have two or three girls, and the fact that he faithfully got rid of one and married another is just a circumstance of this recently past era.' Mary herself was something of an authority on this subject, having watched the same Ernest dally with women right before her eyes, in effect putting it up to her to say 'Desist or I'll kick you out'. The fact that she never did was either a testament to her undying love for her husband of a pathological fear of being left alone.

Hemingway always seemed to marry women he had sexual relations with, whether out of some thinly-disguised Victorian guilt or moral scruple. He had many one-night stands with women he didn't marry, and probably a great number of short term affairs as well, but anything longer than this seemed to qualify for a trip to the altar - with the exception, perhaps, of Jane Mason.

He always had sexual double standards with his women as well. When courting Hadley he slept with Kate Smith (who introduced him to her) and an Armenian prostitute he met in Turkey when researching an article for the *Toronto Star*. He felt Hadley would like to have slept with the bullfighter Cayetano Ordonez, whom they met in Pamplona (he was the model for Romero in *The Sun Also Rises*), but disapproved heartily of this notion. His own infidelity was 'merely' physical, he reasoned, whereas hers would be a betrayal of the heart. Such a doublethink was carried over into his relationship with Pauline Pfeiffer. When he divorced *her,* as mentioned already, a part of him felt it was no less than she deserved because she had 'stolen' him from

Hadley.

Even though he was always 'Papa', the surrogate father, many of the women in his life were markedly older than him: not only Duff Twysden, Agnes von Kurowsky and Pauline, but also Hadley, who was eight years his senior. Was he looking for a mother figure in the absence of having had any love from his natural one?

It's curious that he never referred to Kurowsky or Twysden in his letters or interviews, as if they hit him at a sensitive point that went too deep for words. In his fiction he was more confident addressing such issues, because he could practise a form of concealment at which he was a past master. Here he could give them different names, and invent reasons why certain romances never materialised. Jake's emasculation was a convenient manner of avoiding Twysden having to write him a 'Dear John', for instance. Kurowsky's letter of rejection only appears in a very short story (called precisely that) and it took Hemingway four years before the pain of that letter was out of his system enough so that he could actually address it in print.

When he did so, it was in an ironic fashion. There's nothing noble about being jilted, but there's a certain dignity in losing your love by death. Hemingway was sensitive about Agnes' rejection but didn't like to publicise his emotional vulnerability. He preferred the image of himself as a rake.

'I have fucked every woman I wanted to fuck,' he told Malcolm Cowley, in a quote that carried a degree more wish fulfillment than reference to his actual experience.

He liked to boast to people not only that he had caught frequent doses of 'the clap', but that a prostitute once waived her fee thanks to his 'performance'. And then there was that romance with Mata Hari. Boasts about boudoir exploits with Montmartre prostitutes rolled as trippingly off his tongue as tall tales about killing Krauts mercilessly in the war.

Scott Fitzgerald's heaven, he said once, would be comprised of wealthy monogamists heartily drinking themselves into the grave, whereas his own was holding two *barrera* seats at a bull ring with a trout stream outside and two houses nearby. One would be for his wife and children...the other for his nine nubile mistresses.

The reality of the situation was that he generally felt uncomfortable sleeping with women if he didn't intend to wed them - or had already done so. His voracious sexual appetite posed insuperable problems for him in this regard. If it weren't for this, he may have been happy with Hadley forever and a day. Some biographers have suggested he ought to have stayed married to Hadley and had his affairs on the side, but that wasn't his style. Neither would it have been practical over a lifetime span.

His literary creations also reprised this streak. Frederic Henry feels obliged to marry Catherine after he has slept with her - and Robert Jordan sees Maria as his wife when they commingle.

If he hadn't married Pauline or Martha it's unlikely he would have stayed long with either of them, but some puritanical guilt always made him waltz his sex partners up the aisle. As Hadley put it in one of her more impish moods, 'If Ernest had not been brought up in that damned stuffy Oak Park environment, he wouldn't have thought that when you fall in love extra-maritally, you have to get a divorce and marry the girl.'

'I'm a fool with women,' he said once, 'I always marry them.' But he was a dangerous friend with wives too...

He had the ability to convince himself that the woman he was with was his ideal love. When married to Hadley he said, 'I wish I had died before I ever loved anyone but her', but six years later he said of Pauline: 'I would sooner have the pox than fall in love with another woman' - words that must have stuck in Hadley's throat.

He wrote to Mary Welsh in 1945: 'If anything happened to you I'd die the way an animal will die in the zoo if something happens to his mate.'

One of the preconditions of being Mrs Hemingway - apart, it seems from having to hail from St. Louis - was the willingness to be one of the boys. This meant being able to hold one's drink and cuss and whoop it up when the occasion called for it. To be fair to Hemingway, he wasn't the kind of chauvinist who liked to have one life in the bar (or on the ocean, or in the jungle) and another one at home with his little lady. He preferred his little ladies to accompany him wherever he went, and to take at least some of the risks he took. 'Any girl who marries Papa,' as Mary once commented, 'has to learn how to carry a gun.' He liked his wives to be sporty, but not to the extent that they would threaten his own expertise. On the other hand, if they became too house-bound, as happened with Hadley, he became bored.

He once described Hadley as 'the best guy you ever saw on a trip', serving notice of exactly what he wanted from his women. They had to be Boy Scouts in the outback, and perhaps harlots in the boudoir. It also helped if they could lower a few daiquiris and tell salty yarns...so long as they weren't funnier than his own ones.

He loved his wives in the same way he seemed to love everything else in life: feverishly, but unpredictably. A man who always had to be on the move to greener pastures, he was never going to be a candidate for monogamy no matter how great his devotion to a spouse. Even in the early days of his marriages he was a raw nerve, forever seeking challenges that would be commensurate with that high octane brain. Hadley tagged along with him as best she could until age caught up with her, as did Pauline, but as the years went on he seemed to want to be away from these women. Martha seemed to go her own way from the off, so this marriage was doomed almost before it started. The marriage to Mary lasted because she soaked up everything he threw at her, remaining by his side through every safari and corrida he attended, even when he abused her like a deficient housemaid. The highs were incredibly high with him, but the lows were equally low, and it was a test of Mary's character that she never gave him less than 110% commitment.

The difference between Hadley and Hemingway's other wives

was that he still loved her when he left her, and she him. The other marriages were dead when he left, if not before, which meant there was more rancour brewing. Hadley was also grateful to him for the time they spent together, even if it wasn't to be forever. She met Paul Mowrer at a time of her life when she was slowing down so he was a timely arrival for her, whereas she met Hemingway when they were both full of a kind of nervous energy combined with resentment about their respective pasts. Watching Mowrer indulge his fascination for chess wouldn't have ranked anywhere near running with the bulls in Pamplona on the emotional Richter scale, but Hadley could never have matched Hemingway's energy in the thirties even if she was of an age with him; being eight years older made their long term compatibility almost unthinkable.

Hemingway gave Hadley herself by marrying her, and then saved her from *him*self by leaving. These were hardly his motives for either act (he was far too self-obsessed for that), but they were nonetheless the upshots of them. Perhaps this is why she forgave him for what he did, and never resented anything about him afterwards. She actually told Bumby once that his departure from her life was like 'the lifting of a great weight' from her shoulder.

Perhaps the greatest friendship Hemingway ever formed was with Marlene Dietrich, whom he met aboard a transatlantic liner in 1934. The circumstances could hardly have been more romantic. The superstitious Dietrich refused to sit a table with twelve diners, because she would be the thirteenth, whereupon Hemingway came to the rescue and said he would make it fourteen. The friendship took off from there. It never developed into an affair, largely due to logistical reasons, and was probably stronger for that.

He once told A.E. Hotchner that there might have been a romance between them but it was scuppered by the fact that when they met she was linked with 'that worthless R—', which is probably a reference to Erich Maria Remarque, the author of *All Quiet on the Western Front*, a book he had no time for...arguably for that very reason.

'He never asked me to go to bed with him,' she complained, intimating that her answer would have been yes if he had done so. As time went on, however, they became more like sister and brother.

This was one of the purest relationships he ever had with a woman. He doesn't appear to have ever entertained the idea of marrying her but they were always there for one another at any hour of the day or night when depression struck either, or both. She kept all his letters and refused to allow them to be published after his death. If he wrote something that pleased her, her approval meant more to him than that of any critic. She, for her part, said that Hemingway was 'my anchor, my sage, my best advisor, the pope of my personal church.' His huge body, she said, 'seemed to emit sparks whose light fell on us and was reflected in our eyes.' Even though she was horrified by his suicide, she didn't want to go to his funeral. She knew he would have understood. It's tantalising to speculate whether they would have made a good marriage, despite their contrasts. Dietrich herself felt they would. 'I've met many wonderful men like ships that pass in the night,' she said, 'but I believe their love would have been more constant had I dropped anchor in their port.'

Something else that appealed to Hemingway about Dietrich was her androgynous appeal. Women who had this - his mother apart - always attracted him. Pauline had it, and so did Duff Twysden, Jane Mason and Mary Welsh.

Dietrich and Mary were arch-rivals for Hemingway's affections. In 1944 he escorted both women to official receptions simultaneously in Paris, afterwards entertaining them in the Ritz Hotel where Dietrich sang and Mary seethed. His suite he called 'the Paris command post for all veterans of the 22nd Infantry Regiment.' It's probably safe to say Dietrich was more amused by the comment than Mary, who wanted her escort to be more solemn. Dietrich flirted with him in an inconsequential manner, but Mary was more anxious to know if his recent marriage proposal to her was based on sound principles or merely uttered on the spur of the moment.

He called Dietrich 'a good General.' She would sit on his toilet seat or the edge of his bathtub as he was shaving, crooning 'Lili Marlene' as he showered her with praise. 'If she had nothing more than her voice,' he wrote in a much-quoted *Life* essay on her, 'she could break your heart with it.'

Maybe Dietrich was more androgynous than all Hemingway's wives and girlfriends put together. 'Her name begins with a caress,' said Jean Cocteau, 'and ends with the crack of a whip'. Hemingway experienced more of the former than the latter, having touched a nerve of empathy in 'the Kraut'.

'It's the friends you can call up at 4 a.m. that matter,' Dietrich would say, and Hemingway was one of these. She also said of him, 'I honestly think if more people had friends like Ernest, there would be fewer analysts.' What a pity, though, that the physician couldn't heal himself. She said he was the most positive life force she had ever encountered.

Dietrich's daughter Maria Riva claimed her mother never really knew Hemingway the man, only the image. For her, according to Riva, he was 'the dashing war correspondent in the turned-up-collar raincoat; the hunter, shotgun cocked, standing strong in the path of charging rhino; the lonely philosopher of the bleeding hands, clutching the fishing line.' When he killed himself, Riva says her mother was incredulous, blaming Mary, or surmising that he might have had some terminal disease. She knew nothing of his inner demons according to Riva. This is unlikely, however, considering the intimate nature of their lengthy phone calls, not to mention the letters.

Dietrich became like an adoptive daughter to him in time. In this she resembled people like Ava Gardner and Ingrid Bergman. Bergman would never become as dear to him as Dietrich, but she was somebody to whom he formed a deep attachment.

Hemingway was insistent that she play the part of Maria in *For Whom the Bell Tolls* just as he had insisted on Gary Cooper for the male lead. He had, after all, once called her 'the best actress in the world'. When she was undergoing press problems in Hollywood many years later as a result of being pregnant outside wedlock with Roberto Rossellini's child, he publicly stood by her. What was the problem, he wondered aloud: they were both in love so where was the sin? He hoped she had twins. He would be the godfather, he said, and carry them into St. Peter's Church with him, one on each arm.

When she expressed a desire to leave films and concentrate on being a housewife as a result of feeling unwanted by the top Hollywood brass, Hemingway took her to one side and dispensed the following fatherly caution. 'Listen, daughter,' he expounded, 'I have looked into Dr Hemingstein's crystal ball and a housewife is one thing you ain't gonna be. When they are starved enough for you they will come to get you. In the meantime, anything I can do with my cheque-book or my 16-gauge Winchester or maybe just to cream a couple of characters that need creaming, you only have to say the word.'

Hemingway liked Gardner because she was tempestuous, unlike some actresses of his ken. She smoked like a chimney, drank like a fish and cussed like a longshoreman. She also liked to throw wild parties and dance barefoot in the streets in the small hours. In other words, she was a Hemingway type of woman. And of course she was an *aficion* of the bullfight - which was like a ticket into his heart. The two never became lovers, though he had a strong physical attraction to her.

In these relationships we see Hemingway in his natural state, open and jovial as he had been before success turned him in on himself, being a friend instead of a spouse. Marriage always seemed to take away his spontaneity. In fact it may well have tarnished the Dietrich/Bergman friendships. He was never really cut out for it, as Mary suggested. He was much better at putting women on pedestals and adoring them. That's difficult when you're living with somebody twenty-four hours a day.

Adriana Ivancich was another woman he adored from afar. He

never slept with her, but despite that fact - or maybe because of it - he never lost his devotion to her. Adriana, for her part, never got over the experience of being the love object of America's supreme literary stylist, so the scar tissue cut both ways.

She became famous for her association with Hemingway like many another before and after her. (Morley Callaghan would often lament that he was remembered more for the fact that he had a punch-up with him than anything he ever wrote in his life). In this she was like Agnes von Kurowsky, another woman who had rejected the writer but still became something of a celebrity from his reflected glory. Agnes wouldn't commit suicide like Adriana, but at the end of her life she became a librarian in, of all places, Key West. Tour guides pointed her out as the inspiration behind *A Farewell to Arms*, which caused her more distress than comfort. It may have only been a 'boy-girl' thing, but it stayed with her right through life, though not in a way she welcomed.

After the dalliance with Hemingway, Ivancich married twice but both marriages were unhappy. She even wrote an autobiography, but it suffered the same fate as *Across the River and Into the Trees* and promptly disappeared from the bookshelves. Whether as a result of this or a general feeling of depression, she hanged herself in 1983, another member of the extended Hemingway circle who could never quite recover from his electric presence.

So was he hero or villain, sinner or saint? Probably both. In his alter ego Nick Adams we have echoes both of the devil and the Garden of Eden even in his name. Hemingway also straddled both extremes - often at the same time.

If his war exploits are exaggerated, so are his demonic rages. Everything was always writ large with this man. Part iconoclast and part prophet, nobody quite knew what side of the fence he was coming from. The only thing one could be sure of was that he wouldn't sit on it. Most people who knew him agreed that only John F. Kennedy and Franklin D. Roosevelt had the same kind of magnetism when they entered a room.

It's easy to criticise him, however. Easy because everything in his life (and work) is so bald. The maltreatment of his mother, for instance - at least as far as, say, Marcelline was concerned. The backstabbing of friends who had put him on the road to success. The selfish, self-indulgent carousing. The sexual perversions - real or imagined. The boozy excesses. The sadistic putdowns. The trite pugilism. The desertion of wives. The wallowing in shoddy glory. The failure (or refusal) to work at relationships. The wearing of false hair on his chest. The exploitation of pain (his own and others) for art's sake. The woeful temper tantrums. The fake sweetness and light. The slushy, sermonising style. The final descent into a paranoid, self-piteous nightmare.

And so on. The irony is that the people who generally indulge in this kind of mudslinging fail to place it in the perspective of his overall character, preferring to indulge in such gratuitous jibes for the sensational effect. The point is that Hemingway was well aware that he was no angel, but his virtues were as huge as his vices, and they came from the same tortured heart. If he was obnoxious, he was also magnanimous; if he was unforgiving of slights, it was because he set such rigorous standards. He didn't always meet such standards in his own life, but that was beside the point. He loved and hated with more passion than the average soul, and was finally overcome by that very passion. The man who had said he was 'fraid o nothing' at the age of five, ended up being 'afraid of just one thing: his own mind. And no amount of combat training could assuage that.

'Living was a field of grain blowing in the wind on the side of a hill,' he wrote in *For Whom The Bell Tolls*, and maybe it was as simple as that for him at the end of the day, as simple and beautiful and pagan as that.

What casual readers of his books didn't realise was that beneath the swagger he had a heart like putty: the tip of the iceberg didn't conceal ice so much as molten lava.

He was a braggart, but braggarts are often innocent, needing approval from others. If you scratch one you might find a soul too sensitive to admit its vulnerability. For such a successful writer, he displayed an incredible insecurity that made him feed off adulation like oxygen. And react against criticism with vitriol.

If we wish to be crass about it we may say his priorities were lopsided, that he had more of a conscience about betraying his typewriter than he did about betraying his friends. Gertrude Stein was right: his eye was on posterity rather than on the people who lived across the way. As he put it himself, he knew his stuff would last. His character might be bowdlerised by posterity, but his work would always be there. Nobody could take that away from him, not even the shrinks.

Robert Manning put it well. 'He made himself easy to parody', he said, 'but he was impossible to imitate. He sometimes did or said things that seemed almost perversely calculated to obscure his many gallantries and generosities and the many enthusiams and enjoyments he made possible for others. He could be fierce in his sensitivity to criticism and competitive in his craft to the point of vindictiveness, but he could laugh at himself, and enjoy the pure pride of believing that he had accomplished much of what he set out to do forty five years before in a Parisian loft.'

Henry Strater was frequently irked by Hemingway, but always said that, no matter how much he hated him, 'of all the friends I've had, now dead, the one I most wish were alive today is Hemingway.'

He also had a huge impact on the lives of people who never even knew him. One such is James Mitchell Lear, an actor who has toured the world with his one-man show *Hemingway Reminisces*. In the late seventies, Hemingway's grand-daughter Margaux asked Lear to act as 'The Spirit of Hemingway' for a collection of photographs she was appearing in for *Town and Country* magazine as a result of being struck by his uncanny resemblence to her famous grandfather.

After posing for the shots Lear became obsessed with the man he resembled and over the next few years visited Hemingway's haunts in such far-flung locales as Pamplona, Key West, Paris and Austria in an attempt to get inside his skin.

There's been so much written about him,' Lear said to me when I interviewed him backstage during the Dublin run of his play, 'it gets difficult to separate fact from fantasy. What I try to capture in my show, though, is his *joie de vivre*. We hear a lot about his dark side these days, but that only came at the end of his life, after the electric shock treatment robbed him of his creativity and self-esteem.'

Lear's show is set in a cafe in Havana where Hemingway waits for a reporter. As he does so, he brings up details of his life, speaking at length about politics, literature, love, war and death. He interviewed Mary Hemingway to write the play, and also Madelaine, who showed him many letters Hemingway had written to her during the twenties when he was in Paris. 'I'm in the bucks,' he said in one of them, 'come visit me'. She never did, she told Lear (mainly because she didn't get on with Pauline) but regretted the decision all her life.

Lear has little truck with those who interpret Hemingway's life backwards from the way ended rather than forward from the way it began. The latter attitude, he believes, smacks of sensationalism - a sin of which A.E. Hotchner ('a kind of adult groupie', according to Lear) is particularly guilty.

He never met Hemingway, but doesn't regret that fact. 'If I had,' he told me, 'my performance would have been more of an impersonation than anything else. The fact that I never knew him gives me freedom to improvise, to say and do things I think Hemingway might have said and done rather than knowing for sure. At the end of the day, my show is James Mitchell Lear doing Hemingway. Maybe there are as many Hemingways as Hemingway actors......'

Lear doesn't only have the beard of Papa Hemingway, but the bearing as well. Offstage as well as on it he makes you feel as if you're in the presence of The Great Man as he denounces upon life, love and the whole damn thing.

'Luck has played a big part in my life,' he admits, sipping the red wine he also drinks in his show as we sit in a hotel room looking down over the city of Dublin discussing a man who is nearly forty years dead. 'It still amazes me that he exerts such a fascination,' he says. 'Everything he did attracted attention, and I'm sure that was part of the reason he did it. But people like John Steinbeck drank more and cussed more. What is it about Hemingway that everything he did was automatically news?'

He's not too sure of the reason, putting it down to the man's essential mystery. It's like the gag about the two psychiatrists who pass one another on Fifth Avenue in New York. One says to the other 'Good morning' and the other says 'Good morning, how are you?' Then they both walk on a bit and stop. 'I wonder what he meant by that?' each says. For Jim Lear, Hemingway is somewhat similar: people are continually wondering 'what he meant by that.'

Hemingway Reminisces was never meant to be as obtuse. Lear continually insists he's an actor rather than a writer, and isn't shy to admit that if he didn't look like Hemingway it would probably never have happened. The fact that he grew *that* beard for *that* play in *that* year and had *that* person recognise him as a dead ringer for the deceased playwright meant a sea-change in his life and art. Providence moves in strange ways for journeymen actors.

Beginning its run in Key West (where else?) after Lear cried off a gig in the Kennedy Centre ('Hemingway wouldn't have been caught dead there,' he opines), the play subsequently toured such variegated locales as Paris (outside Sylvia Beach's bookshop), Prague (Lear actually met Vaclav Havel while there), Havana, Oak Park and even Sarajevo. Each venue gives him a different type of inspiration, spurring him on to different interpretations. It's as if Hemingway is like an onion where he keeps peeling the skin away to reveal some new layer underneath.

'People say he was anti-semite, racist, homophobic and all those things, but they usually ignore his sensitivity. He was an incredibly

315

generous man, and also a very feeling one. How else could he have written all those wonderful stories? Toby Bruce, who was one of his best friends, gave me many instances of his big-heartedness - with down-and-outs, with prostitutes, with people who needed help. He could be a bully too, but I don't think he ever went looking for fights. Fights found *him*.'

Was he a very egotistical man, though?

'Sure he was, but is that a sin?' he says, exploding into laughter. 'If you're not egotistical in some way, you probably think nothing of yourself. But he wasn't a megalomaniac. That's all the difference you need. I'm egotistical, maybe you're egotistical. So what? That doesn't have to mean we treat people badly.'

He pours cold water on some of the academic exegeses trotted out regularly at Hemingway conventions. 'I always go for the most obvious explanation of something. There's too much obscure analysis of him for its own sake. People draw too many conclusions. I merely make suppositions.'

So does he believe, say, that Hemingway had a death wish all his life ?'

'Why - because he went hunting? If that's the case, then you have to say that anyone who ever went hunting had a death wish. Is that not logical?'

His own belief is that Hemingway's fascination with outdoor pursuits was a fairly obvious reaction to his upbringing. 'He came from Calvinist stock. It was all very prim and proper - use the proper knives and forks, sit erect, do what you're told. The fact that he had a tyrannical mother made this even worse for him, as did the fact that she introduced him to people as her little girl when he was young.'

Hemingway was a very average All-American boy, according to Lear, who formed a dream of being a writer because of failing to measure up in other areas. 'He couldn't get on the first team in swimming or football, was unspectacular academically, and had big clumsy feet. He also a bum eye so he couldn't get into the army as a young man, but he joined the Red Cross instead and became an ambulance driver. Then he got that awful wound - because he went to the front line, where he shouldn't have been. Afterwards he fell in love with a woman nine years older than him, and that was another kind of thrill.'

'He was never a good newspaperman,' Lear contends, 'because he put too much of himself into it. He was really just biding his time to write literature when he was a cub reporter.'

It's Lear's ability to empathise with Hemingway's demons that made the last twenty years of his life so resonant. 'He fulfilled a part of every person,' he says, 'They could all dream they were inside him.' And so we all continue to do so, reading his classic novels and stories all these years later, and dreaming his dreams in the Ambos Mundos as a bear of a man arranges an audience with his ghost for us. It's not a patronising odyssey or a whitewashing one, but it cuts a swathe through a lot of the pretentious gobbledygook that passes for Hemingway scolarship these days as Lear - now didactic, now anecdotal - gives us a unique porthole into a much misunderstood and much maligned man.

'He brought a lot of the abuse on himself,' he admits, 'but he was really a pussycat to those who knew him well - a sheep in wolf's clothing.'

'He had a lifelong fantasy about being a general,' Lear informs me, 'but I doubt if he would have been able to stand the discipline of that kind of life. He idolised people like General Patton and Buck Lanham, and tried to adopt their lifestyle during his exploits in the Second World War, which almost had him court-marshalled for betraying the Geneva Convention. He couldn't take the charge seriously, though. 'In the next life,' he said, 'I'll have a Geneva Convention rose tattooed on my ass!'

Lear's overall view of Hemingway is of a man with immense courage, immense fear, and immense capacity for pain. 'Did you know,' he asks, 'that he once walked a mile in Madrid with a broken leg?' He regales me with a story about Hemingway's gracious behaviour towards a prostitute called Leopolda in Havana, and then about his daiquiri-drinking competitions. 'He always acted on instinct. I think it grew from that need to be famous. He couldn't help himself - like all of us.'

So was he the brawler of legend? The jury is still out on that one. 'Toby told me he never saw him starting a fight, though he could finish one all right. If people rubbed up against him the wrong way, he decked them. Toby told me he hit a man so hard once, the man somersaulted over a car. He had unbridled energy. It probably came from all his pain - and from the booze, which anaesthetised it. I saw the same energy in Sunny. She was eighty-three when I met her and she had emphysema and an oxygen tank, but she was still able to bring me boating out on Lake Walloon. And she wouldn't let me help her in anything we did.'

When they got to the cottage in Windemere she had a bottle of beer waiting for him. He drank it, then looked out across the lake to Petoskey and the indian camp of Hemingway's first, brilliant story. Beside an outhouse he looked at a sign that said, 'Hemingway Sat Here' - written by the man himself. 'Seeing things like that, to me, is research,' Lear says. It's preferable to sitting for months in a library poring over self-indulgent tomes. 'I saw what Hemingway saw the way he saw it - the cottage, the lake, the way the sun set over Petoskey Bay. How can you match that?'

Sunny told him Hemingway donated the Windemere cottage to her after he inherited it. 'Do you see what I mean? He was incredibly generous. But how many people want to know that? Most of them want to paint him in a bad light. That sells more magazines.'

Lear was indifferent to Hemingway before he met Margaux. After that day, however, he became a seminal part of his life. And now he has developed something of an obsession with him. He spends his time changing the text of the play, putting in an anecdote here, taking out one there, working on it like a jigsaw, or a mosaic.

We talk about the similarity between Hemingway and King Lear, two giants of men who suffered from God complexes, two beautiful, perhaps insufferable patriarchs. Come to think of it, there was something more than a little Shakespearean about Ernest Miller Hemingway.

Hemingway Reminisces doesn't whitewash its subject. It also shows him being tetchy, argumentative, irascible, insecure, volatile and unreasonable. Lear portrays him as a fallen angel, a man of many moods, a dormant volcano. But, in the end, somebody more sinned against than sinning.

Revisionists may quibble at this overtly simple interpretation of the legendary scribe, but Lear, who has been close to many of those who knew his subject, wants to tell it like it is, without frills or ostentatiousness. He wants to give us a man in a cantina sitting astride a carafe of wine, a man with the same failings as the rest of us, albeit writ large. He gives us a man as combative as he's insecure, a man who uses the tavern as both soapbox and confessional. In short: Everyman.

I ask about the relationship between Ernest and Grace. Was it not true that they hated one another because they were both actually very similar in temperament: two controlling personalities who couldn't accept it when things didn't go their way?

'Grace dominated Clarence in the same way as Hemingway liked to dominate his wives,' he allows. 'And both of them always had to be right about things.' Neither of them could suffer fools - or even geniuses - gladly. And both also had to be the best at what they did - and to be *seen* to be the best.

'Hemingway was never friendly with other writers,' he says finally. 'He didn't want to be around them. He was jealous of them, and honest enough to admit that. What other writer made fun of writers like he did? What other writer put them in his books like he did? People like Fitzgerald and Sherwood Anderson - who would be instantly recognised. He turned against most of the people who helped him. In that sense he was a mean man.'

So there you have it. He was mean, he was lovable, he was larger than life, he was obnoxious, he was cruel, he was generous, he was frightened, he was lost, he was brilliant, he was pathetic...and so on and so on.

Why do we still talk about him forty years on? Perhaps for these very reasons.

The Importance Of Being Ernest

To most of us, Hemingway was the gentle giant who scoured the world in search of trophies. Some of these trophies took the form of big fish and jungle beasts, but his women were trophies to him too, as were his books. Hunting, writing, fishing and making love were all embraced under one gigantic umbrella as he recreated himself anew with each safari, or rambling new novel.

Africa was like Michigan to him, just as the Gulf Stream was an extension of the Big Two-Hearted River. The size of his fishing tackle may have increased, and the pop gun his father gave him may have been replaced by a Winchester, but it was in the early years on Lake Walloon that the lust for the hunt was formed. It was here, listening to the woodchucks in the trees and feeling the breaking twigs underfoot, that he mapped out his future in whatever corner of the globe an animal waited to be tracked, or a fish to be hooked.

'Probably of no other man has so much tripe been penned or spoken,' said Dorothy Parker. With some reason. Hardly a season goes by but some new book hits the stand with the 'definitive' insight into his secret demons, or the arcane leitmotifs in his work. He would chuckle at their volume, but also realise he brought such notice on himself as a result of his very visible and transparent image the world over.

'A life of action,' he said when he was sixty, 'is much easier to me than writing. In action I do not worry anymore. But writing is something that you can never do as well as it can be done. It is a perpetual challenge.' Writing cannibalised him until everything else became secondary. He once told Max Perkins that he only went to World War Two so that he would get a book out of it.

George Seldes' wife used to say, 'Forgive him everything - he writes like an angel.' What was more important to him than anything else was the ability to 'tell the truth without screaming.' Screaming, he allowed, may have been necessary to attract attention to suffering, but it was no literary tool. Like sensationalism or the Book-of-the-Month selection, it did anything but guarantee longevity.

He once told his friend Arnold Samuelson; 'I like to do, and can do, many things better than I can write, but when I don't write I feel like shit.' There were many times that it became a duty rather than a vocation to him, a stern following of an inner light. He goaded it along like a recalcitrant donkey, teasing it out tortuously. At such times he felt himself as much victim as protagonist. When he was lucky he found the right sentences but when he was luckier again, they found him. He was just the receptacle, the messenger boy.

The only reason he made any money at it, he said to Samuelson, was because he was a kind of literary pirate. Out of every ten stories he wrote he claimed, only one was any good and he threw the other nine away. 'The editors want my stuff' he boasted, 'and I've got them in a position where they bid for it and I play off one against the other until they pay for the one as if they had bought all ten.'

All the best stories in life are invented, he told Samuelson. In real life only one out of ten people ever have anything happening to them that would make good fiction. If you write about yourself, he said, you die one time and you're through. But if you write about others you could die a thousand deaths, or have your characters do so, and keep on going.

Hemingway always knew that his writing represented the purest part of himself, even when he was dealing with the most callous species of being. His writing, in a sense, was a way of atoning for past (and even future) sins. It was his purification ritual. That was why he worked so hard at it. The discipline wasn't only therapy for him, but also exorcism. This is how he put it to Samuelson: 'A writer has to be made up of two different persons. As a man you can be any kind of a son of a bitch you like. You can hate and condemn a person and shoot his head off the next time you see him. But as a writer you have got to see him absolutely as he is, you've got to understand his viewpoint completely and learn how to present him accurately without getting your own reactions mixed up in it.' In this sense the artist wasn't only a see-r but a seer. He was a moralist in civilian clothes; an unofficial guardian of virtue.

'Any good man,' he wrote once, 'would rather take chances with his life than with his livelihood'. That was what differentiated the professional from the amateur. The true professional always had to live on the edge, pushing the boat out like Santiago until one day he went too far and had to sacrifice himself for his art, or craft.

Though he could never be adept at playing a musical instrument, he inherited from his mother an appreciation for rhythm which he applied to his prose in large measure. It's a prose we read as much for sound as sense, particularly in the early stories where certain words and phrases recur like drumbeats, or metronomes.

He put his talent into his living but reserved his genius for his work, contrary to popular belief. If he inherited nothing else from the Victorian era from which he sprang, he inherited a work ethic. He was happiest at his typewriter when it was going good and his eyes not paining him. Even when they were, he pushed himself to the limit.

There's an old theory of writing that says, 'No tears in the writer, none in the reader.' Hemingway's tears were there, but they were always hidden. He liked to keep his hands close to his chest in writing if not always in life. He tutored his characters to either grin and bear it or bite their lip and bear it. *Il faut d'abord durer.*

He saw writing like a contest, a competition. He claimed he started out very quietly until he beat Turgenev. 'Then I trained hard and I beat Mr de Maupassant. I've fought two draws with Mr Stendhal, and I think I had an edge in the last one. But nobody's going to get me in the ring with Mr Tolstoy unless I'm crazy or I keep getting better'.

He looked on literature roughly the same way he looked on hunting and fishing. The great white hunter had to write the great white novel. Catching the big marlin had to be followed by penning the big blockbuster. For all his posturing, though, he undermined machismo rather than underlined it.

The style he minted was sharp, hard and cool. The sentences were short with few decorations. Repetition created a musical quality that drew you into them almost without you realising it. The sound of his words were almost as important as their sense, especially in the shorter passages, which read like so many prose poems.

Other authors of his time, the Joyces and Thomas Manns and T.S. Eliots, have perhaps garnered more accolades for their work, but few would deny Hemingway's gigantic influence on the writers who followed him. Such an influence hasn't always been for the best, it must be said. All too often, crass talents have imagined they could reprise his magic by apeing his locutions and filling their pages with a coterie of monosyllabic deadbeats who hadn't two brain cells to rub together. The resultant novel (or story, or thumbnail sketch) tends to be little more than a pretentious nickel-and-dime stab at post-modern angst. Or lowbrow sensuality.

Such writers have taken what they wanted from Hemingway and left the rest. They've fallen for his traps, seeing only the simplicity and none of the profundity that made it work. Hardly a week goes by but some would-be clone imagines that he can emulate him by dint of some choice epithets or quasi-pugilistic endeavours. Wherever Papa is, he would be amused; he suffered his share of such aspirants in his lifetime. But then that's the price you pay for being a pioneer, or somebody who becomes larger than what they do.

As his Russian translator Ivan Kashkeen said, 'He liked to try on an eccentric garb only to discard it, while the imitators continued for a long time to parade the clothes he had cast off.' H. E. Bates put it more strongly: 'Little Hemingways, attracted by the easy street-corner toughness of the style, sprang up everywhere, slick copyists of the surface line, not one in a thousand of them understanding that the colder and harder a man writes, as Chekhov once pointed out, the more deeply and more movingly emotional the result is likely to be.'

Such imitators, Bates said, took his language 'straight off the earth, the saloon floor, the café table, the factory bench, the street and the drugstore counter, not bothering to wipe off the colloquial dirt or the spittle, the common dust or the colour, the wit or the fantastically apt metaphor, the slickness or the slang.' But too many of them achieved *only* the primitiveness and the flip quip; what they missed was the circumambient richness of texture. That came from places less easy to pinpoint.

A mixture of the romantic and the lyricist, the neo-classicist and the hardboiled modernist, Hemingway brought the eye of the reporter to a poetic sensibility, exploiting whatever contrapuntal effects followed thereon. He was loth to ally himself to any school of writing, but this was exactly what he bequeathed to posterity.

What he engaged in more than anything else was the stylisation of the vernacular. He's in that shark-infested domain but not *of* it. You can't be a dumb ox to portray one. But few entered the belly of the subversive beast with as much relish as he did.

He gave readers a new form of tribal poetry, a form of writing bathed in the hot blood of its bewildered, tight-lipped protagonists, a quintessentially modernist sensibility hankering for the tug of the primeval. It was like Babe Ruth written by Tolstoy.

His continuous flouting of the rules of grammer led critics to dub him a mock-primitive scribe who not only wore his learning lightly, but actually seemed embarrassed by it. It was one thing to mix with kings nor lose the common touch, but Hemingway actually brought his common touch *to* those kings.

He was also more fascinated by royalty than he let on, and found it difficult to reconcile this with his simultaneous affection for those who lived on society's fringe. One imagines he never quite reconciled that contradiction - nor wanted to. His Choctaw dialect and air of *negligentia diligens* gave his so-called unvarnished style a subtle affectation after all, but you had to read his sentences twice or three times to see this. On the surface they may have seemed like the verbal equivalent of a camera eye, but Hemingway is always lurking there somewhere, adding in linguistic nuances. But as his creative powers diminished such nuances became more glaring, often strangling the narrative with their coyness.

He created a strong anti-intellectual veneer, but the fact remains that there were almost 5,000 books in his Finca Vigia library, and most of them were well-thumbed. He always boasted that he was read by highbrows and lowbrows alike.

Journalism was the mealticket he used to gain early exposure, but it was always going to be just a temporary mode of expression. He seemed to be somehow above what he was writing about, flexing his muscles for a greater surge. He was a colourful journalist, but not always an accurate one, the novelist's eye for inventiveness often overcoming the painstaking literal recall of the roving reporter.

He had, of course, come to fiction from a tough journalistic school. The rulebook of the *Kansas City Star* stated: 'Use short sentences. Use first short paragraphs. Use vigorous English. Be positive, not negative.' Hemingway took all this advice on board, with the exception of the final directive. He wrote what we today call 'tabloiditis' - but with a cutting edge. It fed into his fiction, annexing itself to it - and vice versa. He was practising the New Journalism before the term had even been coined, creating what Norman Mailer would call 'factoids' in his welding of fact, fiction, innuendo, stream of consciousness and wilful clumsiness. Then he bastardised his own rules. Maybe he was entitled to, because he invented them. Just as Picasso would say that he only developed his non-representational art after he had mastered representational forms, so Hemingway grew tired of the hard clean style that came so easily to him.

He learned how to make every word count as the result of a very pragmatic circumstance: when he was writing despatches, he often had to send them from places which charged up to a dollar a word, 'and you had to make them awful interesting at that price or get fired.' Long after he stopped writing such despatches the discipline he practised here stood him in good stead. Thus was the stark idiom born.

Observation, he often liked to say, was college for a writer. As indeed it was. But you could also take a quantum leap from observation and end up in the fourth dimension. 'In stating as fully as I could how things really are,' he told a group of students once, 'it was often very difficult and I wrote awkwardly, and the awkwardness is what they called my style.'

Warming up for a book to him was the same as getting in training for a fight. He employed the same discipline, even cutting down on his drinking as he got ready to start. He permitted himself a few glasses of wine after a day's work, but only if he did well in his few rounds with Turgenev and Co.

What many people fail to realise about him is the almost samurai-like concentration he demanded of himself when he was writing. It's all very well to talk about the brawling and the athleticism and the safaris, but when he knuckled down to the boring discipline of writing, and he did it most days of his life unless he had a very good reason not to, he did so with single-minded dedication. Nowhere was it more in evidence than in the major novels. The perfectionist in him had to get it right everytime, regardless of the number of re-writes. It was like a mathematical equation that could have only one answer.

The painstaking re-writes weren't so much enjoyable as arduous. 'When a writer first starts out,' he said in 1947, 'he gets a big kick from the stuff he does, and the reader doesn't get any; then after a while the writer gets a little kick and the reader gets a little kick. Finally, if the writer is any good, he doesn't get any kick at all and the reader gets everything.' This is obviously a gross over-simplification of his development but the point is well-taken.

He spent his whole life searching for 'the one true sentence'. Into that sentence he would put, he claimed 'a thousand intelligibles'. There's a line in *Islands in the Stream* that goes,' Even when you break from the straight line of a great painting, it is always there to help you.' So he would return to basics when he found himself in trouble, regressing to rhythmic patterns he could regurgitate almost from memory.

'All my life,' he once said, 'I look at words as though I were seeing them for the first time.'

Morley Callaghan, who described his style of writing as similar to a pool player who lines up the balls with his cue, says 'That one in the corner pocket'... and sinks it cleanly. It had that coolness, that cockiness about it. And that sense of deft control. In some ways it was like chess with words, a domesticated military manoeuvre with everything in its place. Even if the theme was chaos.

He told Charles Scribner that writing wasn't only a disease with him but also, because he enjoyed it, a vice. And because he wanted to write better than anyone who came before him, the vice was an obsession. The critic Emilio Cecchi said he wrote literature 'which has nothing to do with literature, which is not spoiled or weakened by literature.'

His philosophy of writing was simple: delete, delete, delete. It was, again, one he learned from journalism. A common phenomenon among writers, he claimed, was 'guys who think they're geniuses because they have never learned to say no to a typewriter.' (Or as he preferred to sometimes call it, 'a writetyper'.) It wasn't by accident, he said that the Gettysberg address was so short. Only by succinctness could you get the real gen on life.

He told Lillian Ross that the test of a good book was how much you could throw away. He also said to her, 'People think I'm an ignorant bastard who doesn't know the ten dollar words.' He knew these words, he assured her, but there were older and better words which 'if you arrange in the proper combination, you make it stick.' He finished by telling her that 'anyone who pulls his erudition or education on you hasn't any.' One should write to express, not to impress. Art concealed art. If it looked like work, it was wrong. What you had to aspire to was work that wouldn't date, that wouldn't go off, like stale fish.

The main quality that separates him from any other writer of his time - or any other time - is tone. Everytime you read a Hemingway line you feel he's getting at something that he's not quite willing to let you in on. There's also the sense that he's re-written his texts a number of times to come by this effect. Yes, the art conceals art, but if you know your Hemingway you'll see it coming. You'll know he's always being subtle and suggestive in the same way, which dilutes the impact somewhat.

His characters talk a lot, but usually not about things that are important to them - at least in the stories. The manner in which they focus on inconsequential details conceals a multitude. The point is that he never seems to be judging his characters, or even commenting on them, but the reality of the matter is that he does little else. Such judgements are couched in their actions, which makes them difficult to decipher, but those familiar with Hemingway will know all those telling little touches become as preachy as the breast-beating of a fiery fundamentalist in a Sunday morning homily.

You can almost recognise a Hemingway story without even reading the words because of its spatial configuration. One often gets a brief descriptive passage followed by much monosyllabic dialogue, followed by more dialogue, and so on. Obviously the details change, but the pattern remains similar. The stories also tend to begin *in medias res* and end in mid-air, with little if anything being resolved. The abiding impression given is of life going on rather than plots taking place. Such is the laconicism of the endings, even (especially?) in the midst of horrific happenings, one could be forgiven for imagining a page of text had gone missing somewhere. Hemingway would agree with the man who said that all good writing should have a beginning, a middle and an end...but not necessarily in that order.

'With other writers,' as Maxwell Geismar observed, 'the word is a catharsis. With Hemingway it seems rather a weapon of coercion.' And from this springs the technique of concealment.

John Peale Bishop drew an interesting comparison between the characters of Hemingway and those of his contemporary John O'Hara. Nothing from within moved O'Hara's characters, Bishop contended.

'They merely react, like behaviourists' dogs, to certain stimuli. They have appetites, they come into heat, they suffer from sex as from a last disagreement of nature. One imagines their emotional connections as having been put through by the telephone operator of *Butterfield 8*. It is a mere matter of putting in and taking out plugs.' Hemingway's characters seemed to be the same, but were, in effect, precisely the opposite. Such a contrast was marked by a throwaway style that covered a multitude. And that was all the difference you needed.

'The awkwardness they called my style'. Well yes and no. When the awkwardness sprung from some inner dynamic it had a relevance, and sometimes a magnetism, but as Hemingway's creative powers diminished it became an affectation and an encumbrance. To take one example, the fake formalism that accompanies much of his dialogue is fine if the speaker is foreign, but Hemingway spent so much of his time trying to capture foreigners speaking English that he eventually started to make native English speakers possessors of the same awkwardness. It's rather disingenuous to have Americans speaking pidgin English but this is what we often get in the later Hemingway - and even occasionally in some of his early work.

William McFee once said of Joseph Conrad that, even if he wasn't the greatest novelist around, he was undoubtedly the greatest *artist* writing novels. Maybe we could amend that slightly and say that Hemingway may not have been the greatest novelist of his (or our) time, but that he was the most consummate *short story writer* writing novels. If all of his novels have a common fault it's their fragmentary nature.

A Farewell to Arms he claimed he wrote for the simple sake of writing a novel, but this isn't to denigrate the finished product. He may well have been clowning with us here. Even if he wasn't, a writer's motivation is often irrelevant to the finished work. Often the loftier the motivation, the flimsier the finished product. And vice versa. If we look at *Across the River and Into the Trees* we can see the classical corollary to this. He had grand designs for the latter book and most of them came a-cropper, perhaps for that very reason. He was always better when he had little idea where his books were going. And he knew that himself too.

In *Across the River* and even *The Old Man and the Sea* we witness a talent infatuated with its own excesses. The fact that such excesses are filtered through the psyche of a plain and simple man make them less garish in the latter book, but they're still there nonetheless. The tenacious reticence of the early stories and novels may have created a language for our age, but when his muse failed him he continued to rely on such mannerisms to paint himself out of tight corners in the books he failed to finish in the last ten years of his life. The resulting manuscripts are often laughable in their amateurishness, many of them reading like those cheesy imitators of Hemingway that proliferated in 'creative' writing schools after his death.

From 1940 onwards he wrote few stories worth our attention, falling in love with the greater pitch, the one that would put his name in the history books. The pity was that in turning his back on such minimalism he was betraying the very purity that gave him his wings. At the beginning of his career he wrote stories because he didn't feel confident enough to stretch his talent into the longer form, but when he found he could, there were compromises to be made and shortcuts taken. At least three of his novels will live forever, but many Hemingway purists, and they have a point, insist that his most resonant writing was done before 1940. After that date, he seemed all too concerned with imposing himself above his material, with distinctly uneven results.

He was so fascinated by his own outlook on life - which was indeed fascinating - that he found it difficult to create characters who didn't reflect that outlook, or in some way personify it. When he tried to change his approach, the results were often ludicrous or heavily satirical - or both. This is why detractors refer to him as a limited talent. Nobody ever went so far as to dub him a 'minor' writer - the words 'minor' and Hemingway could never be expected to sit commodiously in the one sentence - but this is really what they mean. It has to be said that such detractors have a point, but they're judging him by the most rigorous standards in this regard. Hemingway himself perhaps set such standards in his early career, so there may be a poetic justice there; the fact that he couldn't maintain them is beside the point. Maybe Emilio Cecchi put it best when he said that what he gave was 'a brilliant *half*-vision of life.' I would be prepared to settle for that evaluation, even though I know he would be unspeakably insulted by it.

When George Plimpton asked Hemingway who his influences were in 1958, he replied, 'Mark Twain, Flaubert, Stendhal, Bach, Turgenev, Tolstoy, Dostoevsky, Chekhov, Andrew Marvell, John Donne, Maupassant, the good Kipling, Thoreau, Captain Marryat, Shakespeare, Mozart, Quevedo, Dante, Virgil, Tintoretto, Hieronymous Bosch, Breughel, Patinier, Goya, Giotto, Cezanne, Van Gogh, Gauguin, San Juan de la Cruz, Gongora'. The placing of Shakespeare is interesting, as is the gentle transition from authors to painters to musicians.

He was no starstruck country bumpkin who achieved dreams beyond his wildest expectations. He always knew he was good, which meant it had to be only a matter of time before he became famous. He was equally at ease with a pen as a fishing rod - or a rifle or a pair of boxing gloves. He could outwrite most of his contemporaries, which gave him an enormous cockiness. What he needed to make it to the top fast wasn't mere talent. It was luck - and getting to know the right people.

His prose style swaggered just as he did himself, but behind the posturing there was a kind of panic - as there also was in Hemingway the man. Not only did he bring doubt into the locker-room; he also brought it into the boudoir, the finca, the *Pilar,* the pool-hall, the jungle, the tavern, the brothel and the church. Anywhere there was a thrill to be experienced, a price was exacted. And often it was the ultimate one.

When all is said and done, Norman Mailer claimed, Hemingway was 'a mid-western boy seized by success and ripped out of every root,' and he spent the rest of his life trying to relocate some of his old sense of *terra firma* by following each movement of the wind (and there were many) through his talent and his dread.

As his biographer Michael Reynolds noted, 'He was a child of this century, born too late for the frontier and too soon for outer space, leaving him only the dark country within himself to explore.' Such a country finally proved his undoing.

His brief was the ordinary, often pathetic lives of those living on the fringe, lives that would be anathema to his parents, who had never experienced, or wished to experience, the *ambience* of drunks, misfits, layabouts, prostitutes and disaffected bohemian intellectuals. The language he employed for such characters was one that walked on eggshells. He tentatively threaded his way through the tense, terse sentences the same way as his characters threaded their tentative way through life.

Every time a tragedy presented itself he retreated to his writing desk to try and deal with it. To the casual eye the writing was realism itself, but viewed more closely one could see the experiences had been filtered through the prism of his eclectic mind.

He ached over the loss of his friends, friends he may not have seen for ten or fifteen years, but who still occupied a place in his heart. He used his writing as therapy for such losses. His pain passed into the writing, but in a distilled way, like you would cauterise a wound. It was the way he had always written and always would do throughout the good times and the bad, right down to the day when he knew he couldn't do it anymore, when he knew there was nothing left but to put a bullet through his brain to keep the halcyon memories intact for posterity. 'He caused the complacent man,' Nelson Algren said, 'standing content in his own well-lit door, suddenly to sense the precipitous edge where life drops off into utter dark.'

Today we have the Hemingway lookalike contests in Key West,

the wannabe novelists apeing the hardboiled style but forgetting the tone, the boudoir worthies enquiring of their girlfriends if the earth moved, the purgatorial exegeses on hidden meanings in his books by critics he would have taken great pleasure in decking if he met them. We haven't got the T-shirts or key chains yet because he wasn't that type of guy, but his work will live as long as people read, and he's left us at least three classics.

The central mystery of his life remains the most obvious one: how could somebody who believed in doing everything to excess manage to remain so obsessively reticent in his books?

Possibly, one can only surmise, for that very reason.

The Legacy

What I have written is my family's money in the bank.
Supposing I was to publish everything I had. Imagine
what it would do to taxes. I've got some stuff put away.
Ernest Hemingway

In the fall the war was always there - as were the bulls and the fish and the lions and the books and the frozen daiquiris and the Finca Vigia - but he did not go to them any more. Even if he were alive, it's doubtful he would have wanted to. They had long lost their lustre for him. He was free of his torment, leaving Mary to clean up the physical mess he left, and also the unedited clutter of his writings. He had often said he was vain enough to know 'my stuff will last'. In killing himself he was only nurturing the legend further. The sad wreck of a man would yet have the last laugh.

Gertrude Stein once said, 'Hemingway looks like a modernist, but he smells of the museums.' She was probably alluding to the fact that, even if his main brief was the glorification of the now, he also had an eye cocked to posterity. I think she had a point, and neither would Hemingway have disagreed. He never made a secret of the fact that he liked to deal in big themes, and write literature that would be read long after he was dead. Her remark begs the question: what's so wrong with museums?

He was hardly cold in his grave when the biographies started appearing, some from friends (or so-called friends), some from family members, immediate or extended, and some from literary scholars. It's probably fair to assume he would have been equally unimpressed with all of them, particularly those which were already in the process of composition when he was alive without him knowing it. Leicester claimed he would have abhorred Aaron Hotchner if he knew he was writing about his last years even as they hung about together, but he

335

would hardly have been over the moon to know Leicester would write a book about him too, complimentary or not. He would have been even less impressed to hear of a memoir from Marcelline which she was allegedly putting together as early as his funeral.

Carlos Baker's exhaustive biography was published in 1969. It was a mammoth undertaking, but so cluttered with (often inconsequential) detail that it didn't have much in the way of human interest for anyone but a Hemingway fanatic. There was little humour in it, and little stylistic virtuosity. Neither did it get inside his head at any point. As one wag put it, 'Baker writing on Hemingway is like a virgin writing on sex.' It was all very dutiful and informative, but totally devoid of passion - an unforgiveable sin considering its subject.

Mary wrote *How It Was,* which told us little or nothing about the intimate details of her relationship with her husband, particularly the dark periods. Her book is dull and over-long, with many noticeable omissions. Subsequent biographers have filled in the blanks, sometimes with significant anecdotes, but more often voyeuristic speculation. Such biographers have even fallen out with one another. Jeffrey Meyers sought Hotchner's cooperation for a biography and when he didn't get it, took to attacking Hotchner as more of a servant than a friend. Mary claimed that if her husband twigged Hotchner was writing a book about him, he would have killed him. For all that, Hotchner's book tells us infinitely more about Hemingway than Mary's does. She called it 'a knife-in-the-back job' but it's really an affectionate panegyric to a legend, allbeit a legend in the final throes of self-destruction.

How It Was is choc-a-bloc with trivial minutiae. Her excuse for keeping such details was that Hemingway himself might some day need them for a work of his own. He didn't, as things turned out, having, as she put it, had a tape-recorder in his head, which made nonsense of her putting them in here, and thus losing her readers with her pedanticism. Her editors tried to persuade her to perform major surgery on her book, but unlike her husband she wasn't possessed of an aptitude for this kind of work. So *How It Was* was foisted upon the reading public in all its flabbiness. One imagines few people enjoyed it save incurable Hemingway groupies and equally enthusiastic *National Geographic* readers.

Leicester's book was called *My Brother Ernest Hemingway*. It perhaps exaggerated their closeness but was still a valuable memoir. Leicester's main thesis is that Ernest needed a 'spiritual kid brother' all his life, a function he himself fulfilled for a time (there was a sixteen year age gap between them) and which he then passed on to the likes of Hotchner and Gianfranco Ivancich, Adriana's brother. As with most members of his family, Leicester lost contact with Ernest in the last years of his life so the book is sketchy about this time. Nevertheless, it doesn't stop him theorising about his decline and suicide, though without any startling insights.

Gregory's memoir, *Papa,* is short and to the point, a kind of chronicle of death foretold. It's uncompromising in depicting the abrasive relationship he had to his father, and how it transposed itself as both men changed. There's not much sentiment here but you feel you can trust it for that very reason. It's born out of Gregory's own pain, his own coming to terms with the uneven hand life dealt him. Like Martha he also stood up to Hemingway. And, as was the case with that lady, Papa didn't like it too much. But the pair of them had a grudging respect for one another, even if it ran its course long before Hemingway died.

Marcelline's book, *At The Hemingways*, is bland and rather boring except for the occasional curiosity. There's little to suggest she liked Ernest the man, and even less that she admired his writing. The books by Gregory and Leicester show true warmth, but Marcelline's main interest seems to be herself rather than her famous brother. She also takes her parents' side on any area of friction between themselves and Hemingway over the years. The main question her book poses is why she wrote it at all if she had nothing enlightening to say. Hemingway's life after Oak Park is virtually invisible as far as this book is concerned, but then he disengaged himself from her after he stopped living there so maybe this isn't too surprising after all.

Madelaine's book was called *Ernie*. This reads like so many high school essays on 'Me and My Life' as she regales us with yarns about childish japes herself and 'Ernie' engaged in during the innocent years of killing skunks, hunting squirrels and calling each other names like 'Oinbones' and 'Nunbones' as if to intensify their camaraderie. And yet when Hemingway dies Madelaine seems more concerned about how she got to Ketchum for the funeral than the fact that she had lost a brother. 'I was deeply shaken,' she tells us, but nothing else in the narrative suggests that.

Hemingway did all the outdoorsy things with Madelaine when he was young. As he grew older, she reports, he supported her both emotionally and financially. But if they were really this close, how is it that she hadn't seen him for a long time before he died?

The most telling part of the book is when Madelaine writes of meeting with Hadley in 1927, shortly after Hemingway had divorced her. Hadley told Madelaine on that occasion that she believed she could have held on to Hemingway if she allowed him to burn out his sexual attraction for Pauline rather than commanding him to break off contact with her. Years later, Madelaine met up with Pauline in Key West and told her she herself was in love with a married man. Pauline told her to 'go ahead and get him', regardless of his wife. Madelaine couldn't countenance this, and had little sympathy for Pauline when Hemingway finally deserted her. Like her brother, she felt it was a kind of poetic justice that was at work.

Jack also wrote a memoir. Published in 1986, it was ominously entitled *Misadventures of a Fly Fisherman*.

It's a fitfully interesting book from an anecdotal point of view, and the fly-fisherman comes across as a good sport (in all senses of the term), but it's more about Jack than Ernest. Which means that, by definition, it's cutting off a large section of the book-buying public.

Jack appears as a decidedly good egg in the book. He also shows himself to be a true son of his father in the jock department. But you still leave it down feeling somehow shortchanged, considering his closeness to his subject. People who knew Hemingway less well seemed to get closer to him than the lad who once said 'La vie est beau avec papa.'

Jack's strained relationship with Mary is evident at many stages of the book, but he keeps his feelings on her in check in a manner his father would have admired.

Above all, it's an honest book which pulls no punches, either about his own life or those he was fortunate enough to be surrounded by because of his circumstances. And that applies at *both* ends. 'I spent the first fifty years of my life being the son of a famous father,' he writes wryly, ' and am now spending the last fifty as the father of the famous children.' (Mariel, he says, was thrust into the limelight at the tender age of thirteen when she upstaged her elder sister Margaux in the latter's first movie - a significant coup as later events were to prove).

Hotchner's *Papa* came out in 1966 and became a best-seller because of its lively style and fund of humorous anecdotes, many of them elucidating a Hemingway few knew. The likelihood is that Hotchner goosed it up somewhat, but there's no gainsaying the fact that he was a confidante to Hemingway for the last fourteen years of his life, and privy to many telling outbursts from that fevered brain.

Mary took Hotchner to court pleading (rather disingenuously) that the conversations this pair had were private property! Not surprisingly, the case was thrown out and Hotchner's book got published. Many have accused him of lifting anecdotes from other sources and making out as if they happened when he was in Hemingway's company. Be that as it may, there's still enough material here to give us a vivid picture of Papa in his great highs and lows, a figure of huge mirth and equally large depressions.

Mary's real problem with the book, as Jack wisely pointed out, wasn't the fact that it played around with facts but rather that it went

into areas about which Mary herself felt proprietorial. She believed
Hotchner was muscling in on her terrain so she had a vested interest in
criticising his writing. If Hotchner betrayed his old friend by divulging
more than he should have about the time they spent together, Mary also
went for a cheap shot in trying to suppress a book that was infinitely
superior to her own one.

Hotchner met Hemingway in 1948 and became his friend (and
indeed his Boswell) for life. Author Jose Luis Castillo-Puche called
him a 'toady' and an exploiter of Hemingway's reputation in his book
Hemingway in Spain and was promptly sued by Hotchner for the
allegations. A jury awarded him $125,000 in punitive damages, but an
Appeals Court subsequently reversed the decision on the basis that
denying an author free speech was a more dangerous evil than the
possible defamation of somebody's character. Which was a fine
democratic principle - unlesss your name was Aaron Hotchner.

Castillo-Puche's book is written with a poet's eye - the author
was a prolific novelist - and captures Hemingway both in fire and ice.
His laughter booms, but equally resonant are the cold silences and vast
moodswings, particularly towards the end of his life, when the writing
of *The Dangerous Summer*, the tract he believed would be his best
writing on the finca, wasn't going well. His temper rages and pages fly
about the room as Hotchner and Miss Mary watch on helplessly.

Puche describes him as 'a missionary disguised as a tourist on a
non-stop spree.' He chronicles his obsessive fascination with bullfighting, his deep-seated insecurities about his overall worth, and the fact
that time's winged chariot is forever at his back, taunting him in almost
medieval fashion with notions of his evanescence.

This is a woolly and repetitive book, juiced up with florid
rhetoric to camouflage the dearth of hard fact. In this sense Puche is
even more Hotchner than Hotchner. He ably captures Hemingway's
fascination with things Spanish, as one had a right to expect, but his
frequent comments on the many dark nights of the soul are largely
conjectural and tortuously over-written. The abiding impression one

gets is of a casual friend expanding harmless anecdotes into didactic parables about the price fame exacts on the unprepared. This is all very well, but still only scratching at the surface of the man that was Hemingway.

The book is awash with detail, too much of it to do with the corrida and suicide, and maybe it tells us more about Puche than it does about Hemingway in the last analysis. It also has an inordinate amount of conversation, which suggests that the author was assiduously compiling notes for some time on his relationship with Hemingway. If this is true he's hardly in a position to accuse Hotchner of being opportunistic. The irony is that they were both at the same game.

Peter Buckley wrote a book entitled simply *Ernest,* which was distinguished not only by an enormous set of evocative and revelatory photographs but also a purity in the writing that put one in mind of Hemingway's own Homeric diction. It often errs on the side of hagiography, Hemingway coming across as the arch-sufferer who never seeks sympathy from any quarter, and his mother also comes in for an extremely rough ride. (It's interesting to contrast Buckley's appraisal of the woman with that of Marcelline or Madelaine in their autobiographies). But this is a deeply thought-out book that's deceptively simple in its style, and it's obvious Buckley has read widely on his subject. There are certain biographical gaps - he's very flimsy on the women in Hemingway's life, for instance - but the rhythms of the prose are so hypnotic one finds this easy to overlook, or forgive. One leaves the book down knowing it's a voluime Hemingway would have been proud to read: it's probably the one biography he would himself have authorised if he were alive to see it. (It was published seventeen years after his death).

Buckley writes like a poet, setting much store by Hemingway's perennial search for truth. In a sense it's like an extended elegy to him, a paean both to him and the world of nature he loved so passionately. The collage of graphic images, piecemeal and all they are, accrue to a cameo of a man and his time that's as moving as it is unsentimental. He gets inside Hemingway's soul with insight, intuition and a deep understanding of how his failings made him as loathed as he was loved.

Many other biographies have been written about him. Jeffrey Meyers and Kenneth Lynn investigated him deeply, albeit with certain agendas of their own that fed into the writing. Peter Griffin has written a series of books about him, as has Michael Reynolds, another author who seems to be attempting to unlock Hemingway's soul as a safecracker would a gold vault. Dennis Brian has tried a different approach in *The Faces of Hemingway,* recording telephone interviews and playing them off against one another in a kind of ersatz open forum.

Charles Fenton, like Philip Young - and indeed Griffin and Reynolds - have sought to divine his essence through a rigorous investigation of his early years, while the likes of Hotchner, by dint of circumstantial evidence, present us with the lion in winter. Every book has been explicatory in its way, but they all stop short of omniscience - probably because Hemingway's tactics of concealment were as canny both off the page as on it. He insisted on having the last word here as elsewhere, leaving so many clues that seem to mock the researcher rather than enlighten him.

Every biographer has his take on Hemingway, but too many of them have come to him with preconceived notions about his life and art, and determine to strangle that life and art into twee preconceptions. His war trauma. His purported quarrel with androgyny. The vexed question of his dubious machismo. His inability - or unwillingness - to sustain friendships. His marital and domestic disharmonies...all of these are grist to so many scholarly mills, but in the end do we know any more about the forces that drove this most complex of men? And are his biographers disingenuously selective in their emphases because it makes their own work easier? In an essay called 'Shadow-boxing in the Hemingway Biographies,' Donald Junkins wrote: 'Young probes the sore spots with Freudian simplicities. Baker and Donaldson, enamoured of the fiction but puzzled by the man and wary of his dark side, listen to the gossips. Meyers and Lynn, armed with theories, go in with the knife. Mike Reynolds steps back but slaps wrists. All of them admire Hemingway's art enormously, and all are fascinated by his life, yet each expresses some degree of annoyance with him, as if it would have been better if he'd lived a different life while writing the same stories.' Indeed, but then biographers always like to have it both ways, while denying such complacent felicities to their subjects. And thereby hangs a tale - or many tales.

The above books, in any case, are only a minuscule selection of what has become something of a cottage industry for journalists and dons the world over. And an ever-growing one too.

Posthumous publications *by* Hemingway are as fascinating as anything about him. In the last years of his life he found it impossible to finish anything he was writing - *The Garden of Eden, Islands in the Stream, A Moveable Feast,* even *The Dangerous Summer.* After he died, however, as one might have expected, work that was either cast aside or mislaid found its way onto bookshelves sooner or later.

It was his friend Charles Ritz who found the manuscript of *A Moveable Feast* in a trunk in Paris, Hemingway having deposited it there some twenty years before and forgotten it. This is incredible considering it contains some of his most entertaining sketches and most closely observed character portraits. In the absence of an Oak Park book, it's the closest he came to an autobiography. The pity is that he didn't complete it to his satisfaction before he died. As it stands it's a patchwork quilt of delightful insights and reminiscences, but lacking a final unifying touch. The fact that he couldn't provide this caused him great anguish in his last days, but considering it took him a whole day to compose a paragraph of a tribute to President Kennedy, maybe the surprise is that he was able to work on it at all.

He was going through a kind of second childhood when he tried to revamp it, but if it was a work of fond reminiscing, neither did its author take any prisoners when he got going on his *bête noirs*. Ford Madox Ford comes across as an idiotic fop, Scott Fitzgerald as a hopeless weakling unable to stand up to Zelda, and Gertrude Stein as a solipsistic bore.

Writing *A Moveable Feast* was the classic example of the salmon returning to the stream of his spawning to die. The present had stopped mattering to him, and only halcyon memories of the glory years could spur him on to any kind of creativity. The fact that he brought attitudes of later years to bear upon such memories taints the magic somewhat, but in another way gives it an extra dimension.

'If the reader prefers,' he wrote in the preface, 'this book may be regarded as fiction, but there is always the chance that such a book of fiction may throw some light on what has been written as fact.' This was a pet theory of his, the idea that fiction can even be truer than fact, or at least on a par with it. One imagines his spiritual godson Norman Mailer reading this passage and deriving his notion of 'factoids' (as per his controversial work on Marilyn Monroe) from it.

Casual readers see the book as straightforward reminiscence, but it's anything but that. One suspects the depiction of Gertrude Stein, particularly, would have been more favourable if the manuscript remained untouched in the Ritz Hotel trunk.

Hemingway's portrayal of Hemingway, however, verges on the romantic. The x-ray vision he employs to pull down the likes of Ford Madox Ford and Stein from their perches seems noticeably in abeyance when he comes to discuss his own life. But such is the privilege of the diarist, whether we like it or not. It falls to posterity to fill in the blanks.

According to Gianfranco Ivancich, who slept in Hemingway's house the night after he died, a page from *A Moveable Feast* was in his typewriter on that very day, so maybe it was more important to him than he pretended. Whether it was or not, it deserved to be.

The time frame obviously makes the book a confusing one for the reader, but no less quality-studded on that account. 'The old

Hemingway writes about the young one,' critic Frank Kermode remarked, 'but in the prose of the latter.'

Islands in the Stream came out in 1970, the second posthumous Hemingway book to hit the shelves. This is the protracted story of a painter who struggles against bereavement, family ties and the failure of his art. It isn't prey to the same excesses as some of his latter work, but it leaves one with a curiously empty feeling. Apart from a few rare glimpses of vintage Hemingway it's weighed down by its own dour philosophising, and a plot that fails to reach lift-off.

The character of Thomas Hudson isn't unlike the Colonel Cantwell of *Across the River*, but he's more melancholic by far, and less showy. For those of us who look for Hemingway himself in his increasingly jaded anti-heroes, we have here the beginnings of the depression that would dog him on and off for the last twenty years of his life.

It isn't a poorly-written book so much as an ill-conceived (or even non-conceived) one. It goes on so long in such a dull and linear fashion that it becomes difficult to care what happens to Hudson's painting *or* his fishing. It never threatens to be a page-turner because it really has no plot to speak of. Hemingway liked to say his books grew osmotically from a credible germ, and this is fine, but literary improvisation is only a virtue so long as what's being improvised upon is in itself of interest. Here, sadly, it isn't.

As in *A Moveable Feast*, this is as close to autobiography as we were ever going to get from this man, probably because he died before he could doctor the text sufficiently to disguise himself in it, or disappear behind the lyricism. It's got everything we've come to expect from Hemingway: the fishing, the shooting, the hunting, the drinking, the practical jokes, the clipped dialogue, the internal monologue, the loneliness, the elegant, eloquent fatalism, the autumnal warmth...but above all the necessity (self-imposed) for a gung-ho lifestyle to shore against the ruins of hinted-at inner torment. Such torment is less bald when Hudson is busy, but it's difficult not to see a vestige of Cantwell in the manner in which he tries to apprehend the U-boats. Overall, the book isn't as important for anything in the text itself as the atmosphere it radiates, and the after-taste it leaves as we pine for the dented dreams of the main character.

Maybe the most interesting posthumous publication has been *The Garden of Eden*, notwithstanding its poor literary quality - and the fact that two-thirds of it was deemed unfit for publication seeing as it didn't jibe with the main thread of the plot. This was an unfortunate decision because it was never going to be read for its plot *anyway*. Its main value is to give us an insight into a man who is more bemused by his literary success than anything else.

Telling the story of a World War One veteran honeymooning through France and Spain with his sexually adventurous wife - she likes to swap identities with him during lovemaking - the plot, for what it's worth, takes off when they meet a woman called Marita, who fancies both of them. The novel isn't pornographic, but, even worse, it's boring. It's hardly surprising that Hemingway couldn't see a way to finishing it as it has little meat in it, and few memorable pages. Catherine Bourne is an interesting creation - her jealousy of her husband's writing puts one in mind of Zelda Fitzgerald - but David, her husband, is singularly unattractive. Hemingway might have got away with him in a short story, but he fails to hold the novel together. Catherine is more a flesh and blood character, but equally unlikeable. Maybe Hemingway felt the same way about both of them. The anaemic tone certainly seems to suggest this.

As was the case with *Across the River*, a lot of ink is spilled on issues like ordering the 'right' food and drinking the 'right' drinks. This is done in the kind of monotonous, self-satisfied style that makes you wonder whatever happened to the Angry Young Man who wrote all those pulsating stories about characters who lived on the edge rather than sating their palettes with *haute cuisine*.

Hemingway began it in 1946 and continued to tinker with it until 1958, but really only in a cursory fashion. It explored a fascination with androgny (which as we've seen, goes back to his childhood with Marcelline) and also with male/female role reversal, a theme that's apparent in his writing as early as *The Sun Also Rises.*

The book can also be seen as an exemplification of the *ménage à trois* scenario of himself, Hadley and Pauline. It was after he took up with Pauline, after all, that John Dos Passos said to him, 'Aren't we all expatriates from the Garden of Eden?' thus perhaps vouchsafing him a title for his book. Catherine Bourne seems like a composite of Hadley and Zelda Fitzgerald, with Marita as the Pfeiffer character zoning in on the marriage. She's bisexual as well, and sleeps with Catherine. (Interestingly enough there was a rumour that Pauline once slept with Hadley, and that she went on to have lesbian affairs after Hemingway and herself were divorced.) The idea of Catherine and David having their hair cut the same length has echoes in almost every one of Hemingway's major novels, from *The Sun Also Rises* through *A Farewell to Arms* and *For Whom the Bell Tolls* so it's difficult to pinpoint the exact biographical source of this motif.

As well as dealing with a *ménage,* the book investigates the playful undercurrents made possible by the inversion of traditional sexual roles, thereby giving Freudians who had always suspected Hemingway of being a latent homosexual a veritable field day.

Aaron Latham, the author of a biography of Scott Fitzgerald, said Hemingway was a man 'who dreamed about going out and shooting lions all day and then coming home and making androgynous love.' This is a typical overstatement, but Hemingway *was* fascinated by the theme of sexual inversion. He deals with it not only in stories like 'A Simple Inquiry' and 'A Sea Change' but also in almost all of the major novels.

The Garden of Eden almost matches *Across the River and Into the Trees* for trite, self-indulgent conversations that could only be of interest to a very select, erotic readership. (You can only do so much with your hairstyle.) It might be vaguely interesting to potential coiffeurs, fetishists, gourmands and amateur hunters, if not card-carrying members of the writing profession, but that's about it. It's a book which - at least as presented to us in the abridged form - seems neither to have any ideas where it's going, nor care less. As John Updike put it, in a quote that could either be deemed inordinately kind to the book or a discreet trivialisation of its meandering rigours: 'Hemingway reached back from his workroom in Cuba, through all the battles and bottles and injuries and interviews, into his youth on another continent to make mythic material out of his discovery that sex could be complicated.'

More exegeses have devoted themselves to this book than one would be wise to count. Most of these have been done not because it's regarded as a classic, or anything near it, but because it crystallises some dark areas in its author's psyche, even if such areas didn't always make it to Scribners' final cut. It's sad to see university students spending time dissecting it *ad nauseam* for its obscure hermeneutics. At the end of the day *The Garden of Eden* is a quirky confection that has an understandable appeal for anyone interested in kinky sex or Hemingway's bad hair days. Beyond that, however, it shouldn't go.

For literary merit, one would be infinitely better employed surveying his letters, which Carlos Baker collected in 1981. These run to 921 pages and are as close to an autobiography in their way as *A Moveable Feast* was. They portray him in every possible mood but the overall impression that comes through is his richness of spirit. If the stories and novels only show one-seventh of their author, as per his iceberg theory of writing, here's the other six-sevenths of all those icebergs, giving us a man who was always upfront about his feelings in all their delineations. Fiery, melancholy, jocose, idealistic, defensive, depressed, jejune, self-parodic, self-congratulatory - it's all here.

It's a pity Baker only managed to give us three of the sixty letters he wrote to Adriana Ivancich, but otherwise this is a thoroughly convincing portrait of the artist as a young (and not-so-young) man, a larger-than-life icon shooting first and asking questions afterwards as he endeavours to negotiate the convoluted parabolas of his days with a very mixed degree of success.

Hemingway's almost-Herzog-like obsession with writing letters seems to attest to an inability to spend any time alone without putting pen to paper. He could hunt and fish alone, but within the confines of whatever abode he inhabited, be it in Key West or Florida or Spain, he didn't seem to be able to tolerate his own company for very long. If he wasn't working on a book, letters to all and sundry seemed to fill the gap for him. If he *was,* he begrudged the time spent on them, feeling they wasted his creative juice, but otherwise they were therapy, and kept his hand in, as it were. They also gave him a vicarious connection point with friends and colleagues - and even enemies. Hemingway was every penpal's dream - or maybe nightmare. If he'd been born a century later, he might well have become addicted to surfing the internet.

The main reason he wrote letters, he often said, was so he could get replies to them. Such was his tendency towards loneliness that if they weren't being replied to he went into a decline. They became almost his substitute for company. Another reason he was such an inveterate letter-writer, as he mentioned to Scott Fitzgerald in 1925, was because 'it's such a swell way to keep from working and yet feel you've done something.'

According to Gregory, letter-writing helped him unwind from what he called 'the awful responsibility of writing' - or, as the case sometimes was, the responsibility of awful writing. The looser form meant he didn't have to dot his 'i's or cross his 't's. For such an exhaustive craftsman, this was indeed sweet relief.

He doesn't come out of them smelling like a rose, but manifests himself as a man of great passion and warmth, someone who feels he has been poorly judged both by friends and the critical fraternity. He also comes across as a jovial old (and young) bear, and we would have to have a crystal ball to foresee the mind of a suicide at work in them, even down to the one he penned two and a half weeks before shooting himself in the head. That was to Frederick Saviers and it ends with the postscript: 'Am feeling fine and very cheerful about things in general and hope to see you all soon.'

Bernard Berenson's biographer Meryle Secrest put it well when she said that the letters are 'so spontaneous they will banish forever the image of Hemingway as an anguished writer painfully producing a sentence every third day.' She also said they were 'indomitable and life-enhancing, full of whimsical reminiscence and unguarded insights into himself, written in a laboured hand, like a child learning to write.' They betrayed a wistful, tender and loving man, she said, a man whose character was 'transparently insecure, and diametrically opposite to the almost ludicrous image offered to the world.'

All of these books have their moments, whether we view them from a literary perspective or as apprentice Sherlock Holmes clones assiduously looking for clues to their author's mental state. The latter pursuit isn't to be recommended, for Hemingway gave us at least as many insights into himself in his life as he did in his work, right down to his final act.

That was a different kind of legacy...

The curse of suicide would plague the Hemingway family not once but four times. Not only did Hemingway's father shoot himself when life became unbearable for him, but in 1966 his favourite sister Ursula took a fatal overdose when she was told she had inoperable cancer. By now, hara kiri was becoming something of a family tradition. Leicester even felt Marcelline's death in 1981 was suspicious in this regard.

Leicester himself also committed suicide after being informed in 1981 that he would have to have both his legs amputated as the result of diabetes.

One of Hemingway's first sketches features a wounded soldier who has lost both his legs in the war and commits suicide with the words, 'I had a rendezvous with Death but Death broke the date and now it's all over. God double-crossed me.' Leicester may well have been thinking of these words when he shot himself.

The tragedy of Leicester was that he tried to ape his brother every way he knew how - in his appearance, his lifestyle and his writing. Gregory tried that too, but they were both always going to be on a losing ticket. Neither did such behaviour endear either of them to the man they idolised.

Gregory and Patrick had to have electro-convulsive therapy like their father. In our own generation, Margaux, the beautiful daughter of Jack, died tragically in 1996 after a blighted career as an actress, which was overshadowed by her sister Mariel.

Margaux had many well-publicised problems throughout her life, including bulimia, dyslexia, epilepsy and alcoholism. She had been divorced twice and also spent time in the Betty Ford Clinic. In 1990 she modelled nude for *Playboy:* a sign, perhaps, that her career wasn't exactly going in the direction she might have wished.

Jack had the daughters that nature denied his father, and both of them were beautiful and both in love with life. Happiness radiates from their faces in the photographs contained in his book, but reading it now, one has to wonder how everything went wrong for Margaux and everything right for her kid sister Mariel. Their grandfather would have empathised with the absurdity of it all.

We shouldn't focus on such negative phenomena, however, when he left us so much to enthuse about.

His life began with suicide and ended with it, but between the strained subtleties of 'Indian Camp' (where an anonymous Indian slits his throat with a jackknife after watching his wife undergo a painful Caesarean section) and the nervous panic of July 1961, when a bruised and battered anti-hero sealed his own fate on a quiet Sunday morning, he wove stylistic tapestries that dwarfed not only his contemporaries and those who were to follow, but also, in a way, himself.

At the end of 'Indian Camp' Nick Adams sits in the stern of his father's boat feeling 'quite sure' that he would never die. And in a way he didn't, because we're still talking about him, and his creator, some eighty years on.

He once told Malcolm Cowley, apropos his refusal to make excuses for his lapses: 'There are no bad bounces. Alibis don't count. Go out and do your stuff. You can't do it? Then don't take refuge in the fact that you are a local boy or a rummy, or pant and crawl back into somebody's womb, or have the con. You only have to do it once to get remembered by some people. But if you can do it year after year after year, quite a lot of people remember and they tell their children and their grandchildren. And if it's good enough it lasts forever.'

With Hemingway it was. And it will.

Epilogue

He was a bully, a braggart, a sexist and a misogynist; an anti-semite, an adolescent, a masochist and a depressive; an alcoholic, a coward, a closet snob and a pretentious, self-serving homophobe.

Sure, that's Ernest Hemingway all right. He was also, in case you're wondering, a boor, a brute, an unthankful, unforgiving man... and quite probably gay. Leastways as far as revisionists are concerned. And then of course there was that darned death wish that dogged him all his short, unhappy life...

The reality is that he was a noble soul who time and again, pushed himself to the edge of death to test his nerve, and on paper pioneered a brand of prose-poetry that has been bastardised in the generations following his suicide.

The best known writer in American history, he all but invented the cult of personality on his own. Sending out early signals that a man must live the life he wrote about, and write the one he lived, he simultaneously expanded and diminished his craft. Expanded it because he brought literature out of the drawing-room and into the great world outdoors; diminished it because of the abstruse dictates of his macho code.

In a sense he was like an American version of Ireland's Brendan Behan, a man who became iconic after an early (public) brush with violence. Hemingway's war wounds were gallant, whereas Behan gained his in the hotter furnace of a guerrilla act, but each wore them like badges of courage in the years afterwards. Both men also liked to drink to excess, and the fame of both diminished with the passage of time when they became their own best parodists. Both would also become veritably indistinguishable from their public personae....and both would commit suicide, even if one of them went the roundabout way of doing it.

Like Behan he made boozing into a competition in the same way as he did hunting, fishing, writing and making love. The man who could out-drink his colleagues and still stay standing won many brownie points in Hemingway's aggressive academy; the person who, like Scott Fitzgerald, caved in early, got none. (He drank a quart of whiskey every day for the last twenty years of his life according to Patrick. That's not even to mention his fondness for wine, gin, tequila and whatever you're having yourself. Unlike Behan, he didn't become roaringly drunk, which disguised the enormity of his intake when he was younger.)

In later years he became more a sage than a writer, looking much older than his years as the result of the patriarchal beard and raddled skin, and the pedagogical air he exuded as his disciples swooped on him for slivers of advice about 'the craft', or maybe another war story to still their beating hearts. A man who had done everything, including die, he was a God to many and an anti-christ to others. But nobody could totally resist that intoxicating personality.

Morley Callaghan claimed that he was never anything but gracious to him as long as he knew him. Maybe alcohol made him a bad ass in the last decade of his life, he allowed, but it wasn't his nature to be vitriolic or violent. Many of the alleged scandals relating to his life are the product of gossip-mongers hungry for lurid headlines.

Many debunk him today as an ersatz macho man who spent most of his life trying to end it. He loved life with a passion, but that hasn't stopped a plethora of post-modern trick cyclists coming to such a conclusion over 30-some years of long-winded column inches. (Such column inches, incidentally, are guilty of the very sensationalism they brazenly accuse their subject of).

Almost singlehandedly he spearheaded the transmission of a clean, pellucid language onto the collective populist consciousness of the day, all that bargain basement ennui threaded liberally through the heady escapades as the economical reticence of the early fiction gave way to the full flexing of his impressionistic muscles in the major novels.

Hemingway re-wrote most of his work to give it the illusion of spontaneity. His ad-libbed lines, as Rod Stewart might say, were well rehearsed. In his attempt to create a new language he piled all those flat sentences on top of one another to create a hypnotic effect, amplified by the famous repetition and absence of all but the simplest adjectives. Gertrude Stein once told him, apropos his pointillism, that remarks weren't literature - but neither, he might have replied, was her own verbal extravagance.

He learned a lot from Ring Lardner and Sherwood Anderson, and then Gertrude Stein. But Hemingwayese, as it came to be called, eventually took off in its own direction, the characters imploding under the weight of all those gerunds and pared-down clauses. It was like a form of word painting using only primary colours - and a scalpel instead of a paintbrush.

By the time the tank was finally dry he was a shambling wreck of a man, brutalised as much by his own excesses as he was by the mortar wounds and plane crashes. Some critics would suggest that his literary decline began as far back as the thirties, but that it was camouflaged by his iconic status. 'Fame', as Clive James wrote in the book of that name, 'was a way of doing that which left doing far behind.' He certainly 'did' enough, both on paper and off it, but there's an argument to be made for the fact that his genius was eroded by the many compromises he made in his craving for the instantaneous insight, the elucidatory vignette.

The tragedy of his life would seem to have been undercut by a penchant for a kind of literary shorthand that would seek to understand too much too soon, and in so doing debase the nature of the odyssey. Like his good friend James Joyce he was forever searching for epiphanies, but the ambit of his characters' experience frequently precluded these. At his best, however, he gave a voice to a generation of hitherto marginalised folk. Gertrude Stein would call him part of 'the lost generation', but for Hemingway there was really no such thing. There were only people like himself, so many shopsoiled Lancelots looking to reclaim some kind of grubby dignity in a cosmos that seemed bent on their casual destruction.

He only regretted what he didn't do in life, he said, not what he did do, but he made enough mistakes for people to use his buccaneering streak as a stick to beat him with. Deemed naive by some, he had a view on everything and tended to posit it as an oracle. Whatever he did he had to be the best at, because winning was the only language he understood. But life wasn't a game. Life was war and death and injustice and futility and heartbreak. And when Hemingway saw this at first hand, living through the nightmare, a new consciousness was born in him. He became the ambassador for lost souls, the Poet Laureate of the disenfranchised.

But then his personality took over. Whatever he did became hot copy - the marriages, the divorces, the safaris, the deep sea fishing, the bulls, the plane crashes.....yes, even the books. They made a bust of him in Pamplona, and magazines asked his wives for their hamburger recipes. With the trademark beard and swaggering gait, he became the most recognisable writer on the planet.

It had its price, of course. As he told A.E. Hotchner, 'I had a nice private life before with a lot of undeclared, unpublished pride and now I feel like somebody crapped in it and wiped themselves in slick paper and left it there.' But it was still better than seeing his early stories come back in through his letter box when he was struggling in Paris.

The all-American boy had become America's quintessential talent in true Horatio Alger mould. But the fairytale held a dark subtext. His philosophy of life eventually became one that said, 'We are born into the world's hospital, each of us a terminal case.'

To the end he wanted to be the guy who 'fights in all the fucking wars and gets my brains knocked out and never fake or cheat in writing or write crap for all the dough they offer.' His success in the latter ambition, it must be said, exceeded the former - even if it didn't look that way for much of the forties, if not the fifties.

Since he died, many tales of his fondness for brawling in bars or blowing a fuse with friends of yore have been exaggerated out of all proportion. The fact of the matter is he lived quietly for most of the time, and stayed away from the glare of publicity whenever possible.

Hadley said he was one of the most sensitive people she ever met, and also that he had a lifelong inferiority complex. Kitty Cannell thought he 'over-acted the part of a ruthless, hairy-chested he-man in order to suppress his compassion'.

I doubt, in any case, that his contribution will ever be surpassed, despite the sick cynicism that passes for litcrit in the interim since his demise. His works have all the angst and beauty of the post-existential milieu, right down to his last dying fall.

In 1975 I wrote an 18,000 word essay on Hemingway's literary style for an M.A. thesis I was completing at University College Dublin. Since then I've dipped in and out of various Hemingway texts and kept reasonably in touch with theories about him, many of them outlandish. Returning to him now over twenty years later I'm surprised to find that many of his outpourings had lodged in my mind like mantras that were waiting to be re-discovered. The most obvious question that strikes me now, having read so many biographies of him is, how did he find time to write when he was doing so much living? I'm not just speaking about his novels and stories, but also the hundreds of letters he composed with something approaching an obsession.

Hemingway would no doubt hate a book of this nature. He believed there was a special place in hell for literary critics, and probably for biographers too, with a few notable exceptions. When he was in the process of writing a book, he was, on his own admission, 'like a bear with sore toenails.' Neither did he humour those worthies who came up to him on the street, feeling they had 'a right to call me Papa because they had paid a dollar to read *The Dangerous Summer* in *Life* magazine.'

He once told Arnold Samuelson: 'Writers writing about writers are about as interesting as painters would be if they painted painters.' One is reminded of Marlon Brando saying to Richard Schickel that a book about his life would be about as meaningful as 'frozen monkey vomit'. He would have empathised with that.

Another problem with critics, Hemingway said, was that if you shot them - and he was tempted a few times - they would 'bleed footnotes'. That's one of the reasons there are no footnotes in this book. The other is that I believe in them as little as Hemingway did. We also share similar views on literary criticism in general. But when someone fascinates me as he does, I like to read him and write about him and when his work sparks off ideas in me I like to share them. It's out of that simple ambition I wrote this book. I hope he forgives me, wherever he is.

Index

Dorman-Smith, Chink 273
Dos Passos, John 18, 50, 99,
    111, 114, 142, 144, 157,
    216-7, 241, 253, 289, 347

Eastman, Max 85, 144, 217,
    286-7, 289, 291
Eliot, T.S. 58, 78, 152
Ellis, Bret Easton 79
Evans, Robert 105

Farewell to Arms, A 24, 34,
    44-5, 53, 76, 78, 94, 96,
    104, 127, 134-43, 163-4,
    166, 168, 179, 182, 192,
    211, 214, 216, 218, 225-6,
    237, 240, 293, 311, 330,
    347
Faulkner, William 64, 113,
    157-8
Fenton, Charles 229-31, 342
Fielding, Henry 87, 99
Fifth Column, The 173, 201
Fitzgerald, Scott 7, 14-15, 78,
    83-9, 92, 95, 100-2, 104,
    118, 120, 126-7, 163,
    169-70, 173, 175-86, 208,
    213, 216-7, 234, 239, 253,
    258-9, 264, 286, 291-7,
    302, 304-5, 319, 344, 349,
    354
Fitzgerald, Zelda 7, 84-6, 95,
    155, 170, 176-7, 180,
    182-3, 185-6, 196, 286-7,
    302, 344, 346-7
Flanner, Janet 300 -1
Flynn, Errol 104-5, 249
For Whom the Bell Tolls 24, 44,
    53, 56, 68, 94, 103, 131,
    135-7, 139-40, 153,
    155-6, 158, 163-72, 181,
    195, 201-2, 211, 213-4,
    216, 218, 225, 269, 273,
    279, 301, 309-10, 312,
    347
Ford, Ford Madox 63-4, 118,
    253, 262, 294-5, 344
Frost, Robert 124

Gable, Clark 289
Garden of Eden, The 24, 69,
    211, 241, 343, 346-8
Gardner, Ava 62, 105, 153, 211,
    309-10
Gardner, John 297-8
Geismar, Maxwell 223, 329
Gauss Christian 180
Gellhorn, Martha 9, 12, 16-17,
    52, 68, 115, 159-74,
    195-207, 208-10, 219,
    264, 299, 302-3, 305
Gingrich, Arnold 102, 155, 168,
    183, 227, 299-300
Ginna, Robert Emmett 239
Graham, Sheilah 169-70, 183,
    185-6
Gray, James 289
Greene, Graham 48
Griffin, Peter 107, 342
Green Hills of Africa 46, 92,
    131, 149-50, 170, 213,
    259
Guest, Winston 17, 161
Guthrie, Pat 90-1, 95, 107

Hammett, Dashiell 96
Harling, Robert 247
Hawks, Howard 158